STUDIES IN HISTORY, ECONOMICS AND PUBLIC LAW

Edited by the

FACULTY OF POLITICAL SCIENCE
OF COLUMBIA UNIVERSITY

NUMBER 374

THE RETIREMENT OF NATIONAL DEBTS

THE THEORY AND HISTORY SINCE THE WORLD WAR

BY

WILLIAM WITHERS

THE RETIREMENT OF NATIONAL DEBTS

THE THEORY AND HISTORY SINCE THE WORLD WAR

BY

WILLIAM WITHERS, PH.D.

NEW YORK

COLUMBIA UNIVERSITY PRESS

LONDON: P. S. KING & SON, LTD.

1932

PRINTED IN THE UNITED STATES OF AMERICA

To

I. R.

PREFACE

THE generally accepted answers to some of the vital questions of public finance are based upon the most popular theories of value and distribution, that is, the neo-classical and marginal productivity theories. Yet many economists would admit that these older value theories are of doubtful validity in some respects, because of the questionable psychology and sociology upon which they are based, and because disequilibrium is frequently a " normal " economic phenomenon. In specific studies of economic questions, other than those of public finance, and in general economic theory, a great deal of attention has been paid in recent years to the weaknesses of value theory. But these weaknesses have not been adequately considered in the field of public finance. If the work of the past is to be carried much further, it would seem that the criticisms of the older value theories must be considered more fully in their bearing on this subject. It is not enough merely to introduce dynamic aspects in the manner of neo-classical theory or to treat briefly the institutions which affect changes in values. Such matters need to be studied much more thoroughly.

In this book I have tried to demonstrate the importance of this need. The study of any one problem in the field of public finance may lose its significance when the student narrows his treatment to the facts and theories within this field alone. Institutional and dynamic considerations must almost invariably cause him to step over the customary boundaries of the subject. The attempt to study adequately one problem in public finance, the effects of debt retirement, leads us into money, banking and international trade as well as value theory. Indeed, in economics as a whole the introduction of institutional considerations has already done much to bring economics and sociology together. It is possible that in the social sciences the day of rigid specialization is over, and that the problems of social life will henceforth be given a more synthetic treatment.

The most extensive study of the problems of debt retirement is that of the English Committee on National Debt and Taxation, from which I have quoted extensively in this volume. This committee was willing to go into the habits of saving, the distribution of income and changes in the price level in their relations to the public debt, but it did not go far enough. I believe that its work was significant in so far as it takes account of the influence of other divisions of economics than public finance. I believe also that the same statement may be made about this book. I regret that so many questions are raised in it that are not answered. But to answer all these questions requires much more time than the two years of study that I have been able to devote to them.

I should like to acknowledge my debt to Professor Robert Murray Haig, who has sponsored this study and who has given valuable assistance and encouragement at all stages. I owe a great deal also to Professors James W. Angell and Benjamin H. Beckhart for their helpful suggestions relating to the chapters on money and banking and international trade.

WILLIAM WITHERS

NEW YORK CITY,
MARCH 25, 1932.

CONTENTS

PAGE

CHAPTER VI

CHAPTER VII

CHAPTER VIII

CHAPTER I

The Problems of Debt Burden

Important among the manifold consequences of the World War was the increase in the burden of public debt in most of the belligerent countries. Between 1913 and 1925 the nominal public debt principal of France rose 1550 per cent. Between 1914 and 1924 the public debt principal of the United Kingdom rose 1176 per cent, and between 1914 and 1919 that of the United States increased 2144 per cent. With the exception of a few countries, the return of peace did not end the rise in public debt principal but merely retarded it, with the consequence that today most of the countries of the world are being subjected to further increases in already phenomenal burdens. In France and England a new plateau of public debt has been reached, reminding one of post-Napoleonic days but representing burden on a much higher scale. In the United States, the period after the Civil War is suggested.

As in these earlier years, a renewed interest in the retirement and effects of the debt has been aroused. It is true that perhaps a lion's share of this interest has been focussed upon the debts of the Allies to the United States and upon the reparations payments of Germany, and to a large extent only upon the political aspects of these two groups of obligations. Yet not for many years has there been so much interest in the mechanics of debt management, sinking funds, conversions and refunding. In both Great Britain and the United States the public debt has entered parliamentary debate. Problems of debt retirement have hovered over the councils of Treasury Departments and have probably exercised as much influence as any other factor in determining the governmental policies followed since the war. This is particularly true of the United States, where the question of the debt is admitted by Secretary Mellon to be a most important influence.[1]

In England, beginning with Chamberlain's fourth budget, the Exchequer has paid continued attention to the debt, and particularly to plans for its retirement. In the fourth budget it was proposed to devote a sum of £164,000,000 annually to debt retirement. So eager was the administration at that time to reduce the debt that even this sum was considered inadequate.[2] The desire to retire the debt was partly responsible for the movement for the capital levy and the forced loan. It finally resulted in the appointment of the Committee on National Debt and Taxation, more commonly referred to as the Colwyn Committee because of the presidency of Lord Colwyn. This body reported in 1926. Its majority and minority reports and the accompanying volumes of minutes of evidence will probably go down in history as the most important public documents on national debt issued in the years immediately following the war. Many of the most prominent English economists were called as witnesses and almost every possible phase of the debt was considered.

I. ATTEMPTS TO ESTIMATE DEBT BURDENS

In addition to the appointment of Parliamentary committees and the entrance of debt considerations into political policies and discussions, attempts have been made to estimate debt burdens and to compare these estimates with estimates in different countries and times. In England, for example, much interest has been expressed in the relative weights of the burden after the Napoleonic and World Wars. As

[1] *Annual Report of the Secretary of the Treasury*, 1925, p. 2; 1929, p. 11.

[2] Mallet and George, *British Budgets, 1914-21*, pp. 29, 41, 55, 94.

might be expected, the results of these comparisons are variable. Fisk says, "If we had index numbers of prices such as exist today covering the entire period, and could adjust money values accordingly, we would probably discover that today's burden is relatively not materially greater than at other crucial periods."[3] On the other hand, Layton made a comparison of the burden in 1923 with that in 1913 and 1818 and concluded that the burden in England in 1923 was much heavier than it had been in 1818.[4] As was pointed out in the evidence before the Colwyn Committee, however, it is doubtful whether an analogy can be drawn between present and Napoleonic conditions because of the falling rate in the growth of significant inventions and in the growth of the population. Only the bare facts of population and debt capital and interest are known. In England in October, 1715, the public debt was only about £50,000,000, or 200 per cent greater than it had been in Queen Anne's time. This increase in the debt gave rise to Walpole's Sinking Fund. In spite of the retirement of £6,626,000 by 1727, the debt had actually increased, through constant borrowing, by £2,000,000. New levels of debt were reached after the Seven Years' War, giving rise to the Pitt Sinking Fund, which was designed to retire these new increases in forty-five years.[5] According to Bastable, the debt had reached $122,600,000.[6] At the Peace of Versailles the debt had risen to £238,000,000; at the Peace of Amiens, to £500,000,000. At the end of the Napoleonic Wars the debt expenditures were one-third of the total expenditures and the debt was £50 per capita, about one-third of the total estimated wealth of

[3] Fisk, *English Public Finance*, p. 133.

[4] *Colwyn Report*, pp. 235-6.

[5] Fisk, *op. cit.*, p. 118.

[6] Bastable, *Public Finance*, 1st ed., p. 554.

Great Britain. At the end of the American War the debt was only £29 per capita, 25 per cent of the wealth.[7]

In the United States the conditions after the Civil War have been contrasted with those after the World War. The peak of the Civil War debt was reached on September 1, 1865, when it amounted to $2,758,000,000. The peak of the World War debt was reached on August 31, 1919, at $26,594,267,878. Thus the nominal debt was 9.6 times as great in 1919 as it had been in 1865. The per capita debt was, however, only 3.2 times larger, since that for 1919 was $253 and that for 1865, $77.07.

In addition to the discussions of the increased burden of debt, there has been a tendency in England, France and the United States to use the size of debts as an argument for economy. In a speech made by Ogden L. Mills at the University of Virginia in 1926 the influence of the debt as a factor in increasing the burden of taxation was pointed out.[8] Mellon urged in the Treasury Reports the necessity for economy due to the heavy expenses which were in part a result of the service of the debt. Economy was urged in England and France for the same reason.[9]

Since the war there has been very little assurance that the burdens of debt will be reduced by the increase in population and the growth of wealth. The pessimism arising from this prospect itensified the concern over methods of alleviating the burden of debt. After the first interest in the capital levy, nations have turned toward the problem of the repayment of debt. As Shirras says, "The repayment of the debt has been the aim of all well-financed countries since the war." [10] Not one witness appearing before the Colwyn

[7] Fisk, *op. cit.*, p. 93.

[8] *Annual Report of Secretary of the Treasury*, 1927.

[9] See Chapter VIII.

[10] Shirras, *Public Finance*, p. 532.

Committee suggested that no provision need be made for the repayment of the debt.

II. THE THEORY OF DEBT BURDEN AND DEBT RETIREMENT SINCE THE WAR

Most important for this study has been the growing interest in the theory of debt burden and retirement and the increase of the literature on this subject. Since the war, probably the greatest contributions have been made by the Colwyn Committee and by Professor Jèze in the *Revue de Science et de Législation Financières*. Two problems were given particular attention by the Colwyn Committee: the speed of debt redemption and the effects of retirement on saving.

The Committee concluded that there could be no single index of the speed of redemption and that " . . . there is no formula by which one may determine the rate at which debt payment should proceed."[11] As to the effects upon saving, they said, " On the balance, we think taxation propitious to saving."[12] It was concluded, however, that if taxes were raised too high, saving would be reduced, but that these results might be exaggerated; that the debt was not being too rapidly reduced (from 1924 to 1926), and that taxes could be raised much higher with profit. The Committee did not believe that debt payments made with one particular object in view were likely to be suited to the more general requirements of debt management. The majority report of the Committee advocated the retirement of debt by a sinking fund of £75,000,000, the minority report by a sinking fund of £100,000,000. Parliament eventually adopted a sinking fund almost as large as that advocated by the majority report.

[11] *Colwyn Report*, p. 339.

[12] *Ibid.*, p. 333.

When one examines the previous history of the theory of public debts, it appears that the Colwyn Report really breaks no new ground and that its work consists largely in bringing together the existing knowledge and theory that bear upon the post-war problems of debt. Little analysis resulted from the compiling of the evidence in the final report. Many questions were raised by the work of the Committee, and articles have appeared in various economic publications which attempt to answer some of them. But no comprehensive attempt has been made to relate present facts to past theory in order that more light may be cast upon the complicated problems with which this theory deals. Although many witnesses before the Committee state that the problem of rapidity of retirement is most important, they are unable to evolve any theory or set up any plan that will serve as a basis for public policy.

The conception of speed in retirement requires clarification before such progress can be made. This meaning can be found in the relation of the monetary aspects of the problem to those of capital accumulation. Professor Jèze has begun to make the monetary conception of speed in retirement more definite. To him the problem of retirement is essentially the "*répartition de la charge dans le temps.*" [13] It is true that he takes into account the effects of too large a *répartition* on the production of goods. For example, an annual redistribution of income of more than twenty per cent would be too heavy because "*tout ceci les découragerait de produire.*" [14] But it is probable that still further progress can be made by a more analytical relation of the theories of capital accumulation to the theories of prices. As it stands, the mere inclusion of the effects upon saving in a monetary treatment does not fulfill the necessities of inte-

[13] Jèze, *Le Remboursement des emprunts publiques*, p. 34.

[14] *Ibid.*, p. 34.

gration and it is possible that no more definite conclusions about retirement practice may follow from such a treatment than were suggested by the Colwyn Committee. The speed of retirement must then be determined largely on the basis of mere guesswork. It is also possible that the work of Jèze puts too much emphasis on the speed of retirement; in this respect the work of the Colwyn Committee has an advantage through its broader emphasis.

The Colwyn Committee had before it evidence from which much more definite and consistent conclusions might have been drawn. Although they finally concluded that taxation for debt payment was "propitious" to saving, they failed to make any use of the notions of A. M. Samuel and Stanhope-Pitt that too rapid payment of the debt was confiscation. Mr. Stanhope-Pitt and Mr. Samuel failed to make proper use of their own ideas because they looked to certain figures of the volume of savings as a guide for debt retirement. One would assume from their position that savings might not be increased by the payment of the debt. Not knowing what to make of these difficulties, the final report played safe by concluding that although taxation for debt payment was "propitious" to saving, no formula for payment could be devised, and ignored the thread of connection between the monetary and saving aspects indicated by the confiscation notion presented by Stanhope-Pitt and Samuel. From this point the writer hopes to proceed and explore the theoretical potentialities of the idea of confiscation in its relation to the speed of retirement.

The emphasis upon the speed of retirement by H. C. Adams and more recent writers has come, no doubt, from a desire for simplification of the numerous and confusing factors related to debt retirement. There is a danger that too much simplification may be achieved thereby. But there must be some way to bring greater order into the theory of debt retirement and at the same time avoid over-stressing any one aspect of the whole mass of problems. As in the case of better definition of speed in retirement, so also may this order arise from the greater integration of the monetary and saving aspects of these various problems. The object of the subsequent chapters is to work out this integration comprehensively in connection with all the problems which are believed to be of importance. By way of introduction the questions to be taken up are outlined below.

In Chapter V the relation of the debt and its retirement to money will be discussed. Some answers will be attempted for such questions as: Does debt retirement cause deflation? Does deflation really increase the burden of debt for society and for the individual? What relations exist between inflation and borrowing and deflation and saving? In Chapter VI the relation of debt retirement to banking will be discussed. There are problems here of the effect of the retirement of debt upon the changes in bank assets, of the effect of retirement upon the borrowing of banks at central banks and the control of the volume of credit by central banks. In Chapter VII the international effects of debt retirement will be discussed. What light does attention to the integration of price factors and capital accumulation cast upon the advantages and disadvantages of the payment of foreign debts and reparations to the country paying and the country paid? If debts are paid how will this affect the balance of trade? What additional knowledge does our integration throw upon the capacity to pay foreign debts? How will the balance of trade and investments in different kinds of businesses be affected? In Chapter VIII the effects of the debt and its payment upon distribution are discussed. The factors that affect this distribution are outlined and the old question of whether or not the debt maintains an unproductive class is raised again. Particular attention is paid to the question of how the debt service and the repayment of the debt affect the distribution of the burden of debts among the general public and the bond holders. Some attention is also given to the effects of distribution upon production through the reinvestment of the former debt principal. The effects of the debt service upon the volume of saving are considered in Chapter IX along with certain other related matters.

With this foundation in theory, together with the information relating to the management and burden of debts since the World War, it is possible to arrive at new notions about the burden of debt. These notions are essentially dynamic and entail a distinction between the burden of the war and the burden of the debt. The various kinds of burden can be reclassified and the old classifications commented upon. In the light of the new conceptions of burden the methods of retirement now in use may be evaluated and suggestions made as to the procedure and rate of debt retirement.

It is hoped that some light will be thrown upon the nature of taxable capacity. By some this conception is regarded as of little value because of the difficulties of making it concrete and of determining the extent of the capacity.[15] But regardless of scientific caution, the problems of recent years have required the estimation of taxable capacity and the use of these estimates in practice. It is therefore possible that economists have stood too much aloof from this subject and should now turn their attention to it. The examination of the nature of the tax burden is the prerequisite to its determination.

[15] Shirras, *Public Finance*, p. 131.

CHAPTER II

The Post-War Burden of Debt

Since the proper solution of certain problems related to the reparations payments, the methods and time of debt retirement, and the management of the debt during its life depend upon the existence of genuine burdens of debt, the nature of these burdens becomes of the utmost importance. Economists have tried both to estimate and to analyze debt burdens in order to see what empirical treatment could contribute. In this chapter fresh attempts of this character will be made.

I. The Methods of Estimating Debt Burdens

The estimation of the burdens of debt is a problem by itself, but so preoccupied have economists been with theories of burden that they have discussed very little the methods of estimation. Bastable, Shirras and Henry Higgs have given the subject the most thought. Bastable says,

> Very important questions arise respecting the absolute amount of public debts, the pressure that they impose on the borrowing States or other bodies, and the best mode of measuring that burden. For this purpose very different methods may be used. The most obvious is that which takes the nominal capital of the debt as the basis of measurement.[1]

This, he realized, was clearly defective because no account is taken of the rate of interest. Lord Grenville had said before Bastable that " the Public Debt consists not in capital but in annuities." A second measure might be used, that of

[1] Bastable, *Public Finance*, bk. v, ch. v, p. 12.

market values. Bastable saw two objections to the use of this second measure: first, the whole of the debt is not sold at any one time and, second, the market value is constantly fluctuating. So he believed that the amount or rate of the interest itself might be taken as still another measure. Debt per capita was also suggested, but since this had proved unsatisfactory for the measurement of expenses in general, he did not think it would be satisfactory for the measurement of debt expenses in particular. The best measure, he concluded, was capital and income. But, he says, " such comparisons are by no means easy ", and for practical purposes it is convenient to compare the annual debt charge with the total state expenditures. He also thinks that it is necessary to take account of certain specific assets which are available for the debt's liquidation. He ends his treatment with the words:

> Estimates of the real weight of public debts are, it is now plain, by no means easily formed; the considerations to be taken account of are too complex to be dealt with in a ready and offhand manner. The only way of arriving at a satisfactory result is by the use of each of the different methods of calculation and a combination of their results. . . . Where all point in the same direction a conclusion is easily reached. . . .[2]

Shirras, as has been indicated, also discusses the estimation of debt burdens. He gives most of the methods cited by Bastable, and merely eliminates those methods which Bastable criticized most severely. The proportion of debt to total expenses and the proportion of debt to national wealth are considered by Shirras the most useful measures.

Other economists have gone farther. The inequality of wealth, the form of debt and changes in the price level have been considered. For example, Dalton believes that there is

[2] *Ibid.*, 2nd ed., p. 634.

what he terms a direct debt burden when those owning securities are taxed less than the amount paid to them in their service.[3] In other words, the proportion of security holdings to taxes is another index of burden. Since it is also believed that burden increases with external debt, the proportion of internal to external debt may be taken as another estimate of burden.[4]

The effects of external debts have been much more discussed than those of other forms of debt, otherwise proportions between these other forms might likewise have been considered as measures of burden. It would be just as reasonable to estimate the proportions between these forms as between external and internal debts. Thus in both practice and theory the dangers of a large floating debt have been recognized.

It has also long been thought that changes in the price level affect the burden of debt and those making estimates of burden have frequently deflated their figures to give a truer picture. Several witnesses appearing before the Colwyn Committee stated time and again that the burden of debt increases with falling prices, and the final report of the Committee emphasized the necessity of considering changes in the value of money in estimating the burden of the debt.[5] Dalton, for example, believes that a downward movement of the price level would "increase enormously the real burden of . . . debt. . . ."[6] Comparisons were made between the Napoleonic and World War eras by witnesses and attempts were made to rule out price changes. But it was denied in the final report that any satisfactory analogy existed

[3] Dalton, *Public Finance*, p. 191.

[4] The relative burdens of internal and external debts are discussed in Chapter VII.

[5] *Colwyn Report*, p. 29.

[6] *Ibid.*, p. 398.

between modern and Napoleonic times because of a slowing down in the rate of population growth and in the frequency of significant inventions.

The Colwyn Committee believed that before any satisfactory estimate of burden could be given the following things must be known: the proportion of total taxation to total wealth, the amount of taxation per capita, the comparative distribution of wealth or income, the incidence of taxes and the adjustment of them to the distribution of wealth, the general character of a country's industry, especially in regard to the capital equipment needed, the ratio between productive and unproductive expenditures, the relation between local and national finance, the policy pursued in regard to the finance of national and local industries, and the psychology of the people with respect to thrift. It is obvious that to obtain satisfactory measures of all these things at once is virtually impossible.

Silverman says in a recent book that the nature and composition of any taxation are of importance in determining whether it is a burden.[7] This idea is applied to the debt burden by Matsushita and will be discussed at a later point.[8]

Finally, one may end this summary of recent thought on the subject by reference to the work of Henry Higgs. He thinks that in the comparative growth of debt the following things should be considered: local as well as national debts, the sphere of the government, the different assets available for the payment of debt, the growth of population and wealth, the rate of interest and the distribution of internal and external debts.[9]

The opinions of these men do not afford much encouragement for the estimation of the burdens of debt. They

[7] Silverman, *Taxation, its Incidence and Effects*, pp. 2, 3.

[8] Matsushita, *Economic Effects of Public Debts*, p. 155.

[9] Higgs, *Primer of National Finance*, p. 83.

show quite clearly that the nature of these burdens is not well understood, and that no one thing is generally conceded to represent burden. It would seem that the burden of debt arises from an alteration of the whole economic state, and therefore may require many kinds of measures. If this is true it is impossible to determine the burden by accumulating such measures, because the totality of economic conditions is affected by many influences and this procedure does not isolate those of the debt itself. It also appears that the attempts of some of the men cited above to estimate the whole burden of debt were unreasonable, not only because of the great difficulties involved in the attempts but also because there is no one burden of debt. Their efforts arose, however, from a realization that there must be an interrelation of the many elements in the economic influence of the debt and that the problem of debt burden has some common aspects. These aspects relate mainly to quantitative considerations. There are questions of the general level of taxation which raise corresponding questions of the amount of burden. Thus because of the interrelations of economic factors in their bearing upon debt problems, and because of the quantitative aspect of these burdens, attempts to estimate the whole burden of debt are not entirely unreasonable.

II. MEASURES OF DEBT BURDENS

It is necessary to realize, however, that burdens are both quantitative and qualitative, and that in making use of any data concerning the debt these distinctions must be kept clearly in mind. Such distinctions will promote an appropriate use of the facts about the debt and will justify the employment of estimates of the kinds of burden without any attempt to estimate the burden as a whole. The following types of measures might be of some value, if they could be properly computed: the ratio of wealth per capita to debt per capita, of income per capita to debt per capita, of external to internal debt, of unfunded to total debt, and of debt service to total public expenditures. These measures are satisfactory for international comparisons in that they are proportions and not absolute amounts. When these proportions are compared as to their rate of change they are a type of measure suited to the conception of debt burden as an altered economic state. This conception will be discussed at a later point.[10] In the remainder of this chapter tables of measures of debt burden for a number of countries will be given. They may be classified as direct and indirect measures.

TABLE I

TOTAL NATIONAL DEBTS* IN NATIONAL CURRENCIES

Year	Czechoslovakia (000,000 crowns)	France (000,000 francs)	Germany (000 marks)	United Kingdom (£'s)	India (000,000 rupees)
1912					
1913		32,594			
1914		39,530		649,770,091	5,513
1915		62,390		1,104,967,076	
1916		88,980		2,133,147,644	
1917		128,688		4,011,445,908	
1918		173,293		5,871,850,637	
1919		252,703		7,434,949,429	
1920		324,321		7,828,779,095	
1921	13,390	325,388		7,574,358,486	
1922	19,050	352,423		7,654,301,176	
1923	22,218	416,194		7,742,233,287	8,789
1924	24,627	428,367	2,406,100	7,641,046,952	9,148
1925	26,586	505,448	2,787,700	7,597,848,053	9,561
1926	27,784	497,100	7,841,800	7,558,644,299	9,686
1927	27,775	479,577	8,072,900	7,554,617,647	9,751
1928	28,327	470,037	7,890,600	7,527,816,878	9,916
1929			8,949,900	7,620,800,000	10,742
1930		482,179	10,375,100	7,596,200,000	11,317

* The debts of national governments are here given. The statistics are not strictly comparable since some European governments are more centralized than others. The statistics given in the *Memorandum* of the League of Nations appear under the title of public debts.

10 See Chapter X.

TABLE I—*Continued*

Year	Italy (000,000 lire)	Japan (000,000 yen)	Spain (000,000 pesetas)	Switzerland (000,000 francs)	United States (000 dollars)
1912 . .			10,033		
1913 . .				1,710	
1914 . .	15,766	2,584			1,188,235
1915					1,191,264
1916					1,225,145
1917 . .					2,975,618
1918 . .					12,243,628
1919 . .					25,482,034
1920 . .		2,794	12,974		24,297,918
1921 . .		3,244	15,357	4,414	23,976,250
1922	92,836	3,544	15,201	4,487	22,964,079
1923 . .	95,544	3,809	15,405	4,705	22,349,687
1924 . .	93,163	4,198	16,877	4,789	21,251,120
1925 . .	90,847	4,330	17,217	4,855	20,516,232
1926 . .	93,789	4,999	17,453	4,832	19,643,183
1927 . .	85,596	5,172	18,064	4,914	18,510,174
1928 . .	87,787	5,398	19,032	4,953	17,604,290
1929 . .	88,942	5,831			16,931,197
1930 . .	89,875	5,959			16,185,308

Sources: The *Memorandum on Public Finance* of the League of Nations (1926–28) was used for all the countries except the United States, France, United Kingdom and Germany. For the United States the *Annual Reports* of the Secretary of the Treasury were employed, for the United Kingdom the *Finance Accounts*, for France the figures of Haig in *Public Finances of Post-war France* and the *Annuaire Statistique*, for Germany the reports of the "Execution of the Experts' Plan." The figures for the Swiss debt include the total Debt of the Confederation and the Federal Railways.

(*a*) *Direct Measures*

Among the most important of the direct measures is the nominal amount of the debt principal. It is interesting to see what changes have occurred in this principal, as indicated in Table I.

From the above table it can be seen that if any adequate comparison is to be made between the various countries the computation of indices of change with some year taken as a base will be required. In Table II, which follows, the year

1923 is taken as a base, and the percentage variations in the debt since the war are given. If the data of Table I are used, the rather interesting fact is brought out that of the five countries, the United States, France, United Kingdom, Italy and Japan, the United States shows the greatest increase in the absolute amount of debt as a result of the war, i. e. from the beginning of the war to the year of maximum debt. Even in spite of the great amount of debt retirement that has taken place in the United States since 1920 the total amount of the national debt in 1929 was 14.7 times the total national debt in 1914. In France in the same period the debt had increased only 12.2 times, and in the United Kingdom only 11.6 times, in Italy only 5.5 times and in Japan only 2.1 times. This condition may be explained by the fact that the national debt of the United States in 1914 was small relatively to the total wealth. In absolute amount, also, the base from which the United States started to increase her debt was much smaller than that of Italy, France and the United Kingdom. Converted into American dollars the absolute amounts of the debt in these three countries in 1914 were $3,042,838,000, $7,629,290,000 and $3,157,882,642. The amount of the Japanese debt in dollars was $1,386,832,000.

It is interesting to note just what has happened to the debt in terms of dollars since the war, as shown by the figures for the year 1928. The American national debt had become $17,604,290,000. But converted into dollars the debt of France, owing to the revaluation of the franc, had become $18,425,450,400. This was actually an increase of the debt in terms of dollars of more than one hundred per cent, as can be seen from the fact that France's debt in 1914 was only a little less than 8 billions of dollars. The 1928 dollar figure for Italy, although it is not less than that for 1914, is at least not proportionately higher, only $4,617,576,200. That for Japan is $2,688,204,000. The debt of the United Kingdom

TABLE II

INDICES OF THE RATE OF CHANGE IN THE PUBLIC DEBT SINCE 1912

Year	Czecho-slovakia	France	Germany	United Kingdom	India	Italy	Japan	Spain	Switzer-land	United States
1912 . .								65		
1913 . .		8							36	
1914 . .		9		8	63	17	68			5
1915 . .		15		14						6
1916 . .		21		28						8
1917 . .		31		52						13
1918 . .		42		75						59
1919 . .		61		96						114
1920 . .		77		101				84		109
1921 . .	60	78		98			85	99	94	107
1922 . .	86	85		99		97	93	98	96	102
1923 . .	100	100		100	100	100	100	100	100	100
1924 . .	110	103	(100)	99	104	97	110	110	101	95
1925 . .	119	121	(116)	98	108	94	114	112	103	92
1926 . .	125	119	(326)	98	110	98	131	114	102	88
1927 . .	125	115	(335)	97	111	90	138	118	104	83
19 8 . .	127	113	(328)	97	112	91	141	124	105	79
1929 . .			(372)	98	122	93	152			76
1930 . .		116	(431)	98	129	94	159			72

Source: Data of Table I are used and converted into simple index numbers.

becomes the heaviest in the world in terms of absolute amounts. It was $34,585,180,027 in 1928. All this shows that some attention must be paid to changes in the price level, although such methods as the above may give misleading impressions.

From Table II one finds that the nature of the increase or decrease in national debts since 1923 has been variable. Czechoslovakia, France, Germany, India, Japan, Spain and Switzerland showed a rise in the six years ending in 1928 and all these countries showed a tendency toward a constant rise in the absolute amounts of the debt during these years. The United States, Italy and the United Kingdom showed a fall in the amount of the debt and they may be listed in this order to represent the rate of the decrease. In France from 1924 to 1928 there was also a constant decrease in the debt. It is interesting to note that the two nations whose burdens of debt in terms of absolute amounts were most increased by the war (the United States and the United Kingdom) made the most progress in the retirement of debt in the post-war period.

As pointed out above, price changes must be considered in estimating the altered burdens of debt. In view of what is to follow it may be desirable to note that the influence of price changes upon the burden of debt is by no means certain, and the greatest caution should be employed in interpreting the importance of these changes.[11] There is, however, no question but that price changes may have some influence upon the burden of debt and for that reason it is of interest to apply to the absolute amounts of the debts given in Table I index numbers of prices for the respective countries. The results of this process are given in Table III.

[11] See Chapter V.

TABLE III

ABSOLUTE AMOUNTS OF PUBLIC DEBT IN TERMS OF PRE-WAR PRICES

	1912	1913	1914	1915	1916	1917	1918	1919	1920
Czechoslovakia. . (000,000 crowns)									
France* . . . . (000,000 francs)			39,530	43,629	47,324	47,139	50,376	70,984	64,085
Germany . . . . (000,000 marks)									
United Kingdom . (000,000 pounds)			649.8	917.15	1,343.9	1,965.6	2,583.6	2,948.3	2,661.8
India. . . . . . (000,000 rupees)			5,512.8						
Italy . . . . . . (000,000 lire)			15,766						
Japan . . . . . (000,000 yen)			2,584.1						1.078.6
Spain. . . . . . (000,000 pesetas)	10,032 9								
Switzerland . . . (000,000 francs)		1 710							
United States . (000 dollars)			1,188,235	1,167,907	980,116	1,730,010	6,343,847	12,552,726	10.751,291

* During the war years in France the prices of many goods were controlled. Professor J. H. Rogers thinks that there is no way of allowing for these regulations, hence the indices of the Annuaire Statistique Générale are used without any modification in his study of French inflation. Since Professor Rogers has made a very thorough study of the changes in French credit and prices, I have felt justified in also using the prices of the Annuaire Statistique Générale. *Cf.* J. H. Rogers, *The Process of Inflation in France*, p. 94.

TABLE III—*Continued*

	1921	1922	1923	1924	1925	1926	1927	1928
Czechoslovakia. . (000,000 crowns)	799	1,899	2,242	2,357	2,752	2,838	2,828	2,972
France . . . (000,000 francs)	96,554	106,091	100,288	85,207	88,831	58,209	75,763	73,773
Germany . . . (000,000 marks)					2,787.7	7,764.1	7,521.6	7,239.1
United Kingdom . (000,000 pounds)	4,165.9	4,975.3	5,109.9	4,661.0	4,786.6	5,064.3	4,212.7	5,269.5
India. . . . . . . (000,000 rupees)			4,855.7	5,110.8	5,691.1	6,410.0	6,019 1	6,159.1
Italy . . . (000,000 lire)		17,853	18,734	18,196	16,398	15,632	18,160	19,002
Japan. . . . . . (000,000 yen)	1,698.4	1,763.1	1,943.2	1,989.4	2,122.4	2,717	3,024.4	3,194
Spain. . . . . . . (000,000 pesetas)			9,206.7	8,523.9	9,296.9	9,383.5	10,688.7	
Switzerland . . . (000,000 francs)			2,571	2,801	3,112	3,287	3,366	3,439
United States*. . (000 dollars)	16,766,608	16,171,887	15,308,005	14,757,722	13,497,547	13,454,235	13,321,553	12,310,692

* United States, 1929 (000 dollars)—12,007,941.

The absolute figures of Table I are treated by index numbers of wholesale prices given in the *Memorandum on Public Finance*, pp.26–28, of the League of Nations, and in the statistical abstracts of the United States, France, Germany and the United Kingdom. The base years are 1912, 1913 and 1914. The formula used for this purpose where d is the debt in a given year, x the debt of this year representing the influence of price, p1 is the price of the given year and po the price of the base year or 100, is

$$x = d\left(\frac{p_0}{p_1}\right).$$

TABLE IV

INDICES OF THE RATE OF CHANGE OF THE PUBLIC DEBT TAKING ACCOUNT OF VARIATIONS IN THE PRICE LEVEL

Year	Czecho-slovakia	France	Germany	United Kingdom	India	Italy	Japan	Spain	Switzer-land	United States
1912 . .								109		
1913 . .									151	
1914 . .		39		13	114	84	133			7.7
1915 . .		44		18						7.6
1916 . .		47		26						6.4
1917 . .		47		38						11
1918 . .		50		51						41
1919 . .		71		58						82
1920 . .		64		52			56			70
1921 . .	36	96		81			88			110
1922 . .	85	107		97	98	98	91			112
1923 . .	100	100		100	100	100	100	100	100	100
1924 . .	105	85		91	105	97	102	97	109	91
1925 . .	123	89	(100)	94	118	87	109	105	121	88
1926 . .	127	58	(278)	99	132	83	139	107	128	88
1927 . .	126	76	(269)	82	125	97	155	122	131	87
1928 . .	133	74	(259)	103	127	102	164		133	80

Source: Data of Table III are converted into simple arithmetic mean index numbers.

In order that the rates of change may be compared for these various countries, index numbers of the absolute amounts in Table III have been given in Table IV.

When Tables II and IV are compared it can be readily seen that in most of the countries considered the burden of debt appears to have been increased by changes in the price level since 1923. The United Kingdom, Italy, India and Japan seem to have been particularly affected by price changes. In Italy and the United Kingdom the gains noted in Table II seem to have been effaced by falling prices. The influence of stabilization is particularly marked in the case of Italy.

Thus one very important fact stands out. The decline of prices since the war would seem to have robbed the countries of the world of any decrease in debt burden they might have achieved by the actual reductions in the nominal amounts of debt. There has even been an increase in the apparent burden of the debt much more than necessary to counteract the decrease in nominal debt in such countries as the United Kingdom and Italy. The United States stands alone as the only country studied in which falling prices could not equal the rapid decrease in the nominal amount of the debt.

The use of figures of total debt are insufficient as measures of the debt and should be supplemented by figures of the debt per capita. The debt per capita by years is given below in Table V. This table presents a number of interesting facts. In Czechoslovakia the debt per capita has not risen since 1923 so rapidly as the total debt, showing a tendency for the growing population to offset the burden of debt. (See Table II). In France there has been a tendency for the debt per capita to fall since 1925, but there population increase has not accelerated this fall as in Czechoslovakia. In Germany, however, population increase prevented the burden of debt from rising so high as would be indicated by the

TABLE V

NATIONAL DEBTS PER CAPITA IN NATIONAL MONEY

	Czecho-slovakia (crowns)	France (francs)	Germany (marks)	United Kingdom (pounds)	India (rupees)	Italy (lire)	Japan (yen)	Spain (pesetas)	Switzer-land (francs)	United States (dollars)
1912	. .	. .	. .	.	.	. .	. .	502.9	451	
1913	. .	812								
1914	. .	989	. .	. .	22.5	440	48	. .	. .	12
1915	. .	1,567	. .	. .	. .	. .	.	. .	. .	11.83
1916	. .	2,245	. .	. .	. .	. .	.		.	11.96
1917	. .	3,261	.	. .	. .	. .	. .	. .	. .	28.57
1918	. .	4,409	. .	. .	. .	. .	. .	.	. .	115.65
1919	. .	6,457	. .	. .	. .	. .	. .	. .	. .	240.09
1920	. .	8,323	. .	168	. .	. .	48	. .	. .	228.33
1921	988.46	8,386	. .	161	. .		55	. .	.	221.82
1922	1,386 05	8,985	. .	175	. .	2,387	60	706.9	. .	209.25
1923	1,600.89	10,497	. .	173	35.5	2,425	63	711.9	1,195	200.86
1924	1,758.34	10,689	38.3	170	36.9	2,341	69	775.5	1,210	188.59
1925	1,880.65	12,480	44.1	168	38.6	2,254	70	783.7	1,221	179.80
1926	1,947.34	12,147	123.2	167	29.0	2,299	79	788.7	1,182	170.04
1927	1,922.09	11,699	126.1	166	39.3	2,105	81	804.8	1,225	158.28
1928	1,949 64	11,447	122.3	165	39.9	2,152	83	. .	1,229	148.73
1929*	.	. .	137.7	. .	. .	. .	.	. .	. .	141.34

* United States, 1930: 131.42.

Source: The debt figures were secured from sources given in Table I. The population figures for the United States are those of the *Census*; for the United Kingdom, the *Statistical Tables* 1928–29 prepared by the Board of Trade; and for France and Switzerland, the League of Nations estimates. All other per capita debt figures were taken from the *Memorandum on Public Finance*, 1926–28.

nominal debt figures. In the United Kingdom the debt per capita has fallen continuously since 1924, but it has not reached the point to which it had fallen in 1921. Here also the growth of population has been of assistance, but only to a slight extent. In India the growth of population has kept the debt per capita virtually the same since 1923 and has greatly offset the rise in nominal debt. In Italy the debt per capita has fallen steadily since 1923 except for the year 1928. Here also the fall has been more rapid than that of the nominal amount of the debt, showing some assistance from growing population. The same conclusions may be derived from the figures for the United States. The United States has had its per capita burden of debt reduced more than any of the countries studied. Of the nine countries, the United Kingdom has the highest debt per capita. Their respective debts converted into dollars for 1928 are given below.[12]

United Kingdom	$811.90
France	448.72
Switzerland	237.20
United States	148.73
Italy	113.20
Czechoslovakia	57.68
Japan	40.92
India	10.59

The floating debt constitutes a greater potential burden than the funded debt because of the greater danger to solvency involved in its earlier maturity. A large floating debt is frequently considered in both private and public finance as an indication of an unhealthy state of affairs and a nation usually removes the floating debt as rapidly as possible. The proportion of the floating to the total domestic debt may thus be considered as one measure of burden. Such measures have been computed and are presented in Table VI.

[12] The rates of exchange used were par for each of these countries on November 30, 1931.

TABLE VI

Floating Debt Expressed as Percentage of the Total Domestic Debt

(Floating is defined for the United Kingdom, the United States and France as all debt with a maturity of one year or less. For the other countries the figures of the *Memorandum on Public Finance* of the League of Nations had to be accepted. The debt is that of national governments.)

	Czecho-slovakia	France	Germany	United Kingdom	India	Italy	Japan	Roumania	Spain	Switzer-land	United States
1912	. .	. .		. .	. .	. .	. .	. .	2		
1913	. .	4.	. .	. .	. .	. .	. .	. .	. .	4.	
1914	. .	18.	. .	2.	18.	6.					
1915	. .	20.	. .	9.	. .	. .					
1916	. .	27.	. .	27.	. .	. .	. .	. .	. .	. .	3.
1917	. .	34.	. .	. .	. .	. .	. .	. .	. .	. .	11.
1918	. .	32.	. .	11.	. .	. .	. .	. .	. .	. .	14.
1919	. .	44.	. .	20.	. .	. .	. .	. .	. .	. .	14.
1920	. .	39.	.	17.	. .	. .	. .	. .	. .	. .	18.
1921	57.7	38.	. .	18.	. .	. .	. .	. .	.	. .	17.
1922	47.	37.	. .	15.		39.	. .	. .	23.	. .	19.
1923	42.2	33.	. .	11.	28.	37.	. .	41.	24.	6.	6.
1924	34.1	32.	26.	12.	26.	34.	. .	43.	31.	2.	9.
1925	27.6	33.	22.	10.	26.	30.	. .	2.	33.	1.	9.
1925–26	. .	.	. .	. .	.	30.	4.	. .	. .	. .	
1926	19.5	32.	2.4	13.	28.	. .	. .	2.	33.	2.	11.
1926–27	. .	.	. .	. .	28.	25.	6.	. .	. .	. .	
1927	16.4	26.	2.5	11.	. .	. .	. .	2.	1.	2.	17.
1927–28	. .	. .	. .	. .	30.	1.	4.				
1928	13.8	15.	3.4	11.	. .	. .	. .	. .	. .	. .	14.
1929	. .	. .	13.0	. .	. .	. .	. .	. .	. .	4.	9.

Source: The figures are computed from debt figures obtained from the same sources as those of Table I.

TABLE VII

The Percentage that External Debt is to the Total National Debt

	Czecho-slovakia	France	Germany	United Kingdom	Italy	India	Japan	Spain	Switzer-land
1912	. .	. .	. .	. .	. .	.	. .	10.3	
1913									
1914	. .	2.	. .	. .	. .	67.	59.		
1915	. .	4.							
1916	. .	9.							
1917	. .	16.							
1918	. .	16.							
1919	. .	26.							
1920	. .	32.	. .	17.		. .	46.		
1921	26.6	25.	. .	16.	. .	. .	43.		
1922	21.0	27.	. .	15.	.	. .	38.	6.0	
1923	16.4	33.	. .	.14	. .	46.	35.	5.3	5.8
1924	17.3	33.	. .	15.	. .	47.	38.	5.4	5.8
1925	19.6	42.	3.3	14.	. .	47.	34.	5.3	5.8
1925–26	. .	. .	. .	. .	2.	. .	29.	. .	. .
1926	18.6	41.	12.0	14.	. .	47.	. .	5.2	5.8
1926–27	. .	. .	. .	. .	2.	46.	28.	. .	. .
1927	18.3	37.	11.4	14.	. .	. .	. .	5.0	5.8
1927–28	. .	. .	. .	. .	2.	46.	26.	. .	
1928	15.0	38.	12.7	14.	. .	.	. .	5.8	
1929	. .	. .	9.						

Source: See note for Table VI.

In the United Kingdom the floating debt arising from the war was steadily reduced until 1924, from which date very little progress was made. Czechoslovakia emerged from the war with more floating than funded debt and yet shows consistent progress in its reduction. A steady reduction has also taken place in France. Germany's floating debt shows the effects of the recent financial difficulties by its rise in 1929. India has made no progress with her floating debt; Italy and Roumania, Switzerland and Spain had made great progress up to 1927. The United States presents a totally different picture from the other countries. The policy of reduction adopted in 1921 was abandoned in 1924, 1925, 1926 and 1927. The proportion of the floating to the total domestic debt was higher in 1930 than it had been in 1923.

The external debt has also been singled out as a special source of burden. The proportion that this bears to the total debt may therefore also serve as a special measure of debt burden. The results of such calculations are given above in Table VII. It can be seen from these figures that Czechoslovakia, Germany, the United Kingdom, Japan and Spain have made steady progress in the reduction of their external debt. In France the external debt became of increasing importance after 1922 as a factor in the total debt situation. In India, Spain and Switzerland the proportion of external to total debt has remained constant. A striking difference is shown in various countries in the part played by foreign debt. In France, India and Japan the foreign debt is more important than the domestic.

It is still probably true, as will be demonstrated by the chapters on the effects of debt retirement, that a comparison between the national income and the debt per capita would be very useful as a measure of debt burden. It will be remembered that this was Bastable's belief. Because of the inadequate statistics such a comparison can be accomplished

TABLE VIII

TOTAL PUBLIC DEBT SERVICE EXPRESSED AS PERCENTAGE OF TOTAL NATIONAL EXPENDITURES

	1920	1921	1922	1923	1924	1925	1926	1927	1928	1929
Czechoslovakia					21.6	17.9	17.0	18.7	15.5	
France							41.0[1]	44.0[1]	33.0[1]	31.0[1]
Germany						3.8	1.2	3.5	4.5	5.5
United Kingdom	19.0	24.0	29.0	35.0	41.0	44.0	43 0	44.0	45.0	
Hungary					24.0[2]	14.0[2]	12.0[2]	12.0[2]		
India							26.0[2]	25.0[2]	21.0[2]	
Italy						26.0[2]	29.0[2]	34.0[2]	25.0[2]	
Japan						14.0[2]	14.0[2]	16.0[2]	17.0[2]	
Roumania						18.0	18.0	18.0	15.0	
Spain						22.0[2]		28.0	24.0	
Switzerland						66.0	69.0	68.0	64.0	67.0
United States	36.0[2]		49.0[2]	39.0[2]	40.0[2]	54.0[2]	40.0[2]	47.0[2]	36.0[2]	24 0[2]
Yugoslavia					4.0		7.0[2]	7.0[2]	11.0[2]	

[1] Budget estimates.

[2] Fiscal years.

Source: See note for Table VI.

only for a few countries. Except for the estimate of debt per capita the only way to avoid the use of the concept of wealth and income is through an estimation of the proportion of the debt service to the total national expenditure. The results of such a measurement are given in Table VIII.

From this table it can be seen that in all countries of the world except Germany and Yugoslavia the debt service (interest and debt retirement) is more than ten per cent of the total ordinary expenditures. In the United States, until 1929, the expenditures on the public debt were from 40 to 50 per cent of the total ordinary expenditures. In Switzerland the debt service was on the average over 65 per cent of these expenditures. No consistent tendencies toward a decline can be observed in these countries taken as a whole. In 1928 the four countries having the highest burden measured in this way were, in order of the burden, Switzerland, the United Kingdom, the United States and Italy. Next in order are India, Spain, Japan, Czechoslovakia, Hungary, Yugoslavia and Germany.

The way in which debt holdings are distributed is an important factor in the burden of debt.[13] Recognizing this fact, some economists have attempted to devise measures of burden based on the nature of this distribution. Prominent among these are Dalton and Pigou, whose measures will be discussed in Chapter VIII. Since all reasoning from debt facts about the distribution changes in the funds that pay the debt service depends fundamentally upon the presence of direct taxation, it is desirable to estimate at this point the degree to which taxation is direct. The available information about the countries studied is given below in Table IX.

These various countries may be listed in the following order in accordance with the approximate degree to which

[13] The nature of debt burden that arises from the distribution of the holdings will be discussed in Chapter VIII.

TABLE IX

DIRECT TAXES EXPRESSED AS PERCENTAGE OF TOTAL RECEIPTS OF NATIONAL GOVERNMENTS

	1920	1921	1922	1923	1924	1925	1926	1927	1928	1929
Czechoslovakia. .					20.8	22.5	30.2	18.8	16.1	
Germany. . . .					36.0	31.0	33.0	36.0	37.0	37.0
United Kingdom.	26.0	27.0	35.0	41.0	32.0	34.0	31.0	29.0	29.0	28.0
Hungary . .					10.0[1]	18.0[1]	18.0[1]	22.0[1]		
India							15.0[1]	17.0[1]	18.0[1]	
Italy.						29.0[1]	29.0[1]	29.0[1]	21.0[1]	
Japan						14.0[1]	22.0[1]	20.0[1]	22.0[1]	
Roumania . . .						18.0	17.0	20.0	20.0	
Spain						32.0[1]		32.0	30.4	
Switzerland. . .						7.0	23.0	8.4	5.2	9.5
United States	58.0[1]	57.0[1]	49.0[1]	43.0[1]	47.0[1]	48.0[1]	51.0[1]	54.0[1]	54.0[1]	58.0[1]
Yugoslavia. . . .					3.0[1]		20.0[1]	18.0[1]	18.0[1]	

[1] Fiscal years.

Source: See note for Table VI.

their receipts are obtained from direct taxes: the United States, Germany, the United Kingdom, Spain, Italy, Czechoslovakia, Japan, Roumania, Hungary, Yugoslavia and Switzerland. With the exception of Hungary and the United Kingdom the proportion of the receipts obtained by direct taxes has tended to increase. Thus at least one possible cause of the burdens of debt that arise out of the distribution of its holdings, i. e. indirect taxation, is apparently decreasing in importance.

Perhaps the best measures of debt burden are the proportions maintained between national income and the debt service and between national wealth and the debt principal. Estimates of these proportions by consecutive years are impossible for most countries at the present time because no satisfactory statistics of income are available. The work of Stamp and Bowley for England, of King for the United States, of Gini for Italy and of Colson, Pupin and others for France makes it possible to estimate roughly the amount of income and wealth before and after the World War. Dr. Corrado Gini has employed various estimates of income and wealth to secure comparative statistics for the years 1914 and 1925. The following figures are given for four nations.[14]

TABLE X

(IN BILLIONS)

Country	Middle of 1914		Middle of 1925	
	Wealth	Income	Wealth	Income
Italy (lire)	111	19–20	550	100
France (francs) . . .	300	37–38	1,000	150
United Kingdom (pounds)	14	2.25	24.5	3.9 4
United States (dollars) . .	200	33	380	70

[14] Gini, *A Comparison of the Wealth and National Income of Several Important Nations before and after the War*, p. 36. Rome, Provveditorato Generale Della Stato Libreria, 1925.

If one employs the figures given above, reduced to a pre-war price level (1913-14), to obtain ratios between wealth and debt principal and between income and total debt service, the results are as follows:

TABLE XI

Country	Percentage that debt principal is of wealth based on a pre-war price level		Percentage that debt service is of income based on a pre-war price level	
	1914	1925	1914	1925
Italy	14.2	16.5	3.63	6.53
France *	13.2	50.5	2.61	9.86
United Kingdom . . .	5.0	33.6	1.00	7.98
United States	.59	5.4	.07	1.64

* Figures for debt service in 1925 are budget estimates.

Source: Income figures are those of Gini given in Table X. The statistics on the debt service and debt principal were taken from the *Memorandum on Public Finance* of the League of Nations, the *Finance Accounts* of Great Britain, the *Reports of the Secretary of the Treasury*, the *Annuaire Statistique*, Haig, *Public Finances of Post-war France*, etc. The prices used were the wholesale prices given in the *Memorandum on Public Finance*. The price indices for 1925 were: Italy, 554 (Bachi index); France, 550 (Official); United Kingdom, 167 (Statist Index); United States, 152 (Bureau of Labor Statistics). The method of introducing price changes is that used in Table III.

The percentages computed in the table above show that France now has the greatest burden of debt in terms of wealth and income. The percentage that the debt principal is of wealth in 1925 would indicate that the former was half of the national wealth. In the United States the percentage that the debt principal is of wealth was only .59 in 1914 and 5.4 in 1925, very small figures relative to those of the three other nations. If one does not introduce price changes one finds that in 1920 the debt service was 2.1 per cent of the total realized income for the United States.

Progress in the reduction of the debt burden of the United States is shown by the fact that in 1925 the debt service was only 1.64 per cent of the total income on the basis of pre-war prices and in 1928 was only 1.23. But it is also true that the rise in the national income has tended to hasten the reduction of the burden of debt. Thus between 1920 and 1928 the nominal amount of the debt of the United States had fallen twenty-eight per cent. If the burden of debt is to be measured in terms of income alone, then the burden had fallen over forty per cent as a result of the large post-war growth of income.

Statistics of national income for Germany indicate that the total national debt service was .5 per cent of the total national income in 1925, .16 per cent in 1926, .7 per cent in 1927, and .9 per cent in 1928. The income figures used are those given in the *Statistisches Jahrbuch für das Deutsche Reich* (1931) based on the price level in 1928. Regardless of the differences in the nature of the income estimates used, the American figures indicate a heavier burden of domestic debt.

Such comparisons are impossible for many countries because of the lack of adequate statistics of income. Sir Walter Layton has estimated the proportion of the national income taken by taxation, a similar measure, in the United Kingdom and France.[15] The respective figures for these two nations were 22 per cent and 14 per cent. Reference to Table VIII will show that in 1924 the service of the public debt in the United Kingdom was 41 per cent of the total ordinary expenditures. It is apparent from this fact that the service of the debt was in the neighborhood of nine per cent of the total income. At any rate the debt service constitutes a much greater burden in England than in the United States. Layton has also estimated the proportion of tax

[15] *Economist*, August 2, 1924.

receipts to the total income in the post-Napoleonic period in England (1818). His figure for this period is 14.5 per cent.

(b) *Indirect Measures*

Earlier in this chapter it was stated that there were two types of measures of debt burden, direct and indirect. The most promising examples of the former have been considered. We turn now to measure the burden of debt indirectly. This consists in measuring the effects of the debt rather than in measuring the proportion of the debt capital or the debt service to some other factor closely related to the debt. The indirect measures are suggested by theories of the effects of the debt, and an estimate of their value and place in debt statistics can only be made after the theories of the effects of debt burdens are more clearly understood. Two such indirect measures have been suggested, changes in the standard of living and changes in the volume of savings.

Evidence based on the figures of the Ministry of Labour on the standard of living was presented to the Colwyn Committee in support of the theory that the burden of English debt was excessive. The inference from the figures presented was that " . . . on the average, the total resources of the wage-earning class do not differ much from the pre-war level." [16] Thus an index of real wages shows them to be at 100 in August, 1914, and 99 in August, 1925.[17] If it were normal to expect a rise in real wages in a decade, then the presence of some retarding factor must be admitted. Whether this factor is the burden of debt it would be very difficult to determine. In the United States real wages rose during this post-war decade.[18] This increase, in view of the

[16] *Colwyn Report*, p. 11.

[17] *Ibid.*, p. 7.

[18] See *Recent Economic Changes*, vol. i, p. 76 and Douglas, P. H., *Real Wages*.

fact that in the period from 1900 to 1913 real wages were declining,[19] gives some evidence that the national debt was not a burden to the extent of causing a lower standard of living. It should be obvious, however, that such a measure as the standard of living is at best of little value.

Another measure suggested by the witnesses before the Colwyn Committee was the volume of saving. At least three statisticians, Bowley, Coates and Layton, believed that saving had declined since the war. Pre-war savings were estimated at £350,000,000 to £400,000,000. Coates estimated that in 1924 they were £500,000,000. The items included in this estimate were as follows:[20]

Internal new issues for investment in the United Kingdom ..	£89	million
Internal new issues for investment abroad	135	"
Addition to national savings certificates	3	"
Increase of Treasury holdings of bonds tendered in payment of death duties	9	"
Investments sold by the banks	35	"
New houses	35	"
Undistributed profits of corporations and private businesses ..	194	"

The higher level of prices, it was estimated, made this £500,000,000 really represent an actual decline in real savings by £150,000,000 or £200,000,000 since 1913. Layton believed that the desire to increase the standard of living has slightly reduced the amount of saving.[21] Thus some forces have been at work to reduce the volume of savings in England and these may have included the possible depressive effect of the debt.

In the United States there is no available composite index of the whole volume of saving. If, however, savings and time deposits, life insurance and building and loan association

[19] W. I. King, *Wealth and Income of the People of the United States*, p. 168, 1915 edition.

[20] *Colwyn Report*, pp. 16-30.

[21] *Colwyn Report*, pp. 168-78.

assets be taken into account some picture of the tendencies in saving as a whole can be constructed. In terms of 1913 dollars the rate of increase in savings and time deposits was greatly reduced in 1910 and savings in this form began actually to decline in 1915. This decline was halted in 1918 and in 1920 these deposits increased again, but at a much more rapid rate than that of the years 1900 to 1906, which has the appearance of the sort of trend line that should be fitted to the savings for the pre-war years. This rapid increase falls off between 1921 and 1923, when a rate of increase similar to that maintained in the years 1900-1906 was established.[22] Life insurance assets present much the same history except that their decline in 1913 dollars is much greater than the decline of the deposits and the rate of increase was by 1927 still more rapid than the rate in the years 1900 to 1913. It would appear from these facts that the debt did not retard the growth of savings. But the proper interpretation of these changes in saving may lead to an entirely different conclusion, according to one's theory of debt burden and the effects of debt retirement. It becomes of the utmost importance to reexamine the theories of debt burden and retirement in order to determine, if possible, how these facts should be related to the debt. If, for example, the retirement of debt should increase the volume of saving, then it would seem that the data on savings indicate that debt retirement is having its proper effect. Questions of amount may enter also. If debt retirement should increase saving, how rapidly should it do this? It may be that the data on saving indicate an insufficient acceleration. It is easy to see that none of the measures, either direct or indirect, has much meaning except in so far as the one who uses them holds a certain theory of debt burden. The task in the subsequent pages will therefore be, in part, the analysis

[22] *Recent Economic Changes*, vol. ii, p. 673.

of the various theories of burden in order to show how they may affect the interpretation put upon the objective facts. The ultimate object is, of course, not merely to throw some light upon the meaning of the facts related to the public debt, but to add to the theory of debt retirement. To attain this object it is necessary to examine what has been accomplished to alleviate the burden of debt in recent years through retirement, conversion and debt management.

In Tables I to IV we have noted the amount of debt retirement that has been achieved in several important countries and what presumably becomes of that achievement in terms of burden when price changes are taken into account. If the influence of price is ignored, Italy, France, the United States and the United Kingdom have made some progress in debt reduction since 1925. Germany has retired some of her debts and the great increase in her debt arises largely from the revaluation of old debt.

The total debt of France, as can be seen in Table XII, has declined in recent years from 284,464,000,000 francs to 259,084,000,000. The debt was considerably reduced in 1928 and 1929. In 1929 the *Caisse Autonome*[23] turned to the retirement of *rentes* rather than short-term debt. The total repayments of *rentes* from October 1, 1926, to December 31, 1929 was 8,297,000,000 francs. 5,618,992,800 francs were purchased in 1929. The reduction of the floating debt is particularly marked in the years 1927 to 1930. Table XII presents these facts.[24]

In Germany financial conditions were decidedly abnormal from 1919 to 1923. No progress was made in the reduction of the debt. In Table XIII the changes in the funded debt of the Reich are given, in Table XIV the changes in the floating debt.

[23] The work of the *Caisse* is discussed in Chapters III and IV.

[24] *Revue de Science et de Législation Financières*, 1930, p. 707. Political debts to foreign countries not included.

TABLE XII

NATIONAL DEBT OF FRANCE, 1927-1930

(millions of francs)

	Dec. 31, 1927	Dec. 31, 1928	Dec. 31, 1929	May 31, 1930
Domestic Debt				
Perpetual Debt	101,682	101,788	98,117	96,855
Redeemable Debt	77,206	104,466	107,138	106,236
Short-term and Intermediate Debt	25,885	22,077	22,176	22,175
Floating Debt	79,691	44,565	37,647	33,818
Total.	284,464	272,896	265,078	259,084
Foreign Commercial Debt .	17,739	17,504	6,881	5,342

TABLE XIII

FUNDED DEBT OF THE REICH BEFORE AND AFTER THE WAR

End of March	Loans of the Reich	Premium loan	Interest-bearing treasury bills	Total: Millions of paper marks	Total: Millions of gold marks
	Millions of paper marks				
1913 . .	4,585.8		220.0	4,805.8	4,805.8
1914 . .	4,697.9		220.0	4,917.9	4,917.9
1915 . .	8,276.9		1,220.0	9,496.9	8,240.3
1916 . .	28,299.0		1,936.1	30,235.1	23,089.0
1917 . .	45,582.8		4,716.3	50,299.1	34,089.0
1918 . .	64,122.6		7,792.8	71,915.4	58,515.4
1919 . .	80,988.3		11,408.1	92,396.4	33,745.9
1920 . .	78,723.2	3,627.5	10,679.7	93,030.4	5,424.2
1921 .	69,341.3	3,629.0	9,189.7	82,160.0	5,523.0
1922 . .	55,131.5	3,507.7	7,028.5	65,667.7	903.8
1923 . .	49,127.8	3,880.0	6,565.6	59,573.4	11.92
1923* . .	50,126.0	3,880.0	6,482.0	60,488.0	0.002

* September 30, 1923.

Source: *Execution of the Experts' Plan, Germany's Economy, Currency and Credit*, p. 29.

TABLE XIV

FLOATING DEBT OF THE REICH 1920-23 (DISCOUNTED TREASURY BILLS)

Total in Milliards of Marks

Month	1920	1921	1922	1923
March.	166.3	271.9	6,601.1	
September . . .	138.2	210.4	450.9	46,716,616
October	140.5	217.8	603.6	6,907,511,103
November . . .	147.5	226.5	838.9	96,874,330,250
December . . .	152.7	246.9	1,494.9	1,232,679,853

With the Reichsbank

Month	1920	1921	1922	1923
End of March. .	64.5	146.5	4,552.0	
September . . .	49.6	98.4	349.8	45,216,224
October	48.6	98.7	477.7	6,578,650,939
November . . .	51.4	114.0	672.2	96,874,330,250
December . . .	57.6	132.3	1,184.5	

Held by the Public

Month	1920	1921	1922	1923
End of March. .	101.8	125.4	2,049.1	
September . . .	88.6	112.0	101.1	1,500,392
October . .	91.9	119.1	125.9	328,860,164
November . . .	96.1	112.5	166.7	
December . . .	95.1	114.6	310.5	1,232,679,853

Source: *Execution of the Experts' Plan, Germany's Economy, Currency and Credit*, p. 29.

After the adoption of the Dawes plan Germany incurred new debts, among which were debts to the Reichsbank and the German External Loan, and regular payments were made to retire these debts. For example, in the last half of 1926, 45 million marks were advanced for the service of the German External Loan. In the year 1928-29, 412 million marks (gross) of debt were retired. In the year 1929-30 the amount of the service of the German External Loan was 89,068,000 marks. During these years, 1924 to 1929, payments of reparations, which resemble the payment of a debt, were being made.

III. SUMMARY

In the preceding pages the amount and character of the burdens of debt that arose out of the World War have been set forth and the changes in these burdens outlined. These data represent complex influences. If they are to have any meaning for public purposes, it will be as the result of some kind of theoretical interpretation of them. This theory involves the numerous questions raised in the first chapter and any further use of the data depends upon a much more thorough analysis of these questions. The task is, however, as was pointed out, not solely the analysis of debt burdens, but the analysis of the methods of retirement in relation to these burdens. The latter problem requires a preliminary study of the facts relating to the methods of debt retirement and management employed by the leading world powers since the war. This is the work of the next two chapters.

CHAPTER III

Recent Management of National Debts

In the process of the general increase of debt, due to the World War, many new relationships among debt factors have developed. In addition, certain practices in debt management have appeared as a direct consequence of the budget difficulties experienced under the great weight of the debt charges. Thus, taxes are paid in part with government securities in the United States and England, the forced loan has appeared as a possibility in Italy, France and Norway, as a threat in Australia and New Zealand, and as an actuality in Germany and Holland. There has been a liberal use of premiums in both conversion and the issue of new loans in England and France. The capital levy came into operation in Germany and was seriously considered in many countries; France and Belgium made liberal use of " emprunts à lot "; real guarantees were developed in the case of external loans such as the post-war Austrian loan; and the excessively liberal tax exemption has become an important fiscal problem.

I. Changes in the Forms of Debt

(a) *Forced Loans*

Of these measures the forced loan, the capital levy and tax exemption aroused the greatest popular interest. As early as September, 1917, Premier Ward gave a public warning in New Zealand that if subscriptions for an impending loan were not great enough, a forced loan would be necessary. The threat proved very stimulating and the success in that country led to the same tactics in Australia, where the commonwealth treasurer introduced a law which would allow the use of the forced loan under similar circumstances.[1]

In Germany conditions were sufficiently critical to induce the government actually to attempt such a loan. In November, 1918, Germany was confronted with a consolidated debt of 96 billion marks, a floating debt of 45 billion marks and a fiduciary circulation of 27 billion marks. Lottery loans introduced in November, 1919, failed to yield sufficient returns and the forced loan was proposed as the next alternative. Hagenberg suggested a special body, to be known as the *Vermögenanstalt,*[2] to convert the floating and consolidated debt into the titles of the forced loan. According to Jèze, the wealthy class in Germany preferred the forced loan to the capital levy because as tax payers they would receive titles to some possible future income. In the period immediately after the war, however, the forced loan was not adopted, although the proposal was renewed. Finally, in January, 1922, Chancellor Wirth announced his intention of establishing a forced loan of one billion marks. After having met with considerable opposition, the measure was adopted July 20, 1922. Previously, on January 30, 1920, Holland had introduced a similar loan for the purpose of forcing Dutch capitalists to accept less than the market rate of interest in order that a part of the floating debt, amounting to 574 million florins, might be consolidated. The loan was issued at 5 per cent and levied upon those who paid tax on more than 25,000 florins of capital.[3]

The German loan was similar to this Dutch loan. Since it is probably the most important loan of its kind issued during post-war years it is desirable to mention some of its major

[1] *Revue de Science et de Législation Financières,* 1922 (Jèze).

[2] Translated, "Wealth Institution."

[3] *Revue de Science et de Législation Financières,* 1922 (Wellhoff).

provisions at this point. The German forced loan (*Zwangsanleihe*) was offered to the public at subscriptions rising from 94 on the original date of issue, July, 1922, to 100 in November, 1922, and finally to 206 in March, 1923. It was to be paid for in paper marks. The interest was 4 per cent from November 1, 1925, to October 31, 1930, and 5 per cent from that date onward. Repayment was to be made at par from November 1, 1925, through purchases at the Bourse for a sinking fund. All physical and legal persons, associations and "masses of goods" (*Vermögensmassen*) which were eligible to pay taxes on wealth from January 1, 1923, were obliged to subscribe. Some exemptions, however, were allowed. All those with fortunes of less than 100,000 marks and those with less than 1,000,000 marks capital whose income was principally composed of interest or dividends on this capital were not required to subscribe. The rates for those not exempt were 1 per cent on the first 100,000 marks, 2 per cent on the next 150,000, 4 per cent on the next 250,000, 6 per cent on the next 250,000, 8 per cent on the next 250,000, and 10 per cent on capital in excess of 1,000,000 marks. In spite of the effort devoted to the measure and the long period for which it was discussed, it proved a failure according to Jèze, for by November 20, 1922, it had yielded only 2,810 million paper marks. One has only to refer to the mounting expenses of the Reich to see that this was but a small fraction of its needs.

In France, Italy and Norway the forced loan was also agitated, but without resulting in actual adoption. The movement for the measure was relatively strong in Italy. When Nitti, as premier, expressed his intention on July 9, 1919, of imposing a capital levy to reduce the national debt, there was much opposition and a commission to study the project was set up under the finance minister, Tedesco.[4] Even as

[4] *Revue de Science et de Législation Financières*, 1922, p. 141 (Jèze).

early as December 12, 1918, Rolando Ricci had proposed in the Senate that Italy levy such a tax to the amount of 50 billion lire. The commission, however, proposed a forced loan instead of a capital levy, at 1½ per cent interest and payable in 60 to 100 years. Some members of the commission had favored a combination of a capital levy and a forced loan for the purpose of converting the war loans to a lower rate of interest, but those favoring the loan prevailed.

The government, acting on the advice of the commission, attempted to establish a forced loan, but popular sentiment was against it as the result of an adverse newspaper campaign, and the project was temporarily abandoned.[5] The government had to resort then to paper money, but another commission was selected, which again reported in favor of a forced loan, this time with an interest rate of one per cent and a term of 70 years, the whole measure to be coupled with a tax on accretions of capital value. In the face of another campaign against the measure by the press the government decided to await the general elections of November 16, 1919. Although the Socialists were victorious in the election the opposition to the measure had been so strong as to cause the adoption of a voluntary loan, a tax on war riches and a heavy inheritance tax instead. Nitti had thus yielded again to the pressure of public opinion.

In France there was little interest in the forced loan proposal immediately after the war. The capital levy attracted much greater attention. In March, 1922, when the interest in the forced loan measure was at its highest, Jèze says that there was not a majority favorable to it.[6] The forced loan was again agitated, however, in 1928 for the purpose of effecting consolidation. A forced consolidation loan was proposed by the Socialists and the measure was ardently

[5] *Ibid.*, p. 142.

[6] *Revue de Science et de Législation Financières*, 1922 (Jèze).

supported by Léon Blum. In Norway a forced loan was proposed in 1921 to pay the debts that certain large Norwegian banks had contracted and were unable at the time to liquidate, but here, as in Italy, the project was finally abandoned.

Professor Jéze, who has given this whole subject the most study, has come to the conclusion that a forced loan tends to disorganize production and inflict unequal burdens because of the difficulties involved in valuing the capital or incomes upon which it is based. It is likely to succeed only when the financial and not the general economic conditions of the country are very bad, not when both are bad, as was the case in Germany.

(b) *The Capital Levy*

An interest in the capital levy was another direct consequence of the weight of national debts in the post-war period. It was the debt which led to agitation for a capital levy in England after both the Napoleonic and World Wars. In Italy the government was outspoken in attributing its support of the capital levy to the large size of the national debt. Since the subject has received much treatment elsewhere it is not proposed to discuss it here.[7] But in most continental countries where the capital levy was proposed, the measures were closely associated with those for forced loans. This may be illustrated by the experience of Germany with the *Reichsnotopfer*. This tax, which was voted December 31, 1919, was levied on physical and legal persons. It applied not only to resident Germans but also to those domiciled abroad, and to foreigners living in Germany. The property levied upon was classified into *Grundvermögen* (land and natural resources), *Betriebsvermögen* (capital and trade property consisting of machines, vehicles, etc., serving

[7] For a brief summary of the history see Comstock, *Taxation in the Modern State*, chapter xv.

in the conduct of various kinds of industry, and circulating capital and goods held for sale) and *Kapitalvermögen* (all sorts of *rentes,* titles, credits, patent rights). Certain forms of personal property, however, were not assessed and certain types of debts might be deducted. Capital value was determined through estimates based on sales information. Thus a "pecuniary or current value" was used. Further deductions were also made possible according to the number of dependents in much the same way as under the United States income tax system. There were also deductions for those who had reached a certain age. Those forty to sixty years old whose property did not exceed 150,000 marks received a 25 per cent deduction on the first 50,000 marks and a 20 per cent deduction on the next 50,000 marks. The rates were 12 per cent on 50,000 marks, 15 per cent on 100,000 marks, rising to 65 per cent on sums over 2,000,000 marks. An important feature of the law was that payments could be made either immediately or in graduated annuities from twenty-seven to forty-six years in duration.[8]

M. Badulesco criticized the last-named feature of the tax on the ground that it deprived it of all resemblance to a capital levy by reducing the yearly payments to so small an amount. Because of this weakness and the falling value of money, a year passed without the appearance of any appreciable benefits from the *Reichsnotopfer*; it yielded only 1,357 million marks during 1920. This failure led to parliamentary discussion, in which it was proposed both to modify the *Reichsnotopfer* and to adopt a forced loan, the Conservatives forcing the latter. In 1920 Finance Minister Wirth was advised by the cabinet to secure measures for the rapid collection of the levy.[9] Havenstein, the director of the

[8] For more complete details see *Revue de Science et de Législation Financières*, 1921, p. 23 (V. V. Badulesco).

[9] *Ibid.*, p. 39.

Reichsbank, made a speech on Wirth's behalf to the Reichstag in which he advocated a combination of the forced loan and the *Reichsnotopfer*. This combination was finally adopted, although it was strenuously opposed by Helferrich and the National Party. The People's Party was also opposed to the combination, but the Democrats and Centrists, who were backing the law, insisted that the People's Party either accept the plan or leave the coalition through which it, the Democrats and the Centrists controlled the government. The People's Party yielded and a law was adopted December 18, 1920, modifying the *Reichsnotopfer*.

The new law made the facultative payment under the 1919 law obligatory. Although a part of the tax could still be postponed the delayed payments must be made in no more than three installments and these over a short period of time. Another portion could be paid in annuities. One-tenth of the tax was to be paid immediately if the amount of the property was less than 1,000,000 marks, and one-third to be paid at once in case of larger property. The actual passage of a forced loan act was delayed and, as has been stated above, did not appear until 1922. The law of December, 1920, also turned out badly as a fiscal device. By June, 1921, it had yielded the treasury only fifteen billion marks and ten of these were the depreciated titles of old loans. By this time the money circulation had risen to over 75,000,000,000 marks and one dollar was worth 75.15 marks. It was then that the movement for a forced loan began to gain ground, culminating in its adoption in 1922.

The forced loan of Germany thus grew out of the failure of the capital levy, as was the case in Italy; in fact, the very conception of the forced loan is only a step from the capital levy. It was decided that since public sentiment could not be sufficiently aroused for a levy it might be stimulated by the prospect of a loan. The loan law as passed in Germany resembles the levy. The subscriptions were to be made by much the same persons. Property was divided for the purpose of the loan into *Grundsvermögen, Betriebsvermögen* and *Sonstiges Vermögen.* The expectation that the capital levy would check the rise in the issue of paper currency was abandoned and hope was now placed in the forced loan. It is apparent that the forced loan and *Reichsnotopfer* failed largely for the same reasons, the failure to collect the whole amount in a short time, the rapid rise in the quantity of paper money, and the various difficulties and expenses that made it virtually impossible for the state to balance its budget. In view of these facts it is possible to be too hasty in condemning the forced loan. Where it was applied as a threat under less straitened circumstances, as in New Zealand and Australia, it proved more successful. It is apparent that the measure is needed only in case of great financial difficulty; yet at those times it is most likely to be a failure.

In addition to the forced loan, which, as has just been shown, was closely associated with the capital levy, other new [10] debt forms appeared, the chief examples of which were new forms of treasury bills and of intermediate credit, and debt issued in payment of war damages, loan liquidation debt, debts to state banks, debt issues by special autonomous bodies, and small savings debt.

(c) *The "Small Savings" Debt*

In England, France and the United States the burden of war gave rise to added facilities for the small saver. In the United States, War Savings Stamps and Certificates and Thrift Stamps were introduced in very small denominations in 1917. In July, 1919, the Treasury made a change by adding new certificates with denominations of one hun-

[10] The word "new" is here used relatively since forced loans have been used in earlier times.

dred and a thousand dollars. These were called Treasury Savings Certificates, and were issued on the same discount basis as the War Savings Certificates. Redemption and registration were directly through the Treasury office instead of through post offices, but the new certificates were similar to the old ones in that they could be redeemed prior to maturity. In 1921 the existing forms of certificates were continued, but in addition there were projected three new forms on the same plan as the old but with new names: Treasury Savings Stamps for one dollar, Treasury Savings Cards, and Treasury Savings Certificates with a maturity value of twenty-five dollars. In 1922 the basis of issue for the Treasury Savings Certificates was changed. These were now issued at a fixed rate of eighty dollars per hundred dollars certificate, giving an annual interest rate of about 4½ per cent, since they matured in five years from the date of issue. The old certificates matured at a fixed date. The twenty-five-cent Thrift Stamp[11] and the five-dollar War Savings Stamp were discontinued at the end of 1921 on the ground that the ten-cent Postal Savings Stamp and the one-dollar Treasury Savings Stamp removed the need for these forms of security. On October 1, 1922, the selling price of Savings Certificates was increased to eighty-two dollars per hundred in order to take advantage of the easier money conditions. On September 30, 1922, one-dollar Treasury Stamps were discontinued and withdrawn from sale. In November the Treasury announced that holders of 1918 War Savings Certificates could exchange them at maturity for Treasury Savings Certificates. On December 1, 1923, the sales price of these certificates was changed back to eighty dollars per hundred. The Treasury was able to report at this time that the exchange of 1918 War Savings Certificates

[11] These stamps were non-interest-bearing, as is the new Treasury Savings Stamp.

was gratifying and it now offered to exchange 1919 War Certificates for Treasury Certificates. However, the issue of these certificates ceased in 1924 and they passed out of American public debt on July 15, 1929, when a small amount of the series of 1924 was retired.[12]

In Great Britain the issue of War Savings Certificates began in February, 1916, at the rate of 15 s. 6 d. for every one pound certificate repayable at par five years from the date of issue and free of income tax. This form of debt was retained for the purpose of stimulating savings among the poorer members of the population, although there has been a movement on foot to discard it. Investment in these certificates has proved popular and there has been a very considerable increase of it since the war. Beginning with only £1,387,000 in 1916 the amount increased to £273,541,000 in 1920 and £363,448,000 in 1928.[13]

In France securities similar to those in England and the United States were not issued because the form taken by the *Bons de la Défense Nationale* made this unnecessary. Although these *Bons* were issued in the beginning in larger denominations, the denominations were eventually reduced to as low as five and twenty francs.[14] They were issued at a discount, which closely resembles the practice in the case of English and United States securities. The small denominations, the convenience of purchase and the popular appeals made were the same as in the United States and England and must have produced similar results.

[12] See *Annual Reports of the Secretary of the Treasury*, 1919-23 and 1929.

[13] Fisk, *English Public Finance*; and Great Britain: *Finance Accounts*, 1929.

[14] Fisk, *French Public Finance*, p. 15.

(d) *The Growth of Indirect Borrowing*

In addition to the increase in small loan facilities, there was in both France and Germany, as a result of the war, a growth of indirect borrowing. Loans of this form in Germany ceased to have any importance after inflation, but they now are an important part of French public finance. In Germany during the war there were issued *Darlehenskassenscheine*—"*bons des caisses de prêts de guerre*," according to Rist, which may be translated "bonds of the War Loan Offices". Such loans had been made during the Revolution of 1848, in 1866, and again in 1870. Paper money was issued by these offices in loans based on commercial paper, merchandise, and on industrial titles and deposits in savings banks. The loans were for three months and usually at 5 per cent interest. The minimum amount loaned was 100 marks. Thus in Germany paper money was issued by bodies relatively independent of the state on the basis of ordinary trade obligations. These loans in the form of paper money were made on commercial transactions of the smaller variety, leaving the banks free to make larger loans on government bonds. The practice was ostensibly caused by the law of March 14, 1875, which prohibited the issue of paper money by banks on titles with less than three names. The creation of special offices to do this work seemed a simpler solution than the alteration of the banking law.[15] The result was to facilitate borrowing by the government indirectly by lessening the burden on the banks, an arrangement which amounted in practice to the French measures of actual indirect borrowing. These *Darlehenskassenscheine* attained a large volume. Established by the General Reichsbank Law of 1914, at the end of 1918 they totalled 32,936,700,000 marks.[16] Had

[15] Rist, *Les Finances de guerre d'Allemagne*, pp. 37, 39, 44, 65, 99, 103 *et seq.*, 242, 248, 281.

[16] Graham, F. D., *Exchange, Prices and Production in Hyper-Inflation—Germany.*

severe inflation not occurred later, these debts would have constituted an important factor in German post-war finance.

Indirect borrowing is now of importance only in France, where the government has set up two relatively independent bodies for that purpose: the *Crédit National* and the *Caisse Autonome*. The *Crédit National* was established in 1919 for the issue of loans in payment of war damages—the War Damage Liquidation Certificates.[17] Of it Rogers says: "Although established as a joint stock company with shares held by the general public, in its functions it is little more than a department of the Treasury." The *Crédit National* receives funds from the state to pay the interest on these obligations and the organization, although technically separate, is selected and controlled by the state. Its chief officials are nominated by the president on the suggestion of the French minister of finance and the council of the administration. At the end of 1925 its loans had reached 25,632 millions of francs and the annual charge for these loans was about 1,722 millions of francs.[18] In 1928 the *Émissions* of the *Crédit National* amounted to 5,535 millions and the *Obligations* to 14,429 millions.[19] The total debt of the *Crédit National* had thus shown a decrease from 25,632 millions to 19,964 millions in three years. The explanation of the decrease is a law of August 7, 1926, authorizing the optional consolidation of the bonds of the *Crédit National* issued in 1922, the *Bons du Trésor* of 1923 for 36 and 10 years, the *Obligations Décennales* and the *Bons de la Défense Nationale* into 6 per cent *rentes amortissables* by drawings in 50 years

[17] Rogers, J. H., *The Process of Inflation in France*. See also Fisk, *French Public Finance*, pp. 91-2.

[18] *Revue de Science et de Législation Financières*, 1925 (Jèze).

[19] *Annuaire Statistique*, 1929, p. 275. The debt of this body is of two varieties: *Émissions* and *Obligations*. These forms of debt have maturities varying from one to thirty years, the *Émissions* lasting for a shorter period than the *Obligations*.

and with a premium of repayment of fifty per cent.[20] Jèze regarded the independence of the *Crédit National* as fictitious and useless. "*L'utilité de ce rouage est nulle. Le crédit du Crédit National n'était plus fort que celui de l'état. . . . Pratiquement le Crédit National est devenu, presque tout de suite, une annexe du ministère des finances.*" [21] The minister of finance authorizes the issues of bonds and fixes the conditions of issue and the state funds supply the service of the obligations.

The *Caisse Autonome d'Amortissement de la Dette Publique* is a somewhat more independent body. Besides its greater independence, another important difference between it and the *Crèdit National* is that the latter is a joint stock company of peculiar type. Its statutes are approved by the Administrative Council. The management of its funds is subjected to the general audit of the state. The authority to do its work arises out of a convention concluded at the organization of the body which charged it with the finance of war damages and invested it with certain special financial powers.[22] The *Caisse*, however, is a separate governmental institution virtually on a par with Parliament, because it was created by the National Assembly. The details of the *Caisse's* organization will be discussed more fully in the chapter on sinking funds and the methods of amortization. Its greater independence was acquired partly through the allocation of special revenues to it, such as the net profits of the tobacco monopoly and the products of the taxes on the *première mutation* and the tax on the *droits de succession*. It likewise depends on an annuity from the state and Parliament has the right to modify its charges or to prohibit them. It can also reduce the above-mentioned taxes.

[20] Allix, *Science des finances*, p. 790.

[21] *Revue de Science et de Législation Financières*, 1927, p. 643 (Jèze).

[22] *Ibid.*, p. 641.

Of principal interest are the reasons for the autonomy of the borrowing processes created in these two cases. According to Jèze in the case of the *Crédit National* there were many personal and political influences at work. There was also a strong sentiment in favor of separating the funds intended for war sufferers from the other funds of the Treasury. It was believed that the money borrowed for the war sufferers would not be turned over to them if the Treasury alone was responsible. It was also believed that if the funds really did reach the sufferers, loans would be more readily granted by the public. The *Caisse* and its separation from the state arise mainly out of two needs, compulsory debt retirement and a body to specialize in the management and funding of the great French floating debt. The failure of the state in both of these respects in the years before the *Caisse's* organization naturally led to the desire for a separation of these functions from those of ordinary government. It is also true that France has always been much influenced by the ideas of Price and although in the history of the sinking fund in that country, the Price form of sinking fund has been abandoned for a long period, its influence was so great as to make the idea of a special sinking fund body still popular.[28]

It is interesting to note the similarity between these credit institutions and the War Finance Corporation and Reconstruction Finance Corporation of the United States. Both of these latter bodies are similar to those discussed above in that they are separate and non-governmental, and borrow from certain portions of the public for the benefit of the whole, or at least for the benefit of those who would logically be responsibilities of the general public.

[28] The whole subject of recent sinking fund history will be discussed at a later point.

(e) *The Increase in Central Bank Borrowing*

The burdens of the war and of debt have given rise to a great increase in the amount of borrowing from central banks. Thus in Great Britain there were no Ways and Means Advances in 1915 but in 1916 they were £19,896,000; in 1917, £217,527,000; in 1918, £192,271,000; and in 1919, £454,992,000. Beginning with 1920 the British government made strenuous efforts to reduce the debt to the Bank. In that year it was reduced to £204,887,000, in 1921 to £154,489,000, and in 1922 to £147,302,000. In 1923, however, much of this advantage was lost, for the volume increased to £193,898,000, but from that date onward it declined progressively until 1927, when it had reached £116,601,000. The difficulties of recent years have caused again a considerable increase, and the total amount of these advances in 1928 was £161, 850,000.[24] It is generally believed that they had a tendency to increase the price level in England and it was largely because of the fear of this consequence and the pressure of public opinion that efforts were made to reduce them. The whole problem was thoroughly examined by the Committee on Currency and Foreign Exchanges after the War, headed by Lord Cunliffe. In accordance with the advice of this committee there was introduced a policy of limiting the advances to the sums required for meeting purely temporary necessities. It is obvious from the above data that although this policy may be followed, in practice the amount of borrowing by means of bank advances is far above what it was in pre-war years and that the volume in 1928 was larger than it had been seven years earlier.[25]

In Germany the bank loans of war years have disappeared with inflation, but in more recent years two bank loans have

[24] *Finance Accounts*, 1929.

[25] *Colwyn Report*, p. 34.

been contracted, one to the Rentenbank, the other to the Reichsbank. The debt to the latter was incurred on account of deliveries of foreign exchange to the government. Of this debt, which amounted to 190 million Reichsmarks in 1929, 100 millions are due only in the event of liquidation of the Reichsbank and not before October, 1947. The debt bears an interest rate of 2 per cent. The remainder is payable in 15 installments of 9,030,000 Reichsmarks and bears 3 per cent interest.[26]

The French floating debt consists mainly of bank loans and treasury paper. Advances from the Bank of France were particularly relied upon to meet the immediate needs of the country during the war. This policy was severely attacked by men like Jèze, who believed in a greater use of taxes, but it was advocated by Leroy-Beaulieu, Ribot, and many others of sufficient prominence to get it a wide following.

In France as in Germany a special convention existed, ratified in 1911, of which the government took advantage at the outbreak of the war to borrow 2.9 billion francs from the Bank of France. In return for this loan the Bank was allowed to increase its note issue to 5.2 billions. Legal limits were set to these advances, which during the five years ended June, 1919, were increased no less than eight times. By this time the limit had risen to 27 billion francs. For six years there were no increases and by April, 1925, the limit had actually decreased four billions. Four increases during the Caillaux ministry, however, brought the total up to 39½ billions. After the stabilization of the franc this level was reduced to 32 billions and a convention of December 28, 1927, reduced the limit to 31 billions. The legal limit of note circulation was closely articulated with the advances to the state and it had reached 58½ billions in 1925.[27]

[26] League of Nations, *Memorandum on Public Finance*, 1926-28.

[27] Haig, *Public Finances of Post-war France*, pp. 201-4.

As in England, the government really intended these advances to be temporary, but they became permanent because of pressing public needs. The first great French war loan was floated late in 1915 and yielded only 6,300,000,000 francs, whereas 7.4 billions had already been borrowed from the Bank. Out of this loan the government could repay only 2.4 billions of bank debt. Five months later it was necessary to reborrow the entire amount. Similar results followed in the three other war loans and instead of the government coming more nearly to paying its debts to the Bank it fell progressively behind.[28] But Professor Haig has demonstrated that these remained constant in terms of pre-war francs (1913). He says, " When deflated and stated in terms of 1913 francs these advances of the Bank of France to the State show a tendency to remain remarkably constant." [29] Thus actual purchasing power was not greatly increased by the advances. One important factor tending to increase the reliance of the state upon them was their low cost. The interest was never over one per cent and at times the Bank relinquished from one-fourth to three-fourths of the total interest for the amortization of the loan. As early as September, 1914, the Treasury promised that it would begin to credit the amortization account with 2 per cent of the amount of the advances, making a total debt service of 3 per cent, operative one year after the close of hostilities. This was to be maintained even after the interest had been cut. Since such a program could not be accomplished at the end of the war, a new convention was arranged in which the state agreed to reduce the advances on January 1, 1921, by a sum of not less than two billion francs. The arrangement was postponed for a year. The following year the plan was put into operation and the limit dropped two billions. But it could not be

[28] *Ibid.*, p. 211.

[29] *Ibid.*, p. 211.

carried out consistently and in 1923 the limit dropped only one billion, in 1924 only 800 millions and by January 1, 1925, only 1.2 billions. No further reduction was made until January 1, 1927, when the limit dropped two billions. On June 13, 1927, a convention was agreed upon, to take effect January 1, 1928, providing a reduction of the Bank advances by a sum equal to the face value of the 6 per cent amortizable obligations issued in June and July, 1927. The result of this procedure is to convert short- into long-term obligations.[80]

It thus appears that both France and England have had large and troublesome bank debts which they have made an effort to reduce, but that their progress toward this end has been slow. Hence the bank debt has become a relatively fixed part of the post-war debt of these two important countries.

(f) *The Loan Liquidation Debt*

In addition to the increase in bank debt two new forms of debt have appeared in France and Germany: debt for the reconstruction of devastated areas and the payment of war damages in France, and the loan liquidation debt in Germany. The last of these is of most interest. In the first report of the Agent General for Reparations appears the following statement:

> The present value (September 1924) of the old paper mark debt of the Reich unless it should be increased by revalorization amounts to less than 1000 reichsmarks. The government has recently made proposals for revaluing a portion of this old debt, and a bill is now pending in the Reichstag under which it would be revalorized under certain conditions at about four milliards of reichsmarks. Until further action has been taken, it is impossible to give definite figures as to the effect that this will have either upon the principal of the debt or the annual

[80] *Ibid.*, pp. 217-218.

charge for its service. Whatever the resulting charge, it must be clear, of course, that it will be subordinate at all times to the charge for reparations. This in fact is expressly recognized by the bill which the Government has presented.[31]

The bill was subsequently enacted and in 1925 the old debts were converted by the loan-liquidation debt at rates varying according to the year of issue of the old debt, the basic rate being 25 gold marks to 1000 nominal marks. Those who could prove that they had become owners of their securities before July, 1920, or that they had acquired them before July, 1923, in consequence of a legal obligation to invest in trustee stock were given yearly drawing rights for the retirement of the debt in thirty years, beginning in 1926. The amount drawn will be paid for in cash at the end of the drawing year at five times the nominal amount of the new securities, i. e. at five times 2.5 per cent, or 12.5 per cent of the old nominal amount, plus 4.5 per cent interest running from January 1, 1926, to the end of the year in which the drawing takes place.[32] Necessitous German holders of drawing rights who are domiciled in Germany are entitled to special preferential treatment. They are to receive annuities amounting to 80 per cent of the nominal value of the drawing rights, but subject to a maximum of 800 Reichsmarks annually for any one person. This maximum is increased to 1000 if the creditor definitely renounces his drawing rights and to 1200 Reichsmarks if the creditor is sixty years of age at the date of such renunciation. Social and scientific institutions may receive special relief annuities for fifteen years, the total amount of which is limited to 10,000,000 Reichsmarks annually. In spite of these elaborate provisions the

[31] *Execution of the Experts' Plan, Reparations Commission, First Annuity Year*, p. 39.

[32] League of Nations, *Memorandum on Public Finance*, 1926-28, p. 72.

debt does not yield interest until the reparations liabilities have been discharged.

(g) *The War Damage Debt*

In both Germany and France war-damage debt has been issued. In Germany War Damage Liquidation Certificates are issued to meet claims to the claimants themselves. These certificates bear 6 per cent interest from April 1, 1929, and are to be redeemed in March, 1948, with preferential redemption of smaller claims. It is expected that the total amount of these certificates will be 1,000 million Reichsmarks. In France, although in part the war damages are being met by the work of the *Crédit National*, indemnities to persons have been paid in much the same way by the issue to them of debt in the form of *Obligations du Trésor*.[33]

(h) *Contractual Debt and Guaranteed Loans*

Another important change that has taken place in the form of debt in Europe since the war has been the enormous increase in contractual debt, or debt with fixed rates of interest and dates of maturity. Examination of the financial statements of any important country in Europe before and after the war will demonstrate this. Guaranteed loans have also increased in importance. They have played a significant role in public credit for many years. From the time of the Greek loan of 1829, France, England and Russia have guaranteed the interest and principal of a great number of loans. These have taken the form of both personal and real guarantees, according to Professor Jèze. Real guarantees consist either in the turning over of certain revenues to the creditors for their collection or in the establishment of special guarantee funds. A loan made to France by the Morgan bank

[33] Allix, E., *Science des finances*. Since 1923 the *obligations décennales* have been used instead of money to pay indemnities.

on March 11, 1924, payable in gold, was thought to be an example of the latter, because certain parts of the loan stipulations were interpreted to mean that the gold of the Bank of France was surety for the payment of the loan. The Hungarian loan of 1924 was another excellent example of the latter type, because it had a definite guarantee in customs, tobacco, salt monopoly, sugar tax, and other receipts. An American commissioner general, Jeremiah Smith, was stationed in Hungary to supervise the management of the funds provided for the loans, and was given very wide powers in this respect.

The Dawes Report advocated a guaranteed loan of 800 million gold marks to be based on specified revenues and supervised by a commissioner. It was also suggested that it be given international personal guarantees, and special revenues, such as the receipts from customs, alcohol, beer and sugar taxes, were to be attached. The Agent General for the loan was to receive payments from these sources for the service of the debt.[34] The loan was made in November, 1924, and has been known as the German External Loan. The general revenues, rights to the customs, tobacco, beer and sugar taxes are guaranteed to pay the service of the loan. It was payable in twenty-five years and a sinking fund of one and one-half per cent was provided. The amount of the loan was 800,000,000 gold marks. The object of the loan was to insure currency stability. It might also be added that the Dawes plan itself resembles a guaranteed loan of the type set up in Hungary.

The Austrian loan of 1923 represents the most elaborate of these post-war guaranteed loans and has personal guarantees. The amount of the loan was 650 million crowns. It was issued in ten countries and guaranteed for its principal and interest in the following proportions: 21.8

[34] *Revue de Science et de Législation Financières*, 1925, p. 54 (Jèze).

per cent each by France, England and Czechoslovakia, 18.6 per cent by Italy, 2 per cent by Sweden and Denmark, 1 per cent by Holland and 4 per cent by Spain. A committee of control was established. If this committee was notified by the Austrian government of that government's inability to pay interest or principal, it informed the guaranteeing countries, which within the next ten days were required to issue to the committee their own bonds, to be placed in the National Bank of Switzerland to guarantee the defaulted amounts. Interest at one-half per cent more than that paid by Austria would then have to be paid by these governments on their bonds, if Austria defaulted for more than fifteen days. Coupons of the bonds so deposited would be sent by the committee to the Austrian bond holders.[35]

(i) *Lottery Loans*

Lottery loans have also increased in importance since the war. In England and the United States they have been attacked on ethical grounds. In England, after they had been praised by several members of Parliament in 1915 as a means of getting the worker to increase his savings, a commission was established to investigate the matter.[36] It reported unfavorably, but the loans were agitated, chiefly by members of the Conservative party, all through 1916. A committee for propaganda was formed and in 1917 the Council of the Chamber of Commerce voted a resolution favorable to them. In 1917 Bonar Law, who was then Chancellor of the Exchequer, consented to have the whole question reexamined by the Select Committee on Premium Bonds. This committee reported unfavorably in January, 1918. A Lotteries and War Charities Bill was introduced, however, but it was finally rejected in August, 1918. After

[35] *Ibid.*, p. 274.

[36] *Ibid.*, 1919, pp. 55-56.

the war the French government was refused the right of offering a lottery loan in the British market.[37]

These loans have long been used in France. In 1919 André Lefèvre, a former undersecretary of state, advocated their use for the payment of indemnities to war victims. Klotz, who was minister of finance, was not opposed to this plan and when the *Crédit National* was created, to facilitate the payment of war damages, it was allowed to emit such loans. Belgium, which had not issued lottery loans prior to the war, also authorized their issue on January 27, 1920, to the amount of 5 billion francs. On January 2, 1921, the Fédération des Coopératives pour Dommages de Guerre was also allowed to issue them.[38]

II. CHANGES IN THE MATURITIES OF DEBT

(a) *The Relative Increase in Short-term Debt*

Turning from these more specific changes to certain more general changes in the form of debts, we find that most of the countries of the world show a growth in the proportion of short-term and intermediate forms of debt as a consequence of the war, and that new types of relatively short-term debt have been devised to facilitate the problems of recurring maturities. These facts are easily seen when one examines the statements of the public debts before and after the war in the leading countries of the world. The debt of the United States in 1914 consisted mainly of the old unretired debt, the Panama Canal loans and postal savings bonds. There was virtually no floating debt, most of the debt being composed of unredeemed titles. In Germany at the end of the war there were 96 billion marks of funded debt and 45 billion marks of unfunded debt, as against 4,698 millions of funded and only 220 millions of unfunded debt before the

[37] *Ibid.*, pp. 55-75 (Jèze).

[38] *Ibid.*, 1923, pp. 191-199.

war. The United Kingdom had about £33 millions of floating debt before the war as against a total of £706 millions after the war. In France the floating debt was only about 6 per cent of the total and in Italy only 5½ per cent just before the war. It is apparent that the various definitions of floating debts make comparisons between countries dangerous, but there is a sufficient degree of similarity to illustrate the point we are making.[39]

In their floating debt most countries have made increased use of the treasury bill, in the United States termed certificates of indebtedness, in France the *Bons de la Défense Nationale,* and in Germany the *Reichskassenscheine.* For many years during the post-war period these titles, mainly for less than one year's maturity, have played an important role in increasing the difficulties of debt management.

In England the treasury bill is the successor of the exchequer bill, which originated in 1696. It was used to effect a more even adjustment between the flow of funds into the Treasury and public expenses. The exchequer bills were similar to the American certificates of indebtedness in that they bore interest. The treasury bill, however, which was introduced in 1877 is sold at a discount to the Bank of England and is then resold to other banks. The rates of discount are fixed through bidding.

In the United States the old form of certificates of indebtedness came into increased use and was issued at fixed rates four times a year at par. On December 17, 1929, the old form was supplemented by the new treasury bill, issued in imitation of English practice. These bills are offered at a discount at indeterminate dates to meet the varying needs of the government, the discount being fixed by competitive bidding. They may have a maturity as great as one year, but the policy of the Treasury has been to limit their maturities

[39] See Fisk, *French Public Finance*, pp. 131-2.

to three months.[40] These bills were made tax-exempt except for gains obtained from their sale, but since in actual practice little or no gain could be derived from this source and unduly complicated bookkeeping was necessary to carry out the law, they were made entirely tax-exempt on June 17, 1930. The Treasury states, " By the close of the last fiscal year (1930) Treasury bills were established as one of the important means for short-term financing. . . ." [41] The amount of these bills outstanding June 30, 1930, was $155,-916,000. On the same date certificates of indebtedness amounted to $1,264,354,500.

In France this form of debt was used to such an extent that it constituted a fiscal problem of the utmost importance.[42] The *Bons de la Défense Nationale* were in very small denominations, as was noted above, as well as in 100, 500 and 1000 franc denominations. They were at first sold at a discount, which was unlike that of the English treasury bill, since it was set by the government and not by competitive bidding. The *Bons* were purchased more widely by the general public than the treasury bills of England and the American certificates of indebtedness and a more strenuous effort was made to further such purchases.[43]

Thus it is seen that England, France and the United States were alike in the increased use of short-term debt and in the attempt to encourage the general public rather than the banks to invest in it. In the United States, where it has been uncommon to issue debt at a discount, the form of short-dated

[40] *Annual Report of Secretary of the Treasury*, 1930, p. 23.

[41] *Ibid.*, p. 23.

[42] Haig, *Public Finances of Post-war France*, chap. xii.

[43] In Germany the floating debt was discounted first at the Reichsbank and then turned over to other large banks, savings banks, cooperatives, and large industrial concerns. The form and procedure were much the same as in England.

debt has differed from that of England, while the French debt constitutes a cross between this fixed date and interest form and the flexible English variety.

(b) *The Relative Increase in Intermediate Debt*

Post-war debt was also characterized by a growth of intermediate debt. This resulted from the greater ease of refunding at such maturities than with perpetual and long-term debt. In France, the intermediate debt is represented by the *Obligations* and *Bons du Trésor*; in the United States by treasury notes, and in England by the treasury bonds. In France the term *Obligation* as applied to the debt has no very precise meaning. In the reports of the French government the *Obligations* are divided between the *Dette perpetuelle* and the *Dette à moyen et à court terme*. In the former category are included *Obligations* of the state railways, which are payable in fifty years, and *Obligations* of the *Caisse Autonome* and the *Crédit National*. Some of the bonds of the *Crédit National* are also payable at long term, such as the 5's of 1919 and 1920, which are not due for seventy-five years from the date of issue. The 6's of 1921, however, were repayable at par in fifteen years. It is not clear at what point these bonds cease to be *Obligations* and become *Émissions*. Yet it is certain that some of the more recent issues of the *Crédit National* have been of the intermediate variety.

The *Obligations du Trésor* are more nearly intermediate in character. They are for two, three, six and ten years,[44] and their maturity may range from one to thirty years. They are issued in denominations of 100, 500 and 1000 francs and have increased in popularity since the war because of the fear of a rise in prices. Allix makes a distinction between *Obligations "à court et à long terme,"* the dividing

[44] Allix, *Science des finances*, pp. 314, 325.

line being at the fifteen-year maturity. There are two types: *Obligations* of fifteen-year maturity, created in 1873 and 1875 by the National Assembly, and the thirty-year *Obligations* of the second empire which were used to obtain railroad capital. Allix points out that there was only one kind of *Obligation à court terme* before the war. These were the *Obligations sexennales* of 1875 which arose from the budget needs of the war of 1870. In 1928 there were several varieties of the *Obligations du Trésor* but in addition there were four varieties of the *Obligations de la Défense Nationale,* with maturities of from six to ten years.[45]

In addition to the *Obligations,* there were in 1927 four types of *Bons du Trésor,* with maturities of three, six, and ten years, and the *Bons décennaux* of 1926.[46] There was, of course, no such variety of maturities before the war.

In addition to these forms, the *Émissions du Crédit National* may be classified as intermediate debt. These include *Bons* of 1921 of 10 to 15 years, *Bons* of February, 1922, at 2, 5 and 10 years, *Bons* of July, 1922, at 3, 6, 12 and 18 years, and two other varieties at 25 years. Although the debt terminology is very indefinite, it can be readily seen from these facts that many types of debt with intermediate maturities have been used.

In the United States the treasury note made its appearance in 1921 and was given a maturity of two years. The Third Liberty loan, with its ten-year maturity, was a similar intermediate form of debt. Some of the treasury bonds now provide this kind of investment as the date of their maturity approaches. The treasury bonds of 1940-43 issued in 1929 are of this form.

In England in 1921 treasury bonds of three kinds were

[45] Palmade Report, *Revue de Science et de Législation Financières,* 1930.

[46] See *Bulletin de Statistique et de Législation,* 1927.

issued: at 4½ per cent payable in 1932, 4½ per cent payable in 1934, and 4 per cent payable in 1931-33.

The war and the post-war financial burdens have thus led to manifold changes in the form of the public debt in the principal countries of the world. These changes have, through increasing the variety of borrowing conditions, afforded much greater opportunities to the investor. This advantage, which has been too much praised, was gained at certain costs, the most important of which is the increase in the floating debt. But not only have changes in the form of debt arisen from the financial difficulties: there has also appeared the practice of tax exemption and the problems that attend it.

III. TAX EXEMPTION

In France loans were issued with tax exemption except from the inheritance tax and the *impôt sur le revenu global*. In 1927, acording to Professor Haig, over half the interest on the public debt was exempt from income taxes, both normal and surtaxes. Almost all of the remainder was exempt from the normal or "*cédulaire*" tax.[47] This policy was initiated during the regime of Ribot, who came into office in September, 1914.

In England at the beginning of the war tax exemption was timidly introduced, being first provided in 1915 by the War Loan Act for small subscribers, under which bonds were registered in post offices. The Finance Act of 1916 extended exemption to all subscribers of exchequer bonds and by degrees the immunity spread to other parts of the debt. After the war, however, a Royal Commission set up in April, 1919, made a report in which it favored the retention of the income tax on all debt interest. The Conversion Loan of April 26, 1921, accordingly lacked immunity clauses. The

[47] Haig, *op. cit.*, p. 199.

Victory and Funding Loan and Conversion Bonds also had no exemption. Immunity was retained for savings certificates in order to induce savings.[48]

In Italy the interest on debt titles was free from taxation of most kinds and in particular from income and property taxes, both present and future, up to the end of the nineteenth century. After 1900 inheritance and succession taxes had to be paid, although there was a legal fiction of universal tax exemption for debt holders. Laws passed in 1919 and 1920 removed this exemption by placing taxes on all nominal titles. A law under Mussolini's regime in 1922 removed such taxes and restored the exemption.[49]

In the United States tax exemption was provided in Section 2 of the Victory Loan Act, which exempted all Liberty Bonds and Victory Notes from all United States, state and local taxes except estate taxes and graduated additional income or surtaxes. The interest on the capital sum of five thousand dollars of the aggregate surtax could be deducted in the case of 4 and 4½ per cent bonds. The interest on thirty thousand dollars was allowed for the first, second and fourth Liberty Loans for two years after the termination of the war. Three and a half and three and three quarters notes are exempt from all taxes except estate taxes.

IV. CONVERSION AND REFUNDING OF THE DEBT

(a) *In France*

The war burden of debt has not only resulted in new forms of debt and tax exemption, both of which were introduced because of the low state of public credit, but also in efforts by those managing the debt to reduce its burden through conversion. In the remainder of this chapter the history of conversion and the short-term debt in four countries, the United

48 See Jèze, *Revue de Science et de Législation Financières*, 1923.

49 *Ibid.*, pp. 581-91.

States, France, Great Britain and Germany, will be briefly discussed.

Professor Haig has estimated that at the end of 1926 the public debt of France amounted to approximately 500 billion paper francs. This was equivalent to about 80 billion pre-war francs. " She has collected from her investors vast sums, the repayment of which she is now in a position partly to escape as a result of the process of inflation." [50] During this period 285 billions of paper francs were borrowed, but only 100.4 billions in pre-war francs were actually received. A glance at the debt figures for France given in Chapter II shows that the total debt, both domestic and foreign, increased from 32,594 millions of francs in 1913 to 324,321 millions in 1920 and to 470,037 millions in 1928. The post-war increase was due mainly to the rise in the funded internal debt and the external debt. The floating debt had reached 85,573 millions in 1920, and although it subsequently rose to the peak of 98,900 millions in 1925, the median amount for these years was about 92,000 millions. Compared to the funded and foreign debt it shows relative stability. But in spite of this, the size of the floating debt constitutes one of the most important debt problems of post-war France. This floating debt consists chiefly of the *Bons de la Dèfense Nationale* and the *Avances Nouvelles de la Banque de France*. In 1926, for example, there were 49,075 millions of *Bons* and 34,000 millions of *Avances* out of a total floating debt of 93,526 millions.

The *Bons de la Défense Nationale* constituted the most difficult post-war problem in internal debt. In 1924, as Professor Jèze points out, 52 per cent of these had maturities of one year, 23 per cent of six months, 11 per cent of three months and 14 per cent of one month. The amount of the *Bons* outstanding in 1924 was 54,723 millions. This meant

[50] Haig, *op. cit.*, p. 184.

that somewhere in the neighborhood of seven billions would fall due each month, since the proportion of one-month maturities was fairly constant during these years.[51] Such large and immediate maturities were obviously a source of great danger to the government and the fact was frequently remarked upon in political circles, although without any effective action being taken.

It must not be supposed that no funding was accomplished. During the war, from 1915 to 1918, *rentes* were issued which were paid for to a large extent out of other loans.[52] About half of the 5's of 1915 were paid for in this way. Even more than half of the 4's of 1918 were thus paid. The payments were chiefly made in *Bons de la Défense Nationale* and the issue of the *rentes* really amounted to the consolidation of these *Bons*. In 1920, 15,940 millions of 5 per cent *rentes amortissables*,[53] and the 6 per cent loan of 1920 were issued. The latter yielded 28,088 millions. More than half of the 5 per cent *amortissables* were paid for with *Bons de la Défense Nationale*.[54] On February 21, 1923, a law was passed authorizing the issue of *valeurs du trésor*, not to exceed ten years maturity, as a means of repaying the short term loans, and also of *Bons du Trêsor* up to 13 billions with ten years maturity. Proposals of forced consolidation were made in 1924.

Difficulties arising from the war and the failure to balance the budget led finally to strenuous efforts at consolidation in 1925 and 1926. Another issue of approximately six billions of 4 per cent *rentes* appeared in 1925. The Herriot government fell in this year and Painlevé became premier, with

[51] See Appendix I for the circulation of *Bons*.

[52] Fisk, *French Public Finance*, p. 20.

[53] This loan was payable in 60 years and was regarded as one of the most onerous loans ever issued in France.

[54] Fisk, p. 18.

Caillaux as his minister of finance. Caillaux advocated three measures: (1) an increase of paper money to the amount of 6 billion francs, (2) the consolidation of the debt by the issue of 4 per cent perpetual *rentes,* (3) the reduction of the allied debts.

One of the most important episodes in the Caillaux Ministry was the Conversion Loan.[55] This was issued June 27, 1925, and consisted of 4 per cent perpetual *rentes* with immunity from taxes on the *valeurs mobilières* and the *revenu global.* The maximum of the floating debt would be fixed at the amount of the debt at the close of the loan. The rate of exchange was guaranteed so that the amount of interest paid would always bear a fixed relationship to the British pound. A further measure taken by Caillaux to strengthen the loan was to remove from the renewed *Bons de la Défense Nationale* the exemption from the tax on the *revenu global.* The loan was a failure in that it yielded very little reduction in the supply of treasury bills, producing only 5,929 millions of francs. At the end of October, 1925, the Cabinet decided to rid itself of Caillaux by resigning in a body and Painlevé formed a new ministry in which he personally took charge of the finances. The government was not, however, successful in reducing the floating debt. By 1926 the situation had become critical and it seemed necessary either to default in the payment of debt or to convert rapidly into *rentes.* During 1925-26 there were no less than six ministries and the value of the franc fell very rapidly. Messrs. Ribot and Klotz had frequent recourse to the Bank of France.

On May 31, 1926, a Committee of Experts was established and in its report opposed the overissue of paper money. It believed that the large volume of *Bons de la Défense*

[55] *Revue de Science et de Législation Financières,* 1927 (Jèze), "La Dette Publique en France de 1914 à 1926," pp. 634-635.

Nationale constituted the chief fiscal problem,[56] but it opposed the use of forced consolidation, forced loans, or the capital levy as remedies. It favored the offer of consolidation loans on more favorable terms than the Caillaux loan, which had failed largely because the rate of interest at the time considerably exceeded the four per cent interest of the loan.[57] It also advocated the formation of the *Caisse d'Amortissement,* which will be discussed at a later point. It advocated that the *Caisse* receive an annuity from the government and the revenues from the tobacco monopoly.

A *Caisse d'Amortissement,* or sinking fund body, was finally set up after one false start and given the management of the *Bons de la Défense Nationale.* The details of its organization will be given in the following chapter. Strenuous measures were needed because in 1925 the debt maturing in one month had increased from 14.1 per cent to 14.6 per cent and that maturing in three months from 10.6 per cent to 15.4 per cent. In 1926, however, the amount maturing in one month had increased to 38.2 per cent of the total debt.[58]

The *Caisse* has proved effective in consolidating the floating debt, but it has not succeeded in retiring any great amount of debt permanently. The *Bons* were reduced from 46 billions in 1927 to 38,268 millions in 1928, but in spite of this reduction the *Caisse* was attacked by some for the slowness with which reduction was accomplished. It was defended by Poincaré on the ground that slow conversion was less disturbing to business. Still others advocated that the *Caisse* be given additional powers, but Poincaré opposed this because he believed it would hinder the work of consolida-

[56] Report of the Committee of Experts, *Revue de Science et de Législation Financières,* 1926, p. 510.

[57] Rates were 10 and 11 per cent.

[58] Jèze, *Revue de Science et de Législation Financières,* 1927, p. 505.

tion. By the end of 1928 the problem of monthly credits had been solved and all debt of less than one-year maturity had been replaced by 33,506 millions of two-year debt and 12,615 millions of debt payable in 40, 50 and 75 years.[59] In 1927 the *Bons* had still a monthly turnover of three and one-quarter billions.

In 1928 there was a conversion of *Bons* into 5 per cent *rentes,* the option of subscription being tendered exclusively to the holders of the former.[60] 5,321,975,200 francs were subscribed and 2,849,900,500 were turned over to the Treasury and used by it to reduce the advances from the Bank of France. The remainder was consolidated in the form of 5 per cent *amortissables* of the *Caisse.* The interest and service were guaranteed by the Treasury.

In 1929 considerable debt retirement was accomplished, altogether about 8 billions. At this time the *Caisse* turned from the repayment of short-dated debt to *rentes,* the reason given being that the evils of the short-term debt are only great when the amount on the market greatly exceeds the demand for this kind of security. This it did not feel was the case in 1929.[61] During this year the confidence in the Treasury had grown considerably and it was able to borrow at 4½ per cent on long-term obligations. Toward the end of the year the interest on the Bons was lowered to 3½ per cent. In addition to the purchases of the *Caisse,* 7,210 millions of *obligations décennales* of 1919 fell due and 6,189 millions of *Bons du Trésor* at 3, 6 and 10 years (second series) were also repaid.

[59] Annual Report of the *Caisse Autonome, Revue de Science et de Législation Financières,* 1929.

[60] Larrieu, Jean, *op. cit.,* p. 186.

[61] *Revue de Science et de Législation Financières,* 1929, p. 484.

(b) *In Great Britain*

In Great Britain the floating debt and short-term debts were less important factors than in France. The total debt reached a peak in December, 1919, and, as has been seen in Chapter II, the so-called floating debt had reached an amount vastly greater than the funded debt. Thus at first the "floating debt" constituted a much larger proportion of the total debt in England than in France.[61a] Discussion of English debt is confused, however, by the narrow use of the term funded debt, which in England means all debt for which there is no fixed date of payment. According to this definition the United States would have scarcely any funded debt. Great Britain's enormous floating debt does not signify any greater liability than that of other countries which nominally have a smaller amount of floating debt. A better picture of the burden from this form of debt was shown in the second chapter. Great Britain was more successful than France, however, in removing her floating debt (defined as Ways and Means Advances and Treasury Bills) and by March 31, 1926, it had dropped to £704,296,000.[62] This was to a large extent the result of the retirement of the Ways and Means Advances. In comparison with France the loans from the Bank of England have been retired more consistently and more immediately. These advances were £774,000,000 in June, 1919 and had been reduced to £204,887,000 the following year.[63]

The reduction of the short-term debt came about largely through conversions. In a written answer to a question of Dalton on May 25, 1925, the government stated that a nominal value of £1,693,292,140 of bonds and stock with an interest charge of £88,130,000, or approximately 5.2 per cent,

[61a] On June 30, 1919, the total floating debt was £1,570,000,000.

[62] *Colwyn Report*, p. 33.

[63] *Ibid.*, p. 33.

had been converted since April 1, 1919, to a nominal capital of £2,007,327,685 with interest of £86,371,000 or 4.3 per cent. The expense of carrying through these conversions was .03 per cent.[64]

The Colwyn Committee also determined that between April 1, 1920, and March 31, 1926, £306,181,000 of 5 per cent National War Bonds were converted into £322,296,000 of 5 per cent War Loan; £13,138,000 of 4 per cent National War Bonds were converted into the same amount of 4 per cent War Loan; and £46,706,000 of 5½ per cent Gold Bonds were converted into £52,872,000 of 5 per cent National War Bonds. The total conversion would thus be £366,025,000 of war titles into £388,306,000 of new titles.[65]

Hence the conversions were accomplished through an increase in the nominal amount of the public debt, and on February 16, 1928, Pethick-Lawrence objected to a conversion that was proposed at that time on the ground that, although it decreased the interest to some extent, it more than proportionately increased the nominal capital. In fact, throughout the entire post-war period objections have been raised to this practice, but the government has defended itself by pointing out that the principal could be reduced by future conversions.[66] In view of this policy, the nominal debt figures in England have a reduced significance, and the various governments have been able to claim with some reason that the "debt" has been reduced. In that country at any rate the debt service best indicates the condition of the debt.

Reduction of the short-term debt was also partly accomplished, as in France, through the process of refunding during the war itself. True, this refunding did not really begin

[64] *Parliamentary Debates*, Official Report, vol. 184, p. 998.

[65] *Colwyn Report*, p. 45.

[66] *Parliamentary Debates*, Official Report, vol. 213, p. 1042.

until 1917 with the government of Bonar Law. Great Britain had relied greatly upon borrowing in war finance, and in the first years upon rather short-term debt. McKenna was the first chancellor of the exchequer to insist upon taxation for financing the war. (Some people in England think that by insisting upon taxation he saved the country from financial ruin.[67]) But McKenna did not begin the refunding of the short-term debt. This really occurred with the issue of the Third War Loan on January 11, 1917, while Bonar Law was chancellor. These bonds were of two varieties, 5 per cent bonds of 1929-47 and 4 per cent bonds of 1929-42. Exchequer bonds which had much earlier maturities could be exchanged for the War Loan at par and treasury bills and war expenditure certificates could be exchanged at discounts of 5 and 5½ per cent.[68] The resulting conversions reduced the short-dated debt. Treasury bills decreased from £552,-326,000 to £450,710,000 between 1916 and 1917. It cannot be said, however, that Great Britain succeeded very well in reducing the short-term debt in the last years of the war, as is shown by the fact that on March 31, 1919, the Ways and Means Advances had reached £454,992,000, and treasury bills £957,236,000.

The floating debt had become a genuine menace at the end of the war. In his first budget speech, Austin Chamberlain called attention to the difficulty of borrowing nearly a billion pounds of treasury bills four times a year, particularly when there was a rising demand for commercial securities. He believed also that the debt was impeding deflation and that the Ways and Means Advances should be repaid as rapidly as possible.[69] In addition to these forms of very short-term

[67] See Mallet and George, *British Budgets, 1914-21*, pp. 91-92.

[68] Grady, *British War Finance*, p. 132.

[69] Mallet and George, *op. cit.*, pp. 185-187.

debts almost all of the public debt with the exception of the War Loan was due for payment not later than 1929.

On June 12, 1919, the first important effort was made to reduce the floating debt, particularly the Ways and Means Advances. It took the form of an issue of the 4 per cent Funding Loan and the Victory Bonds. The original issue of the former was about £409 millions at 80. About £360 millions of Victory Bonds were issued at 85. Both of these issues had sinking fund provisions which will be discussed in the next chapter.[70] The loans brought about a decline in National War Bonds through conversion privileges. The issue of these new loans increased the amount of funded debt. In 1919 and 1920 the Ways and Means Advances were reduced by about £250 millions, but this progress was considerably offset by an increase of about £150 millions in the treasury bills. The chief accomplishment of these long-term loans thus seems to have been a reduction in National War Bonds.

At this time the evils of the large floating debt gave rise to many suggestions for relief. Samuel and Asquith wrote articles in the papers favoring a war wealth levy, Professor Pigou advocated the capital levy, and a Select Committee was appointed by the House of Commons with William Pearce as chairman to study a war wealth levy.[71] It finally reported that such a levy was practicable, but the chancellor rejected the measure in the budget speech delivered in April, 1920. The Labour party then offered a motion in the House of Commons in favor of a new tax on wealth, but Chamberlain paid no attention to it. A similar

[70] For details of these loans see *British Finance Accounts* and Fisk, *English Public Finance*, p. 213.

[71] *Revue de Science et de Législation Financières*, July, 1920, "Le rejet de l'impôt extraordinaire sur le capital comme moyen de liquider les charges financières de la guerre." For Pigou, see p. 408; for Asquith, p. 412; for Herbert Samuel, p. 417.

motion for a capital levy had been defeated by Chamberlain on May 20, 1919, by a large majority.

Treasury bills increased in 1921 from £1,107,318,000 to £1,120,841,000, but the Ways and Means Advances were still further reduced, the amount having fallen to £154,-489,000. Thus in 1920 there was less of a reduction in the floating debt than in the previous year. Chamberlain explained this on the ground that the external debt had been reduced.[72] But he believed that the time had come for a serious effort to reduce the short-term debt, and planned to offer to holders of National War Bonds with maturities to 1925, Conversion Loans at 3½ per cent. Since these War Bonds bore 5 per cent interest, to effect this nominal reduction in the interest the capital amount of the debt had to be increased. The total amount of the bonds to be converted was £632 millions, with a capital increase to about one billion pounds.[73] £163 millions of these bonds were to mature in 1922, £162 millions in 1923, £161 millions in 1924 and £160 millions in 1925. This plan was carried out and the Treasury chose also to continue the conversion of National War Bonds into the 5 per cent War Loan of 1929-47. By these processes the National War Bonds were decreased to £1,200,-624,000 in 1922, to £952,131,000 in 1923, and £820,094,000 in 1924.

The 3½ per cent Conversion Loan next appeared, and constitutes the only funded debt issued by Great Britain between 1914 and 1926.[74] This loan was exchanged for Exchequer Bonds, but principally for National War Bonds, and was payable only at government option. The Funding

[72] The external debt fell from £1,364,852,657 in 1920 to £1,278,713,405 in 1921.

[73] As it actually turned out, £693 millions were issued to retire £463 millions of other securities. See *Colwyn Report*, p. 50.

[74] *Colwyn Report*, p. 52.

Loan was payable in 1990 and the 4½ per cent Conversion Loan of 1924-5 was payable in 1944.

In 1922 Sir Robert Horne reported a surplus for the fiscal year 1921-22 of £45 millions, which was devoted to the debt. In 1923 Baldwin reported that the Conversion Loan cited above had increased the nominal amount of the debt £135,-500,000. He justified this increase by the reduction of interest by £750,000 a year and the saving of £4,500,000 of premiums that would have to be paid since the debt was not issued at par. By 1924, through repayment, conversion into War Loan and the 3½ per cent conversion loan and the issue of the intermediate form of Treasury Bonds, the floating debt had been very much diminished. Treasury bills amounted to only £588,320,000 and Ways and Means Advances to £186,156,000.

In the years 1925-28 much the same policies were followed. The Ways and Means Advances were gradually reduced until in 1927 they were £116,601,000. They were, however, suddenly increased in 1928 to £161,850,000. Treasury bills were slightly reduced so that in 1928 they amounted to only £526,940,000. The War Loan of 1929-47 was kept fairly constant, but had increased to £2,172,373,000 in 1928. The War Loan of 1929-42 was also kept steadily at about £65,000,000, but increased in 1928 by about £15,-000,000. National War Bonds were very considerably reduced so that they amounted to only £777,829,000 in 1925, £705,700,000 in 1926, £555,273,000 in 1927 and £193,-847,000 in 1928. The latter, it will be remembered, fell due on April 1 and September 1, 1928, and February 1, 1929. Treasury bonds, which had entered the field as an intermediate form of debt, increased from £23,153,000 in 1921 to £452,779,000 in 1922. These bonds had maturities ranging from April 1, 1929, to February 1, 1935. They remained steadily at about £450 millions until 1928 when they were increased to £675,371,000 to assist in the payment of the National War Bonds.

During these years there were three more conversion loans: the 4½ per cent Conversion Loan of 1940-44 issued in 1924-5, the issue of consols at 4 per cent in 1927, and the 5 per cent Conversion Loan of 1944-64 issued in 1929. In the latter there were guarantees that the bonds could not be reconverted before 1944. The loan could be paid for in other loans, such as the 5½ per cent Treasury Bonds of May, 1930, or War Loan of 1929-47.

The conversion loan of 1944-64 was resorted to because of the great increase of short-term debt in 1928 and 1929. By 1929 the short-dated debt had reached £855,000,000. Treasury bills had increased from £526,940,000 on March 31, 1928, to £792,985,000 in November 1929. The Conversion Loan of 1929 was a success and £233 millions were subscribed.[75]

Five main facts stand out in the post-war management of the English debt. First, there was continuous and successful conversion, reducing appreciably the rate of interest. Secondly, conversion was accompanied by an increase in the nominal amount of the debt. Thirdly, new intermediate debt forms were called into use to adjust the maturities. Fourthly, the debt could not be naturally reduced, so that in its discouragement the state converted some of its debt into bonds without fixed dates of payment. Finally, the economic depression of 1929-32 caused a great increase in the floating debt.

(c) *In the United States*

The debt in the United States immediately after the war also presented difficult problems of maturities. These difficulties arose mainly from the fact that conversion had not

[75] The *Colwyn Report* gives on p. 45 a table showing the amount of conversion from April 1, 1920 to March 31, 1926.

been conducted during the war as in England with the object of funding the debt. Conversion had been used primarily for the purpose of equalizing the interest rate paid to all debt holders. The approaching maturities faced by the Treasury were extraordinarily large. For example, in 1919 no less than $9,246,000,000 had to be paid in five years, four billions of which fell due in one year. In 1921 over seven billions were due in two years.

During the war years the following conversions occurred: in 1916 thirty millions of 2 per cent bonds with the circulation privilege were converted into three per cent bonds, also with this privilege. In 1917 3½ per cent First Liberties were converted into special 4 per cent First Liberties, to equal the interest on the Second Liberties.[76] The privilege of conversion was recurrent for all subsequent issues of Liberty Bonds. The Second Liberties could also be converted into subsequent issues at a higher rate of interest,[77] but they could only be converted once into the Third Liberties between May 9 and November 9, 1918. With the issue of the Fourth Liberties, First and Second Liberties were converted into them from October 24, 1918, to April 24, 1919. Victory Notes were interconvertible with all other forms of debt during their life. The following is a summary of the conversions between 1917 and 1921 as given by the Secretary of the Treasury.[78]

November 15, 1917 to May 15, 1918—1st 4's	$568,318,450
As of June 30, 1921—1st 4½'s	$542,387,650
October 24, 1918 to April 24, 1919, 1st and 2nd 4¼'s	$3,492,150
2nd 4¼'s as of June 30, 1921	$3,650,936,150
Victory 4¾'s as of June 30, 1921	$293,111,250
Victory 3¾'s as of June 30, 1921	$495,668,150

[76] Love, *Federal Financing*, p. 149.

[77] *Ibid.*, p. 156.

[78] See *Annual Report of the Secretary of the Treasury*, 1921, p. 261.

Because of the large short-dated debt the Treasury set about to reduce the loan and tax certificates and to issue short-term treasury notes maturing in from three to five years. These notes had maturities distributed over the period 1923-28. From August 31, 1919, to March 31, 1921, the short-dated debt (five years or less) was reduced from $9,248,188,921 to $7,578,954,141.

There were $2,743,334,000 of treasury notes issued between June 15, 1921, and August 1, 1922. These securities extended the maturities of the Liberty Bonds and allowed the government to take advantage of the declining interest rates. The last of the loan certificates of indebtedness were retired on October 16, 1922, leaving only tax certificates. Their number in 1922 was abnormally small in comparison with the Victory notes. With the retirement of these two forms, the short-dated debt consisted of Third Liberties maturing in 1928, treasury notes and tax certificates.

During this early post-war period the Treasury was faced with three important problems in connection with maturities: the reduction of the loan certificates, the heavy maturities of the Victory Loan, and the large maturities of the Third Liberty Loan. The Victory Loan maturity was met to some extent through actual retirement, but largely through the increases of treasury notes. These amounted to only $311,191,600 in 1921, but had increased to $2,246,596,350 in 1922 and to $4,104,195,150 in 1923. The Third Liberty Loan, which amounted to $3,904,313,017 in 1919, was gradually retired until in 1928, the year of its maturity, it amounted to only $1,288,848,600. The surplus and sinking fund were devoted to this purpose, but the Treasury was assisted by the increase of treasury bonds. These rose from $2,790,638,650 in 1928 to $3,136,986,600 in 1929.

Two facts that stand out in American experience in comparison with that of England and France are the greater use of relatively short-dated debt in post-war funding and the ease with which the maturities could be met by large budget surpluses. Until 1923 no long-term bonds were issued. In that year $763,954,300 were issued for the purpose of facilitating the retirement of the Victory Loan.[79] These were 4¼ per cent bonds maturing in the years 1947-52. In December, 1924, a second issue was made, this time of bonds maturing in 1944-54 and bearing only 4 per cent interest. The amount issued was $1,047,488,500. Three other issues of treasury bonds have been made, one issue of $494,898,100 at 3¾ per cent maturing in 1946-1956, a second of $494,854,750 at 3⅜ per cent maturing in 1943-47, a third of $359,042,950 at 3⅜ per cent maturing 1940-43.

Of considerable interest is the refunding of the Second Liberty Loan in 1927. The amount of this loan was $3,807,865,000 on November 15, 1917. By February 28, 1927, it had been reduced to $3,104,520,050. Of this amount $1,976,990,200 was exchanged for other issues at a lower rate of interest, $580,149,750 was redeemed for the sinking fund, $524,450 was redeemed from miscellaneous sources, $527,170,500 was paid on presentation pursuant to call, and only $19,685,150 remained outstanding in 1928.

The Third Liberty Loan was also disposed of in 1927-28. On January 9, 1928, the holders of this loan were offered 3 to 5 year 3½ per cent treasury notes, Series C, 1930-32, at par. To compensate for the premium on the Third Liberties, interest was prepaid in full to March 15, 1928, without deduction for earlier redemption. $697,399,650 was thus converted. At this time $160,062,000 worth of Third Liberties were purchased by the government. Some months later $314,993,300 worth were purchased from the surplus. Thus out of the $5,264,526,950 of Second and Third Liber-

[79] Tables of the maturities and the kinds of debt issued by the United States are given in Appendices II and III.

ties outstanding in March, 1927, $2,794,732,200 were refunded through direct exchange for other bonds, $700,-067,100 were purchased for the sinking fund and $567,401,-750 were purchased with surplus revenues, $5,900,000 were retired through miscellaneous accounts and $1,196,425,400 were retired with the proceeds of other loans, these consisting mainly of treasury notes and treasury bonds.

(d) *In Germany*

In Germany inflation has created abnormal conditions since the war. There has been nothing which might be termed a conversion and only very recently has any refunding of the short-term debt occurred. It will be recalled from Chapter II that the German debt was 5,158,000,000 marks at the beginning of the war and that in 1919 it had risen to 156,452,000,000 marks. The floating debt had become an increasingly larger portion of the total and had risen from 4.26 per cent to 48 per cent in 1919.[80] Thus Germany was confronted with an even more embarrassing floating debt at the end of the war than any of the principal Allies, in spite of the constant efforts of the government during the war to fund the debt. Two kinds of loans had been issued for this purpose, *Deutsche Reichsanleihe* and *Deutsche Reichsschatzenweisungen.* In France these two forms would be called *rentes* and *obligations* respectively. They were both issued to take up the treasury bills, which in Germany, as in other countries, were the initial source of war funds. These bills were discounted with banks and thence passed on to the general investor in much the same manner as the English treasury bills.

The German *rentes* mentioned above were little different from the French except that they could not be converted before October 1, 1924, and were issued at a price very little

[80] See Fisk, *French Public Finance,* p. 138.

below par. The Treasury *obligations* were also issued near par, the first series payable in the years 1918-20, and the second series in 1921-22. The first of these issues was limited in amount to one billion marks. Altogether there were nine issues of *rentes* and nine of Treasury *obligations*. These occurred virtually every six months and the date of payment of the later *obligations* was extended to 1967. Approximately 98,188,000,000 marks of *rentes* and 13,738,000,000 marks of *obligations* were issued from September 10, 1914, to November 8, 1918. Long-term loans thus had a much more important place in the German war debt than in the United States and England.[81] The total floating debt was estimated by Rist at 45 billion marks in 1918. This figure included the *obligations* since the amount of the floating debt was nearly half of the total.[82]

Thus the issues of long-term debt in Germany did not succeed as well in funding the debt as they had in the other principal nations. But the monetary and budgetary difficulties that followed still further increased the floating debt. Such financial measures as the payment of customs taxes in gold, the tax reforms of Erzeberger, the turnover tax and the *Reichsnotopfer* eventually seemed incapable of meeting the needs of the budget. According to Professor Graham, taxes covered 91.2 per cent of the domestic expenses in 1921 but in 1923 only one to two per cent were derived from taxes.[83] By November 15, 1923, the total floating debt of Germany had reached the ridiculous sum of 191,580,465,422 milliards of marks. Of this sum nearly 100,000,000,000 milliards

[81] See Jèze, *Science des finances*, p. 388, and Rist, *Les Finances de guerre de l'Allemagne*, p. 86 *et seq.*

[82] *Ibid.*, p. 241.

[83] Graham, *Exchange, Prices and Production in Hyper-Inflation—Germany—1920-23*, pp. 38-39.

were paid off between November 16 and November 30.[84] By the time stabilization had been established the Agent General for the Reparations Commission was able to state that the remaining debt, both funded and floating, amounted to only one thousand stabilized Reichsmarks. This would be in the neighborhood of 250 dollars. By 1924, therefore, no refunding of the war debt had taken place and none was now needed. The revalorization of the old debt, however, might by some stretch of the imagination be considered as a conversion. The details of this measure have already been mentioned above.

The revalorization began in 1925. In September, 1927, the German Finance Ministry divided the Loan Liquidation Debt into its two parts, 4,742,500,000 marks with drawing rights and 700,000,000 marks without these rights. Previously it had been carried in the reports to the Agent General as a single figure, much smaller because the debt with drawing rights was not included.

After the institution of the Dawes plan there was some increase in the amount of the debt, and with it, in the floating debt. On April 1, 1924, the public debt consisted only of the Reichsbank and Rentenbank loans contracted for the assistance of these bodies in supporting the currency, of treasury certificates issued in 1923-24 in gold and Rentenmarks, various obligations contracted in the United States and guarantees undertaken toward Turkey during the war.[85]

The first important addition to the debt was, as we have seen, the German External Loan of 1924 amounting to 800,000,000 gold marks. This, of course, was not floating debt. Following this loan came the German Internal Loan of February, 1927. It amounted to 500 million Reichsmarks at 5

[84] Committee of Experts, *Germany's Economy, Currency and Credit*, p. 29.

[85] Reparations Commission, *Execution of the Experts' Plan*, 1927-28.

per cent and matures in 1959. Earlier redemption may be made at par in whole or in part after February 1, 1937. A loan of 100 million Reichsmarks was also received from the post office in August, 1926. A second Internal Loan was issued in 1929. This loan is for the shorter period of fifteen years. It bears 7 per cent interest and is exempt from almost all taxes. The subscription amounted to 180 million Reichsmarks. Short-term credits were also received during this year from German railways.

The fiscal year 1928-29 was marked by a considerable increase of debts of many varieties. In this year there was the issue of war damage liquidation certificates. Bonds were also issued to the Social Insurance Institutes, to the banks and to Roumania in connection with the Roumanian agreement. The first form of bonds was repayable in the years 1930-32; the bonds issued to banks were for seven and eleven months; the Roumanian bonds were repayable one-third in each of the three years 1929, 1930 and 1931. In addition to these forms of short-term debt Reichsmark bills increased in that year by 343 million marks and short-term loans by 145 millions.

The fiscal year 1929-30 brought a still further increase in short-term debt. In this year 1,216 millions of treasury bills were issued, 200 millions to the German banks, 350 millions to the Reichsbank syndicate, 125 millions of treasury bonds, another 180 millions to the German Railway Company and 36 millions to the Agent General for Reparations Payments in compliance with the Hague Protocol of 1929 and the Hague Agreement of 1930. None of these debts had a maturity later than March 15, 1931. Thus the floating debt increased considerably in 1929-30. As we have seen in Chapter II, the total amount of floating debt was only 171 million marks on March 31, 1927. On the same date in

1928 it was 226 millions, in 1929, 990 millions, but in 1930 it was 1,888 millions.[86]

It may be concluded then that after 1923 there was no problem of conversion and funding arising from the war, and that with the exception of the Loan Liquidation debt and the German Internal Loan of 1927 there have been no important internal long-term loans and no conversions. The floating debt has increased constantly since 1925, and in recent years this tendency has become alarming.

(e) *Summary*

It can be said by way of summary that there is very little similarity in the history of debt management in these four countries. Great Britain and, before 1923, Germany probably may be said to have made more systematic efforts to fund the floating debt than either the United States or France. All four emerged, however, with very heavy debts of this character. The United States reduced the floating debt by retirement and by the issue of treasury notes and bonds. Great Britain and France made a greater use of conversion loans. Germany was relieved of her floating debt by inflation.

V. CHANGES IN INTEREST RATES

Turning now to interest rates, it is doubtful whether any safe comparisons among these countries in this regard can be made. It is dangerous to compare nominal rates of interest and the computation of yields would be a difficult if not impossible task. A reference to nominal rates of interest, however, does indicate certain broad tendencies.

Germany was able during the war to issue *rentes* near par at 5 per cent and *obligations* at 5 and 4½ per cent. Rates of interest during the inflationary period of 1921-23 were,

[86] Reparations Commission, *Execution of the Experts' Plan*, 1929-30.

of course, much higher. After stabilization had taken place the government was able to issue the large Internal Loan of 1927 at 5 per cent, but in 1929 the second Internal Loan bore 7 per cent, and 7¼ to 7½ was paid to banks for loans made to the government.

In France in April, 1927, after stabilization, *rentes* of the *Caisse Autonome* were at 6 per cent and *obligations* also at 6 per cent. In May, 1928, *rentes* were issued by the *Caisse Autonome* at 5 per cent and in February, 1929, *obligations* were lowered to 4½ per cent. On October 1, 1926, *Bons* of the *Caisse* were issued at 5½ per cent for 6-month bonds, 5 per cent for three months and 3.6 per cent for one-month bonds. By May 6, 1927, these were reduced to 4½, 4 and 3 per cent respectively, and in 1929 the interest on all *Bons* (now two-year titles) had fallen to 3½ per cent. The *rentes* were issued during the war at 5 per cent in 1915-16 and 4 per cent in 1917 and 1918.[87]

In England estimation of the median rate of interest on all forms of the public debt shows it to be 5 per cent in 1919 and 1920, 5 to 4¾ per cent in 1921, 4¾ in 1922, 4¼ in 1924, 4 in 1925 and 1926 and 1927, and 4¼ per cent in 1928. Winston Churchill in a budget speech in 1925 estimated that the interest on the British debt had been reduced from 6 to 4½ per cent since 1920.[88]

Thus after stable monetary conditions had been established in these three countries it appears that there was a gradual reduction of interest in all three. The most success was attained in France, but the reduction was steady in England. In England and Germany the economic difficulties which began to make themselves felt in 1928 seem to be reflected in a rise in the rate of interest.

[87] *Cf. Bulletin de statistique générale* and Haig, *op. cit.*, pp. 264-267.

[88] *Cf. Finance Accounts.* Great Britain has floated during the spring

A great deal has been said by American government officials and others about the success of the Treasury in reducing the rate of interest on United States bonds and certificates. The Secretary of the Treasury presented in his annual report of 1925 a calculation of the yield of the certificates of indebtedness of 4 and 6 months in 1925 in comparison with the yield on similar forms of commercial paper. This comparison showed a rather close correspondence during the years 1924-1925, and the yield of short-term securities showed a tendency to decline with the fall in the market rates of interest. Although there are exceptions, any careful study of the Reports of the Secretary of the Treasury will show also that for every kind of debt the rate of interest has fallen rapidly and fairly constantly from the war period until more recent years.

and summer of 1932 one of the largest conversion loans of her history. This loan has succeeded partly because of the low interest rates and the scarcity of safe investments.

CHAPTER IV

History of the Recent Methods of Debt Retirement

Since 1919, when in most countries the nominal amounts of national debts were at their highest, unusual efforts have been made to decrease the debt as well as to lower the interest rates and adjust the maturities. Sinking funds have again become prominent in political discussions and various forms have been both suggested and employed. It is important to examine these funds and certain other closely related measures to see what light the different practices of the various countries throw upon their usefulness in debt retirement. In doing this it is perhaps wisest to proceed from the most to the least familiar, in other words to begin with the United States and compare its methods with those of Great Britain, France and Germany.

I. THE UNITED STATES

The more recent sinking fund measures of the United States reflect a policy which was adopted very early in American history, namely the payment of debt through the use of both special appropriations and surplus. The United States has not vacillated as much between these two methods as have Great Britain and France, but very early worked out a compromise, which was for a part of the time written into the law and at other times merely carried out in practice. In 1790 Hamilton had urged Congress to allocate certain revenues, such as tonnage fees and import duties, to the payment of foreign debts, the interest on new debts and the payment of old debts. Post office receipts he thought should be turned over to the debt through a Board of Debt Commissioners, the members of which should be the Vice-President, Chief Justice, Speaker of the House, Attorney General, and the Secretary of the Treasury. The first sinking fund law, enacted in 1790, followed some of these suggestions. Surplus revenues from tonnage fees were used by the Board of Commissioners to purchase public stocks if they were below par. The fund was a mere pretense since the President could borrow up to two million dollars to purchase the debt and since there was no permanent fund devoted to the payment of the debt and the fund could be easily violated.[1] In 1792 Hamilton proposed a real[2] sinking fund involving the payment of interest on a given amount of stock purchased by the Debt Commissioners. A law passed in this year altered the old fund so that two new sources of revenue were introduced, the interest accruing on the stock purchased and the unapplied portion of all moneys appropriated to pay the interest on the debt. The first-named, which has sometimes been referred to as " secondary credit ", has been a peculiarity of American finance which at least one country, Germany, has begun to copy.

The altered fund did not provide for a fixed appropriation although the allocation of tonnage fees suggested the eventual adoption of such a plan. The sinking fund law passed in 1802 also neglected to provide for fixed appropriations and merely devoted a large surplus to the payment of the debt. In 1817, however, the compromise mentioned above was finally developed and embodied in a sinking fund law passed in that year which repealed all previous funds and set up an annual appropriation of ten million dollars, which, together with any budget surplus above two million dollars, was to be paid to the Debt Commissioners. There were to be no further violations, borrowing for payment, or attach-

[1] See Ross, *Sinking Funds*, p. 46 *et seq.*

[2] i. e., resembling that of Price.

ment of specific revenues. Under its operation the country virtually eliminated its national debt.

The debt was increased again by the Civil War, and this gave rise to the sinking fund of 1862. This fund provided for the use of customs duties to pay the interest on the debt first and then to pay off one per cent of the existing debt each year. It was considered at the time that the adoption of this fund constituted a contract with the public to pay the debt.[3] The fund was, however, ignored until Boutwell's administration and in practice such funds as were available from surplus revenues were applied to the debt. Thus it may be concluded that, as in the act of 1817, (since under that law borrowing to pay the debt service was illegal) the funds to pay the debt were derived from the surplus revenues, but the amount set aside for this purpose was definitely indicated by law.[4] The theoretical significance of this solution will be discussed more fully in a later chapter. The attitudes of Secretaries of the Treasury point to the above conclusion about the post-civil war debt payment practice. For example, Secretary Sherman, according to Ross, believed that the sinking fund merely imposed upon him the duty of paying the debt out of surplus revenue, and Secretary Plumb regarded it only as a bookkeeping device.[5]

In 1881 an act was passed which authorized the Secretary of the Treasury to apply so much of the surplus moneys to

[3] *Banker's Magazine*, vol. 40, p. 725.

[4] Secretary Boutwell, who is given the credit by Ross for having been the first to discover the sinking fund law of 1862, tried to comply with its provisions. He bought bonds in excess of the needs of the fund and recommended that these purchases be made in such amounts as eventually would compensate for the failure of earlier secretaries to comply with the fund law. In 1870 (July 14) the famous funding act was passed which included a provision that the bonds bought for the sinking fund be cancelled and destroyed and that the interest on them be still paid into the sinking fund. This provision made the sinking fund of 1862 cumulative.

[5] Ross, *Sinking Funds*, p. 83.

the retirement of the debt as he saw fit.[6] This law thus legalized a common policy among Secretaries of the Treasury after the Civil War. It merely put into the law the practice of the times. When most of the debt had matured or had been reduced to the consolidated form, the Treasury was troubled by the sinking fund, which required the purchase of at least some bonds from the annual surpluses. In 1915 the Secretary of the Treasury advised a revision of the sinking fund. He believed that either an "actual" fund should be established with definite and specific appropriations, together with specific provisions for the administration of the fund, or else the existing acts should be repealed and the Secretary directed to purchase and retire interest-bearing obligations of the United States whenever the same could be acquired advantageously and the conditions of the Treasury warranted such action.[7] Similar recommendations had been made in 1911. The total purchases for the fund had come to a ridiculous figure—in 1916 only $35,903.

But these difficulties solved themselves through the increase of the debt with the World War. It became necessary to establish a new fund at this time. Of greatest interest is the fact that the new fund had a definite appropriation. So long as the interest on the debt was small relative to the total government expenditures, it was believed that the rapidity of debt retirement from surplus could be left to the discretion of the Secretary of the Treasury. This was thought undesirable after the war had so greatly enlarged the debt.

The present sinking fund law was enacted as section six of the Victory Liberty Loan Act of 1919 and was in accord with the recommendations of the Secretary of the Treasury in that year. It provided

[6] *U. S. Statutes 1879-1881*, p. 457.

[7] *Annual Report of the Secretary of the Treasury*, 1916, p. 29.

(a) That there is hereby created in the Treasury a cumulative sinking fund for the retirement of bonds and notes under the First Liberty Bond Act, the Second Liberty Bond Act, the Third Liberty Bond Act, the Fourth Liberty Bond Act, or under this act and outstanding on July 1, 1920. The sinking fund and all additions thereto are hereby appropriated for the payment of such bonds and notes at maturity, or for the redemption and purchase thereof before maturity by the Secretary of the Treasury at such prices and upon such terms as he shall prescribe, and shall be available until all bonds and notes are retired. The average cost of the bonds and notes purchased shall not exceed par and accrued interest. Bonds and notes purchased, redeemed or paid out of the sinking fund shall be cancelled and retired and shall not be reissued. For the fiscal year beginning July 1, 1920 and for each fiscal year thereafter until all such bonds and notes are retired there is hereby appropriated out of any money in the Treasury not otherwise appropriated for the purpose of such sinking fund an equal amount to the sum of (1) 2½ per centum of the aggregate amount of such bonds and notes outstanding on July 1, 1920 less an amount equal to the par amount of any obligations of foreign governments held by the United States on July 1, 1920 and (2) the interest which would have been payable during the fiscal year for which the appropriation is made on the bonds and notes purchased, redeemed or paid during such years or in previous years.[8]

According to Glass the old fund had proved unworkable and nothing more than a bookkeeping account; to make the sinking fund effective it must be derived from the proceeds of taxation.[9] Unless we interpret opinions such as those of Glass as implying the need for a Congress-given policy of debt retirement, we cannot see how they have any meaning. It is quite apparent that there is no sense in saying that debt

[8] *Congressional Record*, vol. 57, p. 4294.

[9] *Annual Report of the Secretary of the Treasury*, 1919, p. 85.

retirement must come out of taxes unless the need for such instruction from Congress as to policy is implied.

Thus the increase in the size of the public debt has resulted in the establishment of a sinking fund policy through legislation which is similar in its main essentials to the policy followed after the War of 1812 and the Civil War. It is possible that the lack of discussion that greeted the measure indicates a belief on the part of the members of Congress that it represents no important departure from past practice. The bill was reported out of committee by Claude Kitchin and only one amendment was suggested. This amendment was offered by Mr. Sherley, and provided merely for the presentation of special annual sinking fund reports to Congress. Only three questions were asked in the discussion of the measure: was the payment of the fund necessary; would Congress, in Mr. Kitchin's opinion, impose taxes to pay the credit; and how large would the fund be.

It will be desirable to describe in detail at this point just how closely this sinking fund scheme follows the previous policy of the United States in the retirement of debt. It can be seen first of all that the appropriation is a definite amount, although it is determined by the use of a percentage. It also is definitely assumed that the appropriation is to be derived from taxes. There is of course nothing in section six that would require the payment of the fund through taxes, since it merely states that the appropriation shall come from any money in the Treasury. But that it should be paid out of taxes was certainly the intention of Secretary Glass and of at least a few Congressmen. The silence of the rest of the members would assuredly have been broken if borrowing to pay the fund had seemed very likely. Since taxation for the debt was assumed, the actual source of the funds would naturally be government surplus. But through the establishment of a fixed appropriation the Treasury was directed as to the amount of debt to be retired and the amount of "surplus" to be used. In addition to this artificially created "surplus" any further excess revenues could be devoted to the debt reduction. Thus the policy was one of fixed appropriations paid out of taxes and the use of additional surplus.[10]

In pursuit of the policy set up by the Victory Loan Act the surplus has been as important a factor as the sinking fund, as is shown by the fact that out of the total reduction in the gross debt of $9,788,934,707 between August 31, 1919, and 1929, the surplus accounted for $4,367,624,774.[11] It is thus responsible for about half of the total reduction. The sinking fund, although intended as a guide to the speed of reduction, has not therefore served very satisfactorily as such a guide. It might be said that the Treasury did not allow the technical surplus in the ten years to exceed the amount of this fund but there is no evidence that this policy was consciously followed.[12]

II. GREAT BRITAIN

The post-war debt reduction of Great Britain, though less successful than that of the United States, was at the same time characterized by more varied methods. As in the United States, there is some similarity to the past history of retirement. It will be useful to recall at this point that in 1786 Pitt, as chancellor of the exchequer, brought forward a sinking fund along the lines outlined by Dr. Price. The fallacy of Price's compound interest scheme has often been pointed out. Nevertheless, his measure had the suggestion

[10] In addition to these sources of debt payment there are certain other miscellaneous sources, including the receipts from the Franchise Tax of the Federal Reserve Banks and the Intermediate Credit Banks, the federal estate taxes, gifts and forfeitures and the reduction of the General Fund Balance.

[11] *Annual Report of the Secretary of the Treasury*, 1929.

[12] See Appendix IV for table on U. S. debt reduction.

of a definite appropriation and fund for the retirement of debt and the separation of the retirement funds from the general funds of the Treasury. After Robert Hamilton's criticisms, the sinking fund as originally constituted was abolished and budget surplus was then paid to the National Debt Commissioners. This came to be known as the Old Sinking Fund of 1829. The law allowed only one-fourth of the surplus for this purpose. The Old Sinking Fund Act of 1866 introduced the requirement that a report of surplus be prepared by the Treasury at the end of the fiscal year, a copy of which was to be sent to the Commissioners for the Reduction of the National Debt. During the next year the surplus was issued out of the Consolidated Fund and used within six months to pay off one or more of the annuities, exchequer bonds, bills and advances made by the Bank to the government, but not the Ways and Means Advances.[13]

In 1876 the New Sinking Fund Act [14] was passed. This law set up a definite appropriation and to this extent is reminiscent of Pitt's sinking fund. In 1876 the amount of this appropriation was £27,400,000, in 1877 £27,700,000 and for every subsequent year £28,000,000. This came to be referred to as the annual debt charge. Out of it all annuities, all interest on exchequer bonds and bills with some exceptions, and all interest on the advances of the Banks of England and Ireland were to be paid. Interest on exchequer bonds and bills for the Public Works Loan or for any bonds following the passage of the act that the law did not specify

[13] Great Britain—*Statutes*, Vict. 29 and 30, chap. 39. E. L. Hargreaves has pointed out that after 1860 a change in the attitude of both Parliament and the nation occurred, which he thinks can be attributed to no one cause. There was less interest in the systematic reduction of the debt and terminable annuities were turned to as a compromise between those who desired a systematic reduction and those who did not. See Hargreaves, *National Debt*, p. 175.

[14] Great Britain—*Statutes*, Vict. 38 and 39, chap. 45.

were not to be paid out of this fixed appropriation. Any surplus remaining after the payment of interest was to be used for the retirement of annuities, exchequer bills and bonds, but not advances of the Banks of England and Ireland. The surplus was paid to the National Debt Commissioners, who were to use the money for retirement within six months of its receipt. The surplus was paid to the Commissioners throughout the whole of the following fiscal year and not, as in the Exchequer and Audit Act of 1866, paid within the next quarter after the end of the fiscal year.

Following the war with Afghanistan and the resulting tendency of Parliament in the decade after 1875 to demand the reduction of taxes, the sinking fund was maintained to a large extent by converting bonds into terminable annuities and counting these as part of the sinking fund payments. By 1885 many of these annuities expired and it was feared by Gladstone that the sinking fund would not be maintained by an additional vote of money equal to the amount of the expiring annuities. Childers became chancellor and in 1883 secured a renewal of the annuities and a slight reduction of their total charge. This was accomplished by a conversion of chancery stock and savings bank stock into annuities.

The situation created by these measures remained virtually unchanged until the World War,[15] when the sinking fund payments for redemption were temporarily abandoned. The Finance Act of 1914 states that " All that portion which is

[15] The Public Building Expense Act of 1898 merely increased the total expenditures for the fund by £250,000.

A Sinking Fund Annuity had been created, arising from the reduction of three per cent stocks to lower interest. Thus Section 3 of the 47th and 48th Victoria, chap. 23, states that this three per cent stock should be converted into lower annuities, constituting a reduced rate of interest and that " such annuities shall be charged on the Consolidated Fund and paid out of permanent annual charge of the national debt and shall be applied by the National Debt Commissioners in like manner as if the same were a part of the new Sinking Fund."

not required for the annual charges directed by the National Debt and Local Loans Act of 1887 or any other act to be paid out of that charge or for the redemption of any Exchequer Bonds under section seven of the Finance Act of 1905 which are drawn for redemption on the 18th day of April, 1915, shall not be paid."[16] In subsequent years (1917-19) payments for the retirement of the debt were suspended.

At the end of the World War the debt had grown to such large proportions that it became desirable to set up some mechanism for its payment.[17] Thus special sinking funds were attached to the War Loan of 1919. This established

[16] Great Britain—*Statutes*, 5 and 6 of Geo. V., chap. vii.

[17] Chamberlain, speaking before the House of Commons on October 29, 1919, said that a sinking fund of ½ of 1 per cent was to be provided for that year, which would if maintained remove the debt in fifty years. He estimated that there would be a substantial sum with which the debt could be paid in 1920. (Parliament, *Official Report*, vol. 120, pp. 755-7.) He thought the condition of the floating debt was better than it had been in the previous year. He was opposed to the capital levy and on May 20, 1919, defeated Acland's motion for the capital levy, 317 to 72. In its place inheritance taxes were considerably increased. This did not remove the agitation for the capital levy, which began again in 1929 when a commission was established to study it. The movement for a levy spread and articles appeared by G. W. Curie, H. Wren, A. Hoare, and Pethick-Lawrence in *The Economist*. Articles by Paish and Pigou appeared in other publications. The Liberals, led by Mr. Asquith, wanted to meet the problem by economy but they insisted that the debt be paid and made it a part of the policy of the party.

Chamberlain during these years felt it necessary to point out the progress made by the Government in the reduction of the debt. In his budget speech on April 25, 1921 he estimated that a surplus of 80 million pounds in addition to 23 millions of the debt retirement funds established by law, 20 millions of terminable annuities, 7 millions of new retirement funds and 14 millions for the Victory Sinking Fund could be applied to the payment of the debt. He thought that repayment could proceed rapidly since the price was below par. There had been, however, a deficit for the year 1919-20. *Cf. Revue de Science et de Législation Financières*, 1919-21.

the Victory and Funding Loan Sinking Funds. Paragraph two of the act states that "There shall be set aside at the close of each half year a sum equal to two and a quarter per cent on the nominal amount of any four per cent Victory Bonds or of four per cent Funding Loan 1960-90 originally created under the prospectus dated the twelfth day of June, nineteen hundred and nineteen, and after deducting therefrom the amount required for the payment of interest on these securities for the half year the balance of the sum so set aside shall be issued to the National Debt Commissioners and be applied by them to sinking-fund purposes in accordance with the terms of the above-mentioned prospectuses.

"The Treasury may make arrangements for the redemption of four per cent Victory Bonds at par by means of annual drawings and may make regulations for the drawing of such bonds and the bonds so drawn in any year shall be redeemed on the first day of September in that year." Accounts must be kept by the New Sinking Fund Commissioners in accordance with directions given by the Treasury and the accounts shall be submitted to the Comptroller and Auditor General. The act also provided that securities issued under it shall not mature if paid in to satisfy certain duties but shall be turned over to the National Debt Commissioners who shall use the interest in part payment of the sinking fund set up in the act.[18] In addition to the Victory Loan sinking fund an earlier fund had been set up in connection with the War Loans of 1929-47 and 1929-42.

Between 1920 and 1923 there was a great deal of discussion of the burden of the debt. Some believed that British wealth would not grow after the World War as it had after the Napoleonic Wars.[19] As much was being taken for interest on the debt as had been taken for the whole budget in

[18] Great Britain—*Statutes*, 9th and 10th Geo. V, chap. 37, paragraph 2.

[19] Parliamentary Debates, *Official Report*, vol. 164, p. 123.

1913. The heavy debt burden, it was thought, hampered England in her competition with Germany.[20] Increased credit power would be gained by the removal of the debt.[21]

There were some who favored a much more rapid reduction of the debt, such as Snowden, Pethick-Lawrence, and other members of the Labour party. The party favored the capital levy, but was willing to accept the next best measures. Snowden, for example, believed that no considerable reduction in taxes could be made until the expenses of the debt were diminished. The sinking fund proposed in 1923 would in his opinion require one hundred and fifty years to remove the debt.[22] The discussion centered upon the selection of fifty or one hundred million pounds a year.

As the act applied only to the Victory and Funding Loan and it was obvious that a much greater effort would be necessary if any substantial proportion of the debt was to be retired annually, the Consolidated Loan Sinking Fund was set up by the Finance Act of 1923. The act of 1875 with its New Sinking Fund was repealed[23] and the fixed sinking fund appropriation was raised to £40,000,000 for the year 1924, to £45,000,000 for 1925 and to £50,000,000 for all years thereafter "unless Parliament otherwise determines."[24] This amount was also called the New Sinking Fund of 1923 and was made a permanent charge on the Consolidated Fund. It was used to pay all debt except advances from the Banks of England and Ireland and loans

[20] *Ibid.*, p. 131.

[21] *Ibid.*, p. 133.

[22] *Ibid.*, p. 73.

[23] This act stated that "The provisions contained in the Sinking Fund Act of 1875 and the provisions contained in any acts amending that act with respect to the permanent annual charge for the National Debt and the New Sinking Fund shall cease to have effect."

[24] 13th and 14th, Geo. V, chap. xiv.

raised under an act to meet Ways and Means Advances. All the appropriation was issued to the National Debt Commissioners to pay the debt except such part as the Treasury thought necessary to reduce the external debt.

The amount of the annual contribution to the New Sinking Fund of 1923 was raised by the Finance Act of 1926, by £10,000,000 [25] and by £15,000,000 under the Finance Act of 1927.[26] These increases came about as a result of a growing public interest in favor of debt reduction and the success of the Labour party, which for some time has been in favor of rapid debt reduction. Finally on March 31, 1929, the New Sinking Fund of 1923 was repealed.[27] On that date £369,-000,000 and on March 31, 1930, and every subsequent March 31st, £355,000,000 were to be paid out of the Consolidated Fund. This is entitled "the permanent annual charge for the National Debt". It is devoted first to the expenses of interest and management. This includes interest on terminable annuities but not on savings certificates, or on bonds of any act passed afterwards that does not direct their payment from this act. The balance left, after the interest is paid, is to be used for the sinking funds set up by the War Loan Act of 1919, for the sinking fund of the 3½ per cent Conversion Loan, for the 4 per cent Consolidated Loan, for payments to the United States, for payments as part of the Death Duties under the War Loan Act of 1919, for interest on savings certificates,[28] and for the Depreciation Fund of 1917.[29] The whole act is referred to as the

[25] 16 and 17, Geo. V, chap. xxii.

[26] 17 and 18, Geo. V, chap. x.

[27] 18 and 19, Geo. V, chap. xvii.

[28] Pethick-Lawrence criticized Churchill for estimating this sinking fund at 65 million pounds since interest on war savings certificates had to be paid out of it. With this deducted it would amount to only 38 million pounds.

[29] The actual retirement of English debt has for a long time been vested

New Sinking Fund Act of 1928. The Old Sinking Fund as it accrues will now be paid into the Consolidated Fund rather than to the National Debt Commissioners, and this surplus is to be used to establish a fund known as the Rating Relief Suspense Account. The Treasury may pay out of this fund such amounts as it sees fit and at any time. The New Sinking Fund was supposed to remove the debt in fifty years, according to the spokesmen of the Government. It was desired to introduce the "principle of accumulation". "Although it begins small, it will grow each year until finally it becomes an immense sum, eating up great chunks. . . ."[30] It was defended by one member of Parliament on the ground that it was automatic, cumulative and continuous.[31]

In 1930, when England began to encounter monetary difficulties, the question of the relative importance of debt retirement and the gold standard was raised. Snowden, in spite of his earlier insistance upon strenuous measures such as the capital levy, said, "the suggested remedy (abandonment of the gold standard) would, I am afraid, produce evils far worse than it was designed to cure."[32] In this year a deficit of over 14 millions was incurred and to pay this 5 millions a year have been added to the sinking fund for three years. This measure caused severe criticism. Mr. Strachey, for example, said, "It is not true economy but false economy which attempts not simply as may be necessary to keep up the statutory sinking fund provided for debt redemption but arbitrarily to increase it by 5 million pounds."

in the National Debt Commissioners who purchase debt titles in the market, or from the Inland Revenue Commissioners who have received these titles for the payment of Death Duties. *Cf. Finance Accounts,* 1928.

[30] Parliamentary Debates, *Official Report,* vol. 219, p. 566.

[31] *Ibid.,* pp. 227-30 (Comments of Sir L. Worthington-Evans).

[32] *Ibid.,* pp. 242, 696-7.

The debt retirement laws of Great Britain from 1866 to 1928 show the use of both a fixed annual appropriation and a provision for the use of the surplus. In this respect the situation has been quite similar to that existing under American law. In practice, however, the surplus of the Old Sinking Fund has not been available for the retirement of debt, and the retirement of debt in recent years has been accompanied by the issue of new debt or the conversion of old debt at a higher capital figure. It may also be said that the notion of a fixed debt retirement together with an additional variable amount depending on the size of the surplus, although present in the law, has not figured either in practice or in the discussion of debt retirement. On the contrary, it seems that in the discussion of the sinking fund in 1875 it was assumed that the Old Sinking Fund, which embodied the use of surplus for debt retirement, was a dead letter and that the "surplus principle" was not necessary. Thus J. G. Hubbard favored the new fund because of the unpredictability of a "surplus", and this was also the opinion of the chancellor of the exchequer.[33] Goschen objected that the new fund would remove the principle that a surplus is necessary and would lead to failure in the maintenance of a surplus for that purpose. ". . . the future Chancellors of the Exchequer would be relieved of the necessity of providing a surplus. . . ."[34] Unless the money came from increased taxes no debt would be written off. Study of the subsequent discussion on these points does not throw any more light on the attitudes of British statesmen. They seem to ignore the possibility of raising taxes to the point where the debt would be retired by a fixed appropriation and also by a variable surplus.

Thus England accepted the fixed sinking fund appropri-

[33] Parliamentary Debates, *Hansard*, vol. 224, pp. 1522-30.

[34] *Ibid.*, p. 1556.

tion in practice. The amount of this fund, however, is much below that advised by the Colwyn Committee. The majority report of this body suggested seventy-five millions and the minority report one hundred millions. Since, as Pethick-Lawrence has pointed out, a good part of the present fund should really be considered interest, the sinking fund is now about half what the majority of the Colwyn Committee believed desirable, and this was reduced by fourteen millions in 1930. The amounts attributed to the various sinking funds are given in Appendix V.

III. FRANCE

France as well as Great Britain has changed her sinking fund laws many times, and involved measures have resulted from her attempts to enforce the payment of the debt. The first *Caisse d'Amortissement* was established by the law of the 6th Frimaire of the Year VIII (1800). This was not a real sinking fund. It was merely an office to which money securities were given by tax collectors to guarantee the loan titles issued in anticipation of taxes. Discount of these loans enabled the state to obtain funds immediately. The *Caisse* was later given power to retire its loans and eventually its functions were increased, so that it came to be known as the *Caisse de guarantie, de depôt et d'amortissement.*

In 1816 it was reorganized along the lines indicated by Price and was made a separate government body.[35] It received first 20 million francs and then 40 million francs, which were guaranteed by certain branches of the revenue. It bought *rentes* in the Bourse and kept these in its portfolio. The details of its early history are well described in the writ-

[35] Vidal, Jean, *De l'amortissement de la dette de guerre*, p. 23; also Jaubert, *L'Amortissement de la dette publique*. These books give the history of the early sinking funds in France. See also Lachapelle, *Le Credit publique*, pp. 40-41 *et seq.*

ings of Allix and Jèze.[36] It will suffice to point out here that the *Caisse* was retained in a form similar to that set up in 1816 until September 16, 1871, when its portfolio was liquidated, and amortization was taken over by the general budget from 1870 to 1879.[37] Thiers tried with little success to retire the debt by budget surpluses. At no time, however, was a solution by compromise between fixed appropriations and retirement through surplus worked out legally, and the history of the sinking fund is characterized by an oscillation between these two methods. Finally, in order to support the public credit, which owing to the large war loans was beginning to weaken, a fund was set up by law on October 26, 1917, upon which the *Caisse,* was allowed to draw for purchases of debt first to the amount of 60 million and later 120 million francs a month. The *Caisse* was required to maintain the amount of this fund at 360,000,000 francs and to increase it when the amount held did not reach this figure. It was required to buy 4 and 5 per cent *rentes* which were annulled when purchased. The debt was reduced by a little more than four billion francs by this method between 1917 and 1921. This fund was suspended in 1922. No important steps were taken to remove the debt until the laws passed in 1926. There were during these post-war years a number of proposals that ultimately developed into the present *Caisse.*

In 1920 Doumer and Cheron proposed to set up a *Caisse* with an annuity of one billion francs from the budget. Besides this annuity it was to receive budget surpluses at the end of the fiscal year and the interest of the *rentes* already purchased.[38] These *rentes* purchased were to be retained as

[36] Allix, *Science des finances* and Jèze, *Revue de Science et de Législation Financières.*

[37] Jèze, G., *Cours élémentaire de science des finances,* pp. 575-6; also Levrault, R., *Les Caisses d'amortissement,* p. 8.

[38] Allix, *Science des finances,* p. 854. The early history of debt retirement is covered in some detail in this general work.

if still active and it is here that the measure would have fallen into "*les dangereuses illusions du système du Dr. Price*" according to Professor Allix.[39] It was from this date that the projects for the retirement of debt began to multiply. The similarity between this measure and the Victory Sinking Fund of the United States, except for the slight Pricean twist, is striking. The influence of the past on the forms of sinking funds proved too strong; the later proposals became more similar to the original conception, although there were marked differences.

The adoption of a sinking fund was opposed in these years by those who advised the use of the capital levy, but the legislative group supporting the latter was never very strong and the sinking fund took precedence over its rival. Besides the opposition of those who favored a sinking fund, the budget difficulties made it incredible that any fund set up would go unraided. In spite of this fact Clementel, in December, 1924, proposed a *Caisse*[40] merely on the ground that any sort of retirement program, whether adhered to in practice or not, might slightly improve the public credit. On April 7, 1925, Herriot proposed to place heavy taxes on wealth to support the *Caisse*.

The difficulties encountered with the floating debt first entered the proposals for a *Caisse* in October, 1925, when Caillaux proposed that its work be restricted to the management of the *Bons* and *Obligations*. In his plan the special revenue feature appeared. This was to keep the conditions of the budget from greatly affecting the management of the debt. Caisse funds were to come from a special income tax. The *Caisse* was to support the market for debt titles as well as manage the maturities, and in addition by the use of the

[39] *Ibid.*, p. 854. See also Levrault, *op. cit.*, pp. 8-25.

[40] Jèze, *Revue de Science et de Législation Financières*, 1928, p. 51.

revenue from the income tax it was to retire from one and eight-tenths to two billion francs a year.[41]

On November 6, 1925, Painlevé advocated a poll tax of twenty francs a year to support the *Caisse*.[42] He stressed the necessary autonomy of the *Caisse,* stating that it should have complete independence and be composed of men high up in political circles. It was to receive a fixed annuity of 2,630 million francs and special revenues amounting to 5,417 millions of francs. The funds of the *Caisse* were to be deposited in the Bank. The *Caisse* was to have fifteen members (this number was later increased to twenty-three). The management of the short-term debt as well as its retirement were to be the functions of the *Caisse.*

On December 8, 1925, Loucheur in his proposal for a *Caisse* introduced the idea of industrial representation.[43] Finally on December 29, 1925, Doumer introduced a plan which the Senate adopted in its broad outlines on February 27, 1926. The Doumer plan provided an annual charge of two and a half billion francs which was to be derived from new taxes. The object of the measure was to remove the long-term debt, and it was believed that the difficulties with the franc would eventually disappear, if the reduction of the long-term debt was begun. Emphasis was placed upon the necessity of creating a budget surplus through increased taxes to remove the debt.

On February 27, 1926, the Doumer plan was adopted by the Senate with some modifications. The *Caisse* of April 28, 1816, was retired and a new body set up. There were to be twenty members, including one deputy and one senator, the latter being the president of the *Caisse.* Among the

[41] *Ibid.,* p. 51 *et seq.* Information about these proposals is set forth by Jèze in the *Revue.*

[42] Levrault, *Les Caisses d'amortissement,* p. 59 *et seq.*

[43] *Ibid.,* p. 49 *et seq.*

resources of the new *Caisse* were the following: the appropriation of the budget already devoted to the debt, an annuity of 600 million francs, all budget surpluses, donations, interest on the unclaimed stock of corporations, lotteries and a variety of other small items. The *Caisse* was to purchase debt titles and these could not be renewed.

On April 29, 1926, the Doumer *Caisse* was finally set up. It was autonomous and its management was turned over to the director of the *Caisse de depôts et consignations,* who was responsible to the council mentioned above. The *Caisse* did not, however, have a chance to show what it could do because of the financial crisis that soon followed.

A law passed on August 7, 1926, replaced it with the present *Caisse,* which followed the recommendations of the Committee of Experts.[44] This body had been established by a *Decret* of May 31, 1926. The work of the Committee was directed toward the problems of monetary stability, the conditions for which were definitely outlined. So far as the debt was concerned the Committee believed that the great quantity of *Bons* constituted the main debt problem, and of the various remedies proposed it rejected forced consolidation, the capital levy and the forced loan in favor of offering to the bond holders consolidation loans and rights to exchange them for titles of greater maturity. The Committee advocated the formation of a *Caisse* with a budget annuity equal to the amount of the interest of the bonds managed by the *Caisse,* an annuity for amortization of at least five hundred million francs and the revenues from the tobacco monopoly. It proposed the removal of the *Bons du Trésor à court terme* and the *Bons du Trésor ordinaire.*

The *Caisse* set up by the National Assembly on August 7, 1926, is technically known as the *Caisse de gestion des bons de la défense nationale, d'exploitation industrielle, des*

[44] Larrieu, *op. cit.*, p. 262 *et seq.*

tabacs et d'amortissement de la dette publique. It has civil personality and is financially independent. It is managed by a council of twenty-one members, consisting of members of Parliament and representatives of finance. The council has two committees, the *Comité financier* and the *Comité technique,* the latter including manufacturers and planters. The *Caisse* has charge of the replacement of the *Bons de la Défense Nationale* and the *Bons du Trésor.* Its powers of general amortization were originally limited. In the process of debt management it was given the power to issue new bonds of its own, but not in excess of the maximum fixed by law of 49 billion francs except for a limit of tolerance of six per cent. The maximum was to fall each year as the amount of the *Bons* were retired. The council proposes the interest on the *Bons* and this is fixed by *decrets.* The resources of the *Caisse* consist of (1) the net product of the receipts of the tobacco monopoly, which is used to pay the interest on the bonds managed by the *Caisse* and supplemented if insufficient by (2) a budget annuity, (3) by receipts of the tax on the *première mutation,* (4) and the inheritance tax, (5) gifts, legacies, and voluntary contributions, (6) supplementary funds granted by the Treasury, (7) and the receipts from bonds or debt titles issued on the security of the tobacco receipts.[45]

It is apparent from this history that the *Caisse* of August, 1926, embodies the emphasis upon debt management of the Caillaux proposal, the autonomy and special revenue features of the Painlevé plan and the industrial representation of that of Loucheur. There is a wide gap between the plan finally adopted and that proposed by Doumer and Cheron in 1920. Autonomy and special appropriations make the plan much nearer the *Caisse* of 1816 which followed Price.

[45] Larrieu, *op. cit.*, pp. 264-265; Rogers, *The Process of Inflation in France*, pp. 46-7; Haig, *Public Finances of Post-war France*; Allix, *op. cit.*, pp. 853, 856.

On May 23, 1928, the *Caisse* made its first annual report to the minister of finance as required by law. The numerous maturities had caused the *Caisse* to build up a large fund of floating capital. The retirement of all the bonds of one year maturity or less had been achieved by this time and the total *Bons* had been reduced from about forty-eight to forty-three billions. In 1928 a successful conversion of *Bons* into five per cent *rentes* took place and in February 1929 the *Caisse* began to issue four and a half per cent obligations to consolidate the floating debt, to convert the existing debt to lower rates of interest, and otherwise to facilitate retirement. In 1928 the following amounts were received from various taxes destined to effect debt retirement.

Taxe complimentaire sur la première mutation[46]	665,704,002 f.
Taxe successorale et droit de mutation par décès	2,179,291,976
Contributions volontaires	2,021,065
Timbres surchargés et timbres speciales	1,648,451
Excédents budgetaires	490,000,000
Excédents des recettes nettes des tabacs	768,986,857
	4,107,652,351

The total receipts and expenses of the *Caisse Autonome* for 1926, 1927 and 1928 show that in each of these three years the largest single item among the receipts was the *Émissions* of *Bons de la Défense Nationale* and that the tax receipts and budget receipts in 1927 and 1928 are in the neighborhood of only four billion francs.

On December 30, 1928, the powers of the *Caisse* were further extended to the retirement of all titles as well as *Bons,* and attention was directed now toward the retirement of the long-term debt as a result of the great success which had been attained in managing the short-term debt. Poincaré defended the *Caisse* from criticism in Parliament for

[46] This is a tax on the transfer of real estate for a valuable consideration.

not consolidating the debt more rapidly. He believed that had consolidation proceeded more rapidly business would have been disturbed.

IV. GERMANY

Turning now to Germany, one finds that each of the new loans which have arisen since the war has a special sinking fund. A special sinking fund was set up for the German External Loan. In the first year of the loan 25,584,000 gold marks were provided for this purpose, or a little over three per cent. The whole service of the loan, which included this amount for amortization, was 88,945,000 gold marks.[47] This was a first charge upon the annuities which constituted the reparations. The service of this loan has proceeded regularly. Purchases for the sinking fund were limited to a certain redemption price and the value of the bonds was so well maintained that it was found very difficult to purchase them below the stipulated price except in the United States and Italy. Twenty per cent of the sinking fund money was used for market purchases and with the rest bonds were drawn for redemption and paid. Between 1924 and 1928, 111,788,000 gold marks (nominal) of the German External Loan were retired, making the average rate of retirement a little more than three per cent.

The Reichsbank Loan also has a sinking fund. 135.5 million Reichsmarks are payable in fifteen annual installments of 9.03 million marks. The Reich Loan of 1927 has a sinking fund which, according to the law, is to come into operation in 1934 and amounts to 2.1 per cent of the original principal of the loan.[48] It is therefore a cumulative sinking fund. There was also a special sinking fund for the Rentenbank loan.

[47] *Execution of the Experts' Plan, First Annuity Year*, p. 121.

[48] It was estimated that the amortization would be completed in 1959.

As will be remembered from the preceding chapter, the Loan Liquidation Debt was divided into two parts, one with drawing rights, the other without them. That portion of the debt with drawing rights is to be retired in thirty years, beginning in 1926. This would require a sinking fund of about three per cent.

V. SUMMARY

If one looks at the broad features of the debt retirement programs of these four countries certain important differences appear. Three of them, France, England and the United States, have consolidated their plans. Only Germany has special sinking funds. All four have found it desirable to rely on a definite plan of retirement rather than upon the indefinite use of budget surpluses. Some of the funds in the United States, Great Britain and Germany are cumulative, whereas France has none of this type. In the United States, England and Germany sinking funds are paid out of the general tax receipts and have virtually no special taxes allocated to them. In France even the receipts of a special government monopoly are so allocated. In France there is no set rate of retirement while in the other three countries there are definite rates. The United States and Germany have preferred to express the charges of the sinking funds in percentages whereas Great Britain has set up a fixed annual charge. In Great Britain and France special government bodies with debt payment functions have been retained but in Germany and the United States there are no such agencies. In the last-mentioned countries and in Great Britain the management of the debt is in the hands of the Treasury. In France the management is placed with a separate constitutional body. True, this *Caisse Autonome* is, as Allix points out, subject to the control of the Treasury, but many functions exercised by the United States Treasury

Department, for example, have apparently been left to the *Caisse* by law and the determination of the degree of independence it actually possesses would require a great deal more study than has been given it here. Germany differs from the other countries in the greater size of her sinking funds and the absence of any provision for the use of the government surplus to retire the debt. France is unique in that the prosperity of the country is likely to be directly reflected in the sinking fund through the increase in the proceeds of transfer and inheritance taxes and of the tobacco monopoly.

But of most importance are the facts that in these four countries there is little uniformity in the methods of retirement used or in the speed of retirement projected, and each country seems to have been influenced to a considerable extent by the policies followed before the World War. Thus in the United States the use of both a percentage sinking fund and the budget surplus follows the policy of earlier years. England returned to the fixed annual debt charge and the use of surplus budget receipts, France to a special sinking fund body with the allocation of revenues and Germany to specific sinking funds.

In these first four chapters the history of the laws and policies of the various governments in the retirement of debt has been traced. In order that this history may be understood and evaluated, it is necessary to consider in the chapters that follow the changing theory of the effects of debt retirement, and the conclusions which may be drawn from these theories as to the manner in which debt may be retired.

CHAPTER V

The Monetary Effects of Debt Retirement

In the preceding chapters the problems and methods of debt management and retirement in the years since the World War have been surveyed. Their evaluation and interpretation depend upon the nature of public debt burdens, and in the pages which follow the effects of debt retirement are discussed, in order that some light may be thrown upon the theory of debt burden. These effects have been classified as monetary, banking, international, distribution and production effects, to each of which a separate chapter is devoted.

I. THE RELATION BETWEEN THE PUBLIC DEBT AND MONETARY CONDITIONS

The monetary effects, which will be first dealt with, have interested economists for many years because the relations between money and the public debt have often been very close and very important. In the United States the public debt issued before the war has served as collateral for a large part of the currency. During the World War the government security back of bank deposits was augmented as a basis for increased purchasing media. Member bank promissory notes backed by government bonds were used as security for Federal Reserve notes, as well as for the direct increase of member bank deposits at the Federal Reserve banks. Under the Glass-Steagall Act passed in Congress on February 28, 1932, government bonds owned by the Federal Reserve banks may be used for one year as security for Federal Reserve notes. These indirect methods of simultaneously increasing money and public debt have had the same object as the much more direct methods of England and France, but in the case of the advances by the central banks to the government, in England and France the public debt and money were almost the same thing.

In the first years after the war public attention was almost entirely concentrated upon the inflationary effects of the public debt.[1] But since 1926, owing no doubt in part to the work of the Colwyn Committee, which examined the problems of debt retirement at great length, two other monetary problems of the debt have been considerably discussed. These are the effects of the debt burden upon deflation and the effects of price changes upon the burden of debt, and to them this chapter will be devoted. They are very closely related problems and opinions about one are likely to color opinions about the other.

There are various sources of knowledge as to the deflationary effects of the public debt. Among them are the numerous statements of economists and business men since the war; the data on the way in which inflation was originally caused; the statements of economists on the relation of taxation to saving; and the statistics of prices and investments.

II. THE OPINIONS OF ECONOMISTS ON THE DEFLATIONARY EFFECTS OF DEBT RETIREMENT

A great variety of opinions have been expressed about the influence of debt retirement upon prices in recent years. The opinions of the Colwyn Committee and of several economists will be discussed, since they suggest the factors involved in the effects of debt retirement upon production. The whole matter was vigorously debated by the Colwyn Committee and particular attention was paid to the effects of the capital levy. The committee agreed that the capital levy would tend to depress prices but that this would not occur in the

[1] *Cf.* Rogers, *The Process of Inflation in France*, chap. v; Graham, *Exchange, Prices and Production in Hyper-Inflation—Germany, 1920-1923;* Seligman, *Currency, Inflation and Public Debts.*

same degree as the amount of capital taken by the levy. This conclusion was based on the belief that "the assets that (business men) could pledge for bank advances are in the aggregate far in excess of those so employed."[2] In view of the fact that the supply of collateral for loans was already greatly in excess of the amount of the loans, it was thought that a very considerable reduction of the debt could occur before any great reduction in credit would take place. It was concluded that a capital levy raising £3 billions would not cause deflation of credit "anywhere approaching that sum, even if the levy had grave psychological reactions."[3] Much emphasis was placed on the way heavy taxation, such as a capital levy would involve, would be received. If pessimism was pronounced, any number of serious consequences might result. There would probably be a general disturbance of the money market and a fall in security prices, panic sales, government sales of securities that had been used to pay the levy, and individual sales of securities not approved by the government for the payment of the levy.

In support of these opinions of the majority, some of the witnesses before the Colwyn Committee believed that the levy would reduce prices very much under certain specific conditions.[4] One of these witnesses, W. W. Paine, thought that there coûld be a great fall in prices only where individual wealth was confiscated and bank collateral materially reduced. Credit would not be affected (1) where business is publicly operated, (2) where payments are made in cash, (3) where businesses do not borrow at any fixed ratio to the amount of government securities they possess. Evidence was presented to show that businesses do not so borrow. From these views it is seen that the extent to which taxation to pay debts will

[2] *Colwyn Report*, p. 271.

[3] *Ibid.*, p. 271.

[4] *Colwyn Report, Minutes of Evidence*, p. 380, par. 5218.

reduce prices depends upon the psychological reaction of tax-payers and the fixity of the ratio of collateral to loans.

Another factor was suggested before the Committee by D. H. Macgregor, who stated that the amount of loans and deposits depends in part upon the reserve ratios and not upon the amount of collateral available for loans. This assumes that the proportion of reserves to deposits remains fixed, just as the belief that, if collateral is reduced, credit and prices will fall assumes, among other things, that the percentage of loans to collateral is fixed. Macgregor was, however, evidently aware of this assumption, for he points out that deflation would occur only if the credit with which the government bonds were paid had come from the central banks and had thus been a net addition to the total credit.[5] The fixity of reserve ratios is assumed only for local banks. He says that "the effect on prices of a large and sudden repayment depends on the possible encroachment on the supply of securities as a basis of advances and the extent to which industry after the war has come to rely on them."[6] These opinions thus point to a third factor, the fixity of reserve ratios and the nature of the credit relations between the central and the local banks.

Sir Josiah Stamp has attempted to classify the types of deflation and in so doing covers two of the above factors. He believes that there would first be (1) primary or automatic deflation due to the removal of a part of the credit based on government collateral; (2) secondary deflation, or deflation as a consequence of the first deflation, which would reduce the money value of the remaining collateral; (3) disturbance deflation which would result from the absence of an adequate immediate supply of investment opportunities for repaid government bond holders; and (4) psychological

[5] *Colwyn Report, Minutes of Evidence*, p. 424.

[6] *Ibid.*, p. 424.

deflation resulting from the supposed adverse effects of the taxes levied to pay the debt.[7]

Although it appears that most economists who have considered this question incline to the theory that debt payment causes deflation, there are some who do not hold this view, because of their opinions as to the effects of taxation for debt retirement upon the volume of credit. Keynes, for example, believes that the payment of the debt may even result in inflation if the size of taxes is too great. Thus he thought that "the tendency to borrow would be incomparably stronger than the tendency to hoard, and . . . consequently the net effect would be inflationary rather than deflationary."[8] Keynes would probably not apply this statement to a more gradual type of debt reduction. Professor W. R. Scott also believes that the repayment of debt will cause a rise in prices, but he attempts to supply a source of the borrowed funds. They will be deducted from those commonly employed by business. He thought that a rise in prices would occur not because of inflation but because of a restriction of business resulting from the diversion of loanable funds to borrowing to pay taxes.[9] He seems not to account for the return of these funds into the money market through the attempts at reinvestment by the repaid bond holders. The real effects under these circumstances would be problematic because of the uncertain consequence for business activity of borrowing to pay taxes. It is certain, however, that there is no permanent and therefore effective restriction in the volume of credit in this case.

In the United States Professor W. A. Brown has given considerable study to the effects of debt retirement upon the price level in so far as the latter is affected by fluctuations in

[7] *Contemporary Review*, January, 1924.

[8] *Colwyn Report*, p. 272.

[9] *Ibid.*, p. 272.

the supply of capital funds. While definitely admitting that the origin of the public debt was attended by inflation, he states that the effect of debt retirement upon the price level will depend upon the influence of repayment upon production through the transference of debt funds in the process of reinvestment.[10] He does not think that capital funds are either increased or decreased by the repayment of the debt, but merely transferred. There has been a great deal of confusion on these points. Professor Brown quotes from the quarterly review of a well-known business house which stated that the too rapid retirement of the debt had caused inflation by its premature injection of funds into the money market.[11] He has also remarked the interesting confusion of the federal Treasury on this question in the *Annual Report of the Secretary of the Treasury* for 1925. At one place the report states, "It is clearly demonstrable that the government program of debt retirement has been a factor in bringing about the improvement in credit conditions which now prevails and the improvement in credit conditions is in turn a prime factor in the present prosperous condition of the country."[12] From this statement it might appear that the Treasury believes that the net supply of funds is actually increased by the payment of debt. At a later point pains are taken to show why the payment of debt can only be a transfer of funds. To add still further to the uncertainty of the Treasury's beliefs on these matters, chief responsibility is given to the increasing volume of savings and to gold imports for the improved credit conditions mentioned in the statement just quoted. No attempt is made to show the relationships among these factors. The improved credit conditions are

10 Brown, "The Effects of National Debt Reduction on the Supply of Capital Funds," *Annalist*, August 31, 1928.

11 *Ibid.*, p. 307.

12 *Annual Report of the Secretary of the Treasury*, 1925, p. 48.

indicated by the lower rates of interest and it may be assumed from these statements that the Treasury thought that the payment of debt caused the decline in interest rates. Taxation, the Treasury very definitely asserts, reduces interest rates and increases saving.[13] Virtually then, the Treasury comes to the conclusion of Professor Brown that an increase in the supply of loanable funds comes largely from the increase in the volume of saving resulting from the taxation and reinvestment of the repaid debt funds.

The inclusion of increased savings is probably not justifiable as an explanation of the greater supply of investment funds, although it may partly explain the falling interest rates. These conditions are much too complicated to allow very simple interpretation. They must be viewed more broadly. The supply of new physical capital and the increase in the supply of credit do not by themselves determine the rate of interest, for the rate depends upon the demand and supply for investment funds.

The opinions of economists and business men on the relation of debt payment to deflation provide a number of useful suggestions with which to work. The factors mentioned are the psychological effects, the fixity of the ratio of government collateral to loans, the fixity of reserve ratios, the relation of local to central bank credit, the increase in saving as a result of taxation, and changes in the national supply of gold. No one has apparently accomplished much more than to list and partially to explain the operations of some of these factors in the problem.

Earlier in this chapter it was pointed out that an examination of the manner in which inflation was originally caused by the public debt might throw some light upon its effects in regard to deflation. This will now be attempted, and it is believed that the history of inflation will show to some extent

[13] *Ibid.*, p. 46.

the functioning of the above-mentioned factors, particularly the relationship of local and central bank credit, the fixity of the ratio of government collateral to loans, and the fixity of reserve ratios.

III. THE EFFECTS OF THE RELATIONS BETWEEN LOCAL AND CENTRAL BANK CREDIT

(a) *The Relations Set Up by Inflation*

In the United States inflation was accompanied by the extended use of government bonds as collateral for increased loans. Instead of borrowing directly from the banks the government issued bonds, which were in large measure destined to be bought by individual citizens. As Dr. R. A. Love has pointed out, the First Liberty Bond Act made an important change in the floating of bond issues. "The Act permitted the Treasury to deposit until needed the proceeds from the sale of bonds and certificates of indebtedness . . . in national banks previously designated as depositors, thereby avoiding the disturbance which would have accompanied the transfer of large sums of money either to the sub-Treasury or to a small number of selected banks." [14] This widespread system of special depositories allowed the government to receive for its bonds bank credit which was well distributed throughout the country. The bonds were then sold to individuals by the banks, which were encouraged to extend to individuals any necessary accommodations. Notes for the purchase of government bonds could be discounted at the Federal Reserve banks at a preferential rate of discount.[15] The additional loans granted by the Federal Reserve banks constituted a net increase in credit which formed to a large extent the basis of the general credit expansion

[14] Love, *Federal Financing*, p. 129.

[15] *Ibid.*, pp. 137-140.

during the war. The loans of the Federal Reserve banks to banks and the loans of banks to individuals, based on notes secured by government bonds, created the additional credit which was loaned in turn to the government by the purchase of its bonds by these banks and individuals. These results are generally recognized by American economists.[16] The relation of borrowing to the price level has been very thoroughly discussed by J. H. Hollander in his volume entitled *War Borrowing,* particularly those aspects related to the issue of certificates of indebtedness.[17]

In France inflation was accomplished to a large extent by the advances of the Bank of France to the government. Dr. J. H. Rogers made an extensive study of the conditions surrounding the course of inflation in that country. He found that curves representing the advances of the Bank of France followed fairly closely the curves of prices and exchange rates; in fact, much more closely than the curves of floating debt, government deficits and internal borrowing. It is thus inferred that bank advances had the closest relation to inflation.[18] He also discovered that the increased sales of short-term treasury obligations were accompanied by decreased bank advances and vice versa. The credit resulting from the direct borrowing of the government at the bank and sales of *Bons de la Défense Nationale,* which in their turn were largely made as a result of loans from the Bank of France, greatly increased prices. Whether payments were made to the government by notes or by *mandats,* the result was increased prices. As the government used these funds in purchases they were deposited in banks and were reloaned by the banks for private business purposes. In 1918 they

[16] *Cf.* Ely, *Outlines of Economics,* 5th ed., pp. 309-310; Taussig, *Principles of Economics,* p. 382 *et seq.*

[17] Hollander, *War Borrowing,* chap. v; see particularly his conclusions.

[18] Rogers, *The Process of Inflation in France,* p. 50.

flowed into *Bons de la Défense Nationale* in large amounts because of the fear of defeat in the war.[19]

In addition to the advances to the government the seven great banks of France made large loans to private borrowers. Some of these loans were based upon the *Bons de la Défense Nationale* as collateral and the Bank of France agreed to accept them as security at 80 per cent of their nominal value.[20] It is probable, however, that these advances were less expanded as a result of the advances of the Bank of France than similar advances in Great Britain. The advances of the Bank of France to the government considerably exceeded the advances of all seven banks to the public.[21] In France inflation seems to have resulted directly from the advances of the Bank to the government. In normal times it is understood that the government may not borrow from the central bank, but during war time this custom is altered—in fact, borrowing is provided for in advance.[22] During 1870-71, the bank thus advanced nearly 1,500 million francs to the state.

In Great Britain likewise the government resorted to direct borrowing, with a similar rise in prices but through somewhat different processes. British conditions resemble American conditions in so far as deposits with the central bank constitute reserves; they resemble those of France to the extent that the central bank makes direct advances to the government. The first Interim Report of the Committee on Currency and Foreign Exchanges describes at some length the methods by which war-time inflation came about. These

19 *Ibid.*, p. 82.

20 Fisk, *French Public Finance*, p. 16.

21 *Ibid.*, p. 42.

22 An agreement by which the Bank of France was to put 2900 million francs at the disposal of the government in case of war was made November, 1911. *Ibid.*, p. 13.

methods are also analyzed by A. C. Pigou in his volume on public finance.[23] The key to the British situation is to be found in the relationship of the banks to the Bank of England. Advances to the government by the Bank would be paid out to those firms providing the government with equipment. The latter would then deposit these claims on the Bank of England in other banks. These other banks would then own the deposits in the Bank of England originally created for the use of the government. Since these deposits serve as reserves, four or five times as many new deposits could be created by the banks and the new deposits in their turn would be used either to buy government bonds or to make loans to citizens, who would buy government bonds and use these bonds as collateral for the loans they had received from the banks. The difference between the French and British processes was that, owing to the fact that deposits in the Bank of England caused a great increase in bank loans elsewhere, the Ways and Means Advances did not have to be increased to so great an extent to accomplish the same amount of inflation as was caused by the advances of the Bank of France. It seems possible that the Ways and Means Advances increased the total credit by three to five times.

It is apparent, therefore, that for three of the leading countries of the world inflation was induced by the advances of the central banks and that in the United States and Great Britain these advances formed the basis of still further credit expansion through loans against government securities as collateral.

Earlier in this chapter it was pointed out that psychological reaction, the fixity of the ratio of collateral value to the value of loans, the fixity of reserve ratios, and the credit relations between local and central banks were all important factors in

[23] *Cf. First Interim Report* of the Committee on Currency and Foreign Exchanges, 1918, p. 2. Also Pigou, A. C., *Public Finance*, pp. 260-271.

our problem. The way in which the last factor in particular operates should now be clearer as a result of this brief survey of the conditions surrounding inflation. The extent and nature of any deflation that may result from debt retirement in any particular country will be largely determined by these conditions.

(b) *The Effects of the Bank Relations Set Up by Inflation*

Let us consider how the relations between central and local banks that have evolved out of war-time inflation affect the degree of deflation which may be caused by retirement in the United States, Great Britain and France. In the United States the effects of debt retirement may be considerably influenced by the fact that government securities are an important means of obtaining Federal Reserve funds. As Love has pointed out, even before the war authority could be found for extending credit on the basis of government bonds in sections 13 and 14 of the Federal Reserve Act and in an amendment to that act of September 7, 1916.[24] This special legal relationship of bonds to central bank credit had caused government bonds to have a peculiar scarcity value in the United States and an effect upon the volume of credit which they do not have in either France or England, and which has a decided effect upon the amount of deflation that may result from the debt retirement.[25]

This scarcity value is well reflected by the way in which holdings of government bonds have increased since the war. So great has been the concentration of the holdings of government bonds in the hands of banks and corporations that Professor Brown was justified in saying, "Already the demand of the small investor has been completely eliminated

[24] Love, *Federal Financing*, p. 133.

[25] *Cf.* Brown, W. A., *Annalist*, August 24, 1928, p. 276.

as a factor in the government bond market." [26] The United States securities and other securities held by all member banks of the Federal Reserve system and all reporting banks in millions since 1920 were as follows:

TABLE XV

Year (as of June 30)	Member Banks		All Reporting Banks	
	U. S. Securities	Other Securities	U. S. Securities	State, County and Municipal Securities
1920	2,942	3,125	3,844	643
1921	2,661	3,444	3,872	1,368
1922	3,247	3,815	3,500	981
1923	3,870	3,925	4,211	894
1924	3,608	4,390	4,614	1,401
1925	3,781	1,029	4,182	1,067
1926	3,744	1,149	4,160	1,271
1927	3,796	1,277	3,829	1,724
1928	4,225	1,367	4,153	1,890
1929			4,023	1,746
1930			3,846	1,702

Source: *The Annual Reports of the Secretary of the Treasury* and the *Annual Reports of the Federal Reserve Board.*

When the holdings of United States securities are divided by the total outstanding, it is found that the percentage held by the above classes of banks increased from about 13.5 per cent in 1920 to about 23 per cent in 1927 and 1928. Of the total national debt in 1930 the member banks held 25 per cent. It is apparent that the bank holdings of United States bonds have rapidly increased since the war and that their peculiar value to the banks is responsible for the increase. Professor Brown has even ventured to predict that the banks will, in the not too distant future, own half of the total.[27] Since the

[26] *Ibid.*, p. 277.

[27] *Ibid.*, pp. 276-277.

rate of increase in these holdings is slowing down, however, it is possible that this eventuality may be considerably postponed.[28] This concentration of bond holdings in the banks affects the extent to which a reduction in the debt can decrease bank credit.

If it could be granted that the amounts of government bonds used in borrowing from the Federal Reserve banks remained a fixed proportion of the total of government bonds outstanding, it might follow that a decrease in the total amount of government bonds would cause a similar decrease in the amount of Federal Reserve bank credit. This in its turn would have a considerable effect upon the volume of member bank credit, since the deposits of the Federal Reserve banks are their reserves. Finally, the decline in member bank credit would have a deflationary influence upon prices, if prices depend to any extent upon the volume of credit. In this chain of reasoning there are several weaknesses, however, which must be considered in turn.

First of all, the volume of government securities held by banks or used as the collateral basis for loans maintains a variable proportion to the total government securities outstanding. This is indicated by a comparison of the total volume of government securities outstanding with the increase in the holdings of member banks in the United States. Not only has the absolute amount of these holdings been increasing, but the proportion to the total has also increased. Second, the reserve ratios of member banks are not fixed. Finally, the influence of credit upon prices is by no means certain. But of these three weaknesses the first, it seems, is

[28] In the year 1931 the issue of government bonds has considerably increased. It is possible that the holdings of the general public will be greatly augmented in the future if the government continues to issue a great quantity of new debt. The preceding discussion refers to the conditions existing up to 1930, which it is probable will be reëstablished when the depression ends.

the most important. If the banks could not get an increasing supply of bonds, it is quite possible that the reduction of the total supply of bonds would have a deflationary effect. In the United States, therefore, the low rates of interest on government bonds and the advantages that they have in banking have probably prevented the rapid retirement of the debt from having any very important deflationary effects. In the immediate future the great increase in the debt and the Glass-Steagall Act may also prevent any increase in retirement. But, if business depression does not unduly increase the amount of government debt, it is possible that these effects may be ultimately realized. Tax exemption and the needs of corporations for government bonds will set up strong competition for the bonds and the supply of bonds may be completely cut off from small holders.

In Great Britain the Ways and Means Advances have stood in much the same position as government bonds in the United States. Their reduction has been urged since the war.[29] Treasury bills were objected to not so much on account of the dangers of government insolvency owing to large and frequent maturities, but because in an attempt to meet these maturities the government would be tempted to resort to Ways and Means Advances.[30] But the payment of Ways and Means Advances would have a tendency to reduce the volume of credit as well as to prevent further expansions. Such payment would tend to create claims of the Bank of England upon other banks, with the result that the balances of the latter would be reduced and the proportion of liabilities to reserves increased. The payment of treasury bills or other securities would also tend to reduce credit, since it would reduce the collateral upon which loans could be made. To just what extent this would occur was discussed by the

[29] Pigou, *Public Finance*, p. 277.

[30] *Ibid.*, pp. 276-278.

Colwyn Committee, as has been pointed out above, with the conclusion that it would depend upon the degree to which collateral continued to be used to back up loans and upon the degree of fixity in the ratio of collateral value to loan value. The tendency of debt payment to cause deflation would probably be greater in Great Britain than in the United States owing to the fact that in Great Britain the debt as collateral was not to the same degree a basis for the inflation and can not be concentrated in the hands of the banks in such a way as to perpetuate the inflation. In England the reduction of Ways and Means Advances resembles the reduction of government bonds in the hands of American member banks.

In France it is probable that a reduction of advances made by the Bank of France would have a deflationary tendency, as would a reduction in the securities issued by the government. There is the important difference, however, that since there is not the same credit relation between the branches of the Bank of France as there is between the private banks of England and the Bank of England, the resulting deflation would not be nearly so great. It thus appears that one of the weaknesses in the chain of reasoning mentioned above, namely that the collateral used for loans does not maintain a fixed proportion to the debt outstanding, does not apply to the same degree in either England or France as it does in the United States. In the latter two countries the collateral value allowed as a basis for loans may not remain fixed, however, and this variation might to some extent limit the deflationary effects of debt reduction. It is also true that a debt reduction of a given amount will not cause a reduction in credit of the same amount. Nor can it be estimated what degree of deflation would result. In the United States, as has been shown, the extent to which a reduction in debt would be effective in reducing credit depends upon the extent to which the bond holdings of one group of holders, the banks, are reduced. In Great Britain it would depend upon the extent to which the holdings in general used for borrowing were reduced.

IV. THE FIXITY OF THE VALUES ALLOWED COLLATERAL IN MAKING LOANS

In regard to the degree of fixity of the values allowed collateral in making loans, another factor in the effects of debt retirement upon deflation, there is very little inductive evidence. It seems likely that these values would remain fairly steady for collateral as good as government securities. In the United States the margin on government collateral has been from five to ten per cent for many years.[31] It is very unlikely that the values allowed on this sort of collateral would increase sufficiently to offset completely the reduction in loans possible as a result of a decrease in the amount of the collateral. Furthermore, the effects of the concentration of bonds in the banks upon the volume of credit are far greater than any variation in the value allowed upon government collateral could be.

V. THE FIXITY OF RESERVE RATIOS

Still another factor in the theory that debt retirement causes deflation is the degree of fixity of reserve ratios. It was suggested by Macgregor, and requires some illustration to be understood. Suppose under American conditions that the government collateral is reduced, once the banks have discovered they they can get along with a much greater volume of loans on a given quantity of gold than before the inflation. May not measures be taken to perpetuate this condition? To the extent that eligible collateral has been reduced, however, there will be a tendency toward deflation,

[31] *Cf.* Kniffen, *Commercial Banking*, vol. ii, p. 628, and Kniffen, *American Banking Practice*, pp. 176-190; and Westerfield, *Banking Principles and Practice*, vol. iv, p. 875.

but deflation will not necessarily occur because of the reduction of government bond collateral so long as the banks, the gold reserves not having been reduced, are willing to loan on inferior collateral. In the three countries considered, the system of central banking is such that the central banks are not disposed to loan on other collateral just because the volume of gold reserves remains the same. If the system of making central bank loans is changed, of course we shall have to wait until those changes take place to estimate their consequences. In both Great Britain and the United States the simultaneous repayment of Ways and Means Advances and the securities of the government would reduce the reserves of the local banks. In these countries the fact that central bank gold reserves remain constant during the period of deflation does not mean that the member bank reserves are constant. Where the payment of debt actually reduces reserves in the real sense of deposits with the central bank, the possibility raised by Professor Macgregor [32] is to a large degree unreal. It has reality only when the reserve ratio referred to is that of the central bank. In the United States, however, this ratio is quite variable and the volume of member bank credit does not closely follow the amount of gold of the Federal Reserve banks. The annual monthly averages of the reserve ratios of the Federal Reserve banks show a very considerable variation. In the post-war years they were as follows: [33] In Great Britain conditions before the war

1921	61.6	1926	73.6
1922	77.3	1927	76.2
1923	76.4	1928	68.5
1924	80.0	1929	71.4
1925	74.4	1930	80.2

[32] See p. 135.

[33] U. S. Department of Commerce, *Annual Supplement of Survey of Current Business, 1931.*

would have fitted more exactly Professor Macgregor's thesis that since the gold reserves remain constant, the total credit will remain constant. The conditions of credit creation have changed. Describing the pre-war period, J. M. Keynes says,

> Thus the rate of creation of credit in Great Britain was caused by a simple piece of mechanism faithfully to reflect the inward and outward movements of gold. . . . The new post-war element of "management" consists in the habitual employment of an "open market" policy by which the Bank of England buys and sells investments with a view of keeping the reserve resources of the Member Banks at the level which it desires.[34]

In the case of France, where the payment of debt securities would not reduce reserves, the effects of debt retirement upon credit are not so certain. It would be possible, of course, for the Bank of France to attempt to maintain a war-time reserve ratio. It has, however, been the custom there to maintain very large reserves. Furthermore, the reduction of the advances of the Bank of France to the government would surely have a deflationary effect.

VI. COLLATERAL THAT MAY BE SUBSTITUTED FOR GOVERNMENT BONDS

It is evident, therefore, that the deflationary effects of debt retirement will not be wholly prevented by the maintenance of war-time reserve ratios, or by the peculiarities of the credit relations of local and central banks (at least in the three countries considered), or by the variability of the value attached to government collateral in loans. There is, of course, the possibility that present banking conditions may change during the course of debt payment in such a way as to prevent deflation, but this is a matter for the future. It is evident, however, that in the United States other securities

[34] Keynes, *Treatise on Money*, vol. ii, p. 231.

may be issued in sufficient quantities to serve as collateral in the future and the Federal Reserve Act may be altered so that deflation may be prevented through the substitution of other collateral for United States government collateral. These securities may be issued by local governments or by private corporations. In both England and the United States the amount of local issues has been rapidly increasing since the war. For example, the total debt of American counties was $371,528,000 in 1912 and $1,272,790,000 in 1922. The total debt of incorporated places and all other civil divisions was $3,104,426,000 in 1912 and $6,481,406,000 in 1922.[35] Approximately seven billions of new state and local debt has been issued since 1920. In addition to the increase in public securities there has been a great increase in private securities, especially marked in the United States. In 1920 there were 1,114 bond issues listed by the New York Stock Exchange; in 1928, 1,513. In 1920 there were 613 stocks listed and in 1928, 1,131.[36] However, until these bonds may be used as collateral for loans from the Federal Reserve banks, it would not be possible for them to prevent the deflation that would follow from the retirement of government bonds. Until such a privilege is granted it cannot be said that the local and private issues can prevent deflation.

The opinions expressed by economists and our own analysis of them leads then to the conclusion that to the extent that government bonds or debts serve as effective bases for increased central bank credit their retirement will set up a tendency toward deflation. A sudden or large retirement of the debt may also cause a fall in prices through its adverse psychological effects. It appears further that the increase in private and local debt will not necessarily prevent these tendencies. Finally, there seems to be sufficient evidence to show

[35] *Statistical Abstract of the United States*, 1931.

[36] *Recent Economic Changes*, vol. ii, p. 685.

that deflation may have been slightly accelerated by the retirement of debt in England and France but that the facts do not seem to indicate this in the United States.[37]

VII. STATISTICS OF PRICES AND DEBT RETIREMENT

It is of interest to note that statistics of prices in the three countries considered do not conflict with these conclusions, although they do not provide any satisfactory confirmation of them. The index of commodity prices of the United States Bureau of Labor Statistics shows that wholesale prices fell from 154.4 in 1920 to 96.5 in 1929 (1926=100). The public debt reached its peak in August, 1919, and had declined by about nine billions to $16,931,197,000 in 1929. The decline in debt is in the neighborhood of 35 per cent. It should not be concluded from the rough similarity in these changes that the decline in prices was caused by a decline of credit arising from the retirement of the debt. The volume of bank credit increased rapidly during these years. For example, the loans and discounts of national banks were $13,544,000,000 in 1920 and were $15,160,000,000 in 1929. Demand deposits stood at $9,501,000,000 in 1920 and had reached $11,089,000,000 in 1929. Time deposits show an even more marked increase.[38] It is thus evident that the fall in prices has not resulted from any actual decline in purchasing medium. The figures on the member bank holdings of government bonds cited some pages back constitute still better proof. One may only say that deflationary tendencies have been set up. But these conditions in the United States raise the question of where the credit has gone. Has production not only grown up to the post-war credit but even increased so rapidly that a further expansion of credit occurred without checking a falling price level? In the next

[37] This question will be discussed in Chapter VI.

[38] U. S. Treasury Dept., Comptroller of the Currency.

chapter an attempt will be made to answer this question in part. The explanation possibly lies in the diversion of funds into the stock market and into business activities requiring purchasing media other than those represented in the wholesale price index. In America there is no doubt that other factors than the issue or retirement of debt exist which are most important in bringing about falling prices. In the past year, for example, commodity prices have fallen sharply in the face of a marked increase in the public debt.

The peak year for the British debt was also 1919 and since 1920 England has likewise experienced falling prices. Taking 1920 as the base year of 100, prices had fallen to 46 by 1927.[39] Since that date prices have declined still further; the greatest decrease took place in the years 1920-22 and in recent years as a result of industrial depression. It is obvious that very little may be proved by these figures. The greatest reduction in Ways and Means Advances had taken place between June 30, 1919 and March 31, 1921. This would, of course, allow the Ways and Means reduction to be an important factor in the decline. In regard to France there is no doubt that the decline in prices has taken place in the period of debt reduction, i. e. since 1926.[40] Very little statistical treatment of these problems is possible. These changes, however, do not prove that there was any causal connection between the decline in prices and the retirement of the debt. This question will be discussed later.

VIII. THE EFFECTS OF TAXATION UPON PRODUCTION AND FALLING PRICES

In the preceding pages we have touched occasionally upon the effects of taxation upon production and the effects of production changes in their turn upon the price level. It is

[39] *Cf. Great Britain and Ireland Statistical Tables,* 1928-29.

[40] *Cf. Annuaire statistique générale.*

possible that prices may fall as a consequence of debt payment without any reduction in the volume of credit whatsoever. It is also possible that these price changes, which may be induced by alterations in the rate of production, may be the most important of all.

Prominent among the economists who have dealt with this phase of the monetary effects of debt payment is Professor Seligman. As he points out, certain price changes may occur as a result of the effects of taxation on production.[41] If the general effects of taxation are to restrict production, prices will tend to rise. If the effects of taxes are to stimulate production, however, a fall in prices might occur. J. A. Hobson, when a witness before the Colwyn Committee, took the position that the income tax may be shifted to the consumer, causing a rise in prices. He was challenged on this point by Sir Josiah Stamp, who demanded that he explain his conclusion in terms of the quantity theory of money. Stamp wanted to know how he would explain a rise in prices without a decline in production or an increase in the volume of money. Hobson after some deliberation wrote a reply to the Committee in which he held that the income tax was a check to production. The debate brought forth articles by Robertson and Stamp in England and by Snavely in the United States, but these were concerned more with the effects of taxation upon production than with the problem of price changes resulting from taxation for debt reduction. They will be discussed therefore in connection with the general treatment of the effects of taxation for debt retirement on production in Chapter IX. Any conclusions about the effects of taxation for debt retirement upon the price level must then depend upon the reasoning in that chapter. On the whole, as will be demonstrated, the effects under certain conditions are favorable to increased produc-

[41] Seligman, *Studies in Public Finance*, p. 83 *et seq.*

tion. If properly arranged, debt reduction should consequently tend to reduce prices.[42]

[42] These conclusions about the effects of debt retirement upon deflation suggest a conception of inflation as the extreme of borrowing. According to the degree of difficulty a government experiences in obtaining funds, it passes from taxes to loans and from loans to inflation. Taxes may be first raised to the point where evasion, reduced savings and other difficulties set in. This point is higher up on the tax schedule during war than during peace times because of the greater willingness of people to make sacrifices during a war. With the return of peace this fact is recognized. In his annual message to Congress, December 2, 1919, President Wilson said that "Congress might well consider whether the higher rates of income and profits taxes can in peace times be effectively productive of revenues, and whether they might not, on the contrary, be destructive to business activity and productive of waste and inefficiency. There is a point at which, in peace times, high rates of income and profits taxes discourage energy, remove the incentive to new enterprises, encourage extravagant expenditures, and produce industrial stagnation with consequent unemployment and other attendant evils." When this point is reached or when it becomes apparent that it must soon be reached, the government turns to loans. In any case, the resort to loans is partly to avoid discontent arising from higher taxes. If the funds secured through loans are diverted from other possible uses no inflation will result, but since loans are used to reduce the difficulty of securing funds through taxes they are not likely to be secured entirely through such diversion.

With an increase in taxes the citizen becomes conscious of the expenses of government. It is possible that he does not have the same feeling if loans are used, because he expects repayment. The taxes cut into his income so that they absorb a part of the surplus above his expenses. This reduces either his savings or his consumption. The extent to which he will allow either to occur depends upon his public spirit and upon what he considers necessary for his consumption. The use of loans encourages him to increase his sacrifice because a part of the loss will possibly be recovered. (This of course does not follow in the later stages of inflation.) But there is a limit to his willingness to make sacrifices consciously. The government then has no recourse except the more obvious inflation of central bank advances and government money. Through these means it secures its funds insidiously and since the loss is not sensed immediately it is more readily borne. Sometimes inflation starts as soon as loans are issued, and this largely because governments tend to follow the way of least resistance; they skip over the step mentioned above. Several governments, among them Germany

IX. THE EFFECTS OF PRICE CHANGES UPON THE BURDEN OF DEBT

The second main problem concerning the monetary effects of debt retirement, which was raised at the beginning of this chapter, relates to the changes in debt burden that result

and France, did not make any very serious attempt at taxation during the World War.

The great needs of the government also involve, in addition to these psychological difficulties, certain problems of transferring property. During the period of greatest war expense countries like England, Germany and France, if not the United States, required sums not only in excess of customary savings but in excess of the amount of saving that could reasonably be stimulated by any conceivable means. A transfer of property rights in excess of annual savings thus became inevitable. Under such circumstances, the question arises as to which method is the most satisfactory to accomplish the end: taxes, paper money or borrowing? Both taxes and borrowing will involve the sale of property by individuals making the payment, in order that they may do so. In the case of taxes the sale may be a forced one, and in some instances may be inconvenient, since the taxes cannot be completely adjusted to individual business needs. It is obvious that borrowing is better because it allows those who are most capable of giving up capital to do so. But it has the disadvantage of mounting interest rates and, in the case of large loans, of lack of confidence in the government's capacity for repayment, so that it becomes cheaper and easier for the government to resort to the more exaggerated form of inflation.

Thus it may be that inflation essentially represents an extreme revenue device that is not altogether like taxation or borrowing. But it is similar to taxation because it is compulsory and similar to borrowing because there is usually some intention to return the money to par. It is also similar to borrowing in that it is an easier method of taking capital and savings than is taxation. It represents the last resort of a hard-pressed government after it has tried taxes and loans. It has been said that inflation results when a government's expenses exceed the savings of the country and begin to entrench upon capital. This is only partly true, because capital could presumably be taken also by either borrowing or taxation. Its truth lies in the fact that as a government's needs tend to exceed the savings of a community it becomes increasingly difficult to secure additional funds through the use of other methods than inflation. Thus because it is difficult, although possible, to secure additional funds by these other methods, inflation is finally used. It is therefore clear not only how but why inflation resulted from war financing.

from variations in prices. This whole question may be discussed from two angles: (1) that of the changing burden on debt holder and non-debt holder regardless of the economic classes to which they belong, and (2) that of the changing burden upon various economic classes. The first of these will be discussed here and the second deferred to Chapter VIII. In regard to the first approach, it has long been argued that debts should be retired as early as possible after a war because of the probable fall in prices, which, it is asserted, increases the burden of debt. This argument has been put forth by a number of economists, among them Dalton, Pethick-Lawrence, and J. W. Kempster.[43] R. G. Glenday, in his testimony before the Colwyn Committee, holds to this opinion without any qualification. Dalton testified before the Committee that a downward movement in the price level will " increase enormously the real burden of your debt and it is going to make it a practical impossibility to balance your Budget." [44] By these witnesses the point was offered as one of the main arguments for the use of the capital levy. Among the reasons given for steady reduction is " the risk of the burden of the debt charge increasing beyond the present point should the level of prices fall in the future." [45] No definite trend of prices was noted one way or the other at the time of writing the report and it could not be predicted just when the burden of debt would be increased by changes in prices. The minority report took the view that falling prices would increase the burden even more emphatically. They said that " since the debt is fixed in terms of money, the extent of this injury in the future de-

[43] Dalton, *Public Finance*, p. 195; Pethick-Lawrence, *Public Debt*; Kempster, *Britain's Financial Plight*, pp. 43 and 83-85.

[44] *Cf.* Glenday's testimony, *Colwyn Report, Minutes of Evidence*, p. 348, and Dalton's testimony, *ibid.*, p. 398.

[45] *Colwyn Report*, p. 329.

pends upon the future value of money." [46] Further on they say, " We doubt if it is generally appreciated how seriously the burden of debt has been increased in the past few years owing to the rise in the value of money."

In the United States this point of view seems to have been accepted by the Treasury and serves as a basis for public policy. A fall in prices was believed by Secretary Mellon to increase greatly the burden of debt for the government. In proof of this he stated that during the Civil War we borrowed a 54-cent dollar and paid back an 85-cent dollar. Using a 1913 base he found also that during the World War we borrowed a 51-cent dollar and in 1926 were paying back a 66 cent dollar. Postponement of repayment thus greatly increased the burden of debt because of the fall in prices.[47] On October 6, 1926, Undersecretary Winston, speaking before the American Bankers' Association at Los Angeles, voiced virtually the same opinion, but on other grounds. He stated that it was the government's intention originally to pay off the debt in twenty-five years and that if that policy were followed, the cost, including interest, would be 41 billions. If a sixty-two year program were followed the cost would be 71 billions. Thus it was argued that in order to pay the debt as cheaply as possible it should be retired quickly. In addition to this, he gave the argument of the Secretary for rapid retirement that prices might fall and increase the debt burden. Here again the above figures were cited. It is thus apparent that not only has the Treasury accepted the theory but that it treats the whole problem in a fashion much too static.

No doubt there are many persons in both England and the United States who believe that debts should be retired rapidly because of the probability of a fall in prices. If this belief

[46] *Ibid.*, p. 364.

[47] *Annual Report of the Secretary of the Treasury*, 1926, p. 7.

is held in unqualified form it is likely to cause false conclusions about the burden of debt and excessive haste in debt retirement. It oversimplifies a rather complicated situation. It seems to the writer that even when qualifications are made, they cannot be understood unless they are interpreted in the light of the whole body of theory of debt retirement. Certainly the rate at which debts should be retired cannot be decided on the ground that prices may fall and increase the burden of debt, and in any case the theory that falling prices necessitate a policy of rapid repayment is not necessarily justified.

X. CRITICISMS OF THE THEORY THAT THE BURDEN OF DEBT IS INCREASED BY DECLINING PRICES

Critics of the rapid retirement theory are not totally lacking. On the whole, however, those believing in slower retirement have not attacked the theory itself. There are those who say that since prices have risen in the past, they are most likely to rise in the future, thus lessening the burden. Still others say that no definite predictions can be made as to the course of prices and therefore the influence of prices should be left out of account in determining the policy of the government with regard to debt payment. Several economists, however, have maintained that falling prices do not necessarily increase the burden of the debt. This point of view deserves an attention it has not hitherto received. Professor Edgeworth, as far back as 1896, criticized the rapid retirement theory, as will be found in his *Papers Relating to Political Economy*. His argument is that prices usually fall because of an increase in the volume of production. Assuming a state where population and the supply of money are constant, an increase in the volume of production will allow creditor and debtor to share equally in the increased purchasing power of money. This is true because money income and debt payments remain the same and all that has occurred is an increase in the supply of goods. The debtor will pay the same amounts for interest and the purchasing power of this interest will have increased proportionately to the increase in the supply of goods. On the other hand, assuming that the money profits of the debtor have also remained the same, their goods value will have increased in a like proportion. So Edgeworth concludes that creditor and debtor share equally in the changes in purchasing power. Applying the theory to debts, it must be likewise admitted that the burden of debt as between the debt holders and non-debt holders as a whole is not affected by a change in prices, provided that population and purchasing power are fixed, or provided that purchasing power increases proportionately with population. Given these conditions, Edgeworth concludes that " the creditor does not get the ' whole advantage.' Nor is it true that ' he has contributed nothing ' to the growth of national income. But for his saving it would have been smaller." These conclusions were reached in a discussion of bimetallism.[48]

The first question arising from Edgeworth's theory is whether after all it holds under dynamic conditions. In American experience there seems to be a tendency for deposits greatly to outrun the population. What effect does this have on Edgeworth's conclusions? In order to answer this question it is necessary to return to static conditions for a moment and assume two factors constant at a time. According to the original statement, if money and population are constant and falling prices are induced by an increase in production, debtor and creditor will both gain equally in the increase in real income. Next let it be assumed that money

[48] Edgeworth, *Papers Relating to Political Economy*, p. 429. In defense of the last point he refers to Professor Marshall's remarks in a discussion of a paper by Bowley in the *Journal of the Royal Statistical Society*, June, 1895.

decreases and that production and population are held constant. In this case it follows that debtors will be definitely harmed, and in proportion to the decrease in the supply of money. In the case of a third assumption, that money and production are constant and population decreases, it is not possible to tell definitely whether there would be a fall in prices. To the extent that a decreased population demands fewer goods prices might have a temporary downward movement, but to the extent that this was counterbalanced by a decrease in production, prices would tend to remain constant.

Now two factors, one changing and one constant, will be considered. As a first case assume that money is constant and population and production increase in the same proportion. In this case, as in the other where money was assumed to be constant, there would be a fall in prices and no burden upon the debtor. In case money increased and population increased at the same rate, and production increased still faster, prices would fall again, but the same conclusion would follow about the debtor. However, if population and production decreased more rapidly than money decreased, the debtor would suffer.

It is not intended that the reader should assume from the analysis above or from the citations from Edgeworth that the problems involved have not been faced by others. Professor Pigou deserves credit for having pointed out to the Colwyn Committee that, if a fall in prices is accompanied by an exactly proportionate increase in the productivity of labor, there is no increase in the burden of debt.[49] Layton in his evidence before the Committee made a similar qualification.[50] Among American economists, one may find a very good statement of these qualifications by Professor Taussig.[51]

[49] *Colwyn Report, Minutes*, p. 39.

[50] *Colwyn Report*, p. 66.

[51] Taussig, *Principles of Economics*, 3rd ed., vol. i, pp. 296-7.

If these points are not sufficiently emphasized, however, a false argument for rapid retirement gains too much vogue. Their realization is also important for the analysis that is given to debt burdens in the subsequent chapters.

XI. CONCLUSIONS WITH REGARD TO THE EFFECTS OF DECLINING PRICES UPON THE BURDEN OF DEBT

It may be desirable to summarize the qualifications at this point. They are (1) that it is not necessarily true that the burden of debt increases with falling prices; (2) that it is probable that over long periods of time, since prices fall due to the failure of money to keep up with advancing production, the burden of debt is not increased thereby; (3) that whenever prices fall due to a decrease in the quantity of money either relatively or absolutely, the burden of debt is increased; (4) that the truth of any of these assertions rests upon one's theory of the value of money, and that since there is no certainty as to the theory of prices there is also no certainty as to conclusions about debt burdens; and (5) that the use of price indices as measures of debt burden is of uncertain value.

There are three ways in which price indices may be used in debt measurements. The first of these is the use of the price level as a measure of the burden of the debt. First, as has been mentioned, the comparison of price changes may be used as a measure of the absolute amount of debt burden. Second, prices are used as a measure of the achievement represented by payments of interest and principal. Both of these devices are defective because they ignore the qualifications described above. Third, changes in the price level might be considered to indicate the harmfulness or harmlessness of retirement policy in practice. Thus if one were to take reduction of saving and enterprise as an evidence of too rapid debt retirement, other things being equal, there would possibly be a rise in prices with retirement of the debt. But since other things are not equal it would be exceedingly difficult to determine whether the rise in prices is due to debt factors or to other factors. If it were possible to isolate these influences then one could say that a rise in prices due to debt retirement is an unhealthy sign, whereas a decline in prices is healthy and to be expected.

XII. THE EFFECTS OF DEBT PAYMENT UPON SPECIFIC PRICES

Thus far we have considered the relation of debt payment to the price level. There has been considerable interest in both England and the United States in the effects of payment upon special prices. The degree to which a certain price may be especially affected depends upon the nearness of the good in question to the overflow of repaid funds and the degree to which it may be subjected to special taxes for debt repayment

Let us consider the first. The repayment of debt has the immediate effect of placing funds in the hands of the debt holders. This money may be devoted to consumption but is more likely to be reinvested.[52] In case of reinvestment three consequences are possible. The first of these is a fall in interest rates, a second is a rise in the value of certain classes of securities or investments that are now used by the former government bond holders. A third possibility is an increase in the kinds of securities used for reinvestment. Very little can be said as to the exact results of reinvestment because of the impossibility of eliminating sufficiently other influences than those in which we are interested. In regard to the first possibility it may be that the money market is compartmental and that to the extent that the funds are reinvested

[52] The proof of this assertion rests upon the discussion in Chapter IX. It is based on the fact that the debt in countries like the United States is held to a very large extent by banks and corporations whose practice is to maintain capital intact.

only in certain types of stocks or bonds there will not be a general tendency toward a decline in interest rates. According to Keynes, "the effect of paying off debt is to take money from the body of taxpayers and to place it primarily at the disposal of a particular form of investment. Thus I should say that the main effect of debt repayment at a rapid rate is to divert the surplus resources of the community into the gilt-edged stock market."[53] It is apparent that just what effect upon interest rates the debt payment will have depends on the people who hold the debt and the kind of investors they are. It has been remarked by the Secretary of the Treasury that the experience with war bonds in the United States has increased the amount of investment in securities.

As a result of this education, of more effective bond salesmanship, and of high earnings in America, there has been created an investment demand and the public readily buys large amounts of new security issues, resorting to the banks for loans to assist in these purchases. . . . Business concerns have come to prefer permanent financing as distinguished from commercial loans from the banks and there has been a tendency with a great many corporations through the sale of bonds, notes and capital stock to resort to the public for money to meet their corporate requirements. Partly because commercial bills are not as frequently resorted to for credit and the banks have difficulty in obtaining a sufficient amount of these bills and partly on account of the demand of the public for loans to help carry securities purchased, the banks have to seek investments and loans on securities or loans to customers secured by bonds and stocks.[54]

In the report for 1925 the Secretary of the Treasury further points out that the retirement of debt is one factor causing a decline in interest rates.[55] As was pointed out earlier in this

[53] *Colwyn Report, Minutes of Evidence*, p. 283.

[54] *Annual Report of the Secretary of the Treasury*, 1926, p. 4.

[55] *Ibid.*, 1925, p. 48.

chapter (see p. 137), however, the volume of saving and the gold imports are given chief credit for the decline. Yet the gradual decrease in the amount of the total debt and in particular the decrease in the short term debt, the Victory Loan, treasury notes and certificates of indebtedness, are at least factors in the decline. The main support of the Secretary's argument that debt retirement has reduced interest lies then in his belief that a net addition to the supply of capital has been made. This contention supporting his opinion about interest rates is most important.

A rise in security values, a fall in interest rates and an increase in the amount of securities may all result from debt payment. These results are dependent upon the intentions of the payee and upon the degree to which the market is compartmental. If the debt holder consumes his principal, it of course will not get into the capital market. The nature of his intentions, in turn, depends upon the economic class to which he belongs. To the extent that the higher income classes save a larger proportion of their income, concentration of debt holdings may be desirable since it increases the investment of the repaid debt. At any rate the way in which interest rates are affected also depends in part upon the distribution of the debt. At a later point more will be said of the results of this distribution.

In discussing the effects of retirement upon the money market only the proximate relations have thus far been considered. The effects of retirement are influenced by deeper factors. Those who discuss the possibility of falling interest rates sometimes give the impression that a fall is inevitable in case of reinvestment and that if the fall is not general, it will at least not be compensated for by a rise in other fields. These things are not inevitable. If the government through taxes merely distributes a given supply of funds, the process has caused no general increase and a fall in interest cannot be said to result from it. If interest falls for certain types of investment, one would naturally look for a rise elsewhere. It is true therefore that only to the extent that the debt-paying process results in a net addition to investment funds can it be said that interest rates have generally fallen from this cause.[56] Ultimately then a fall is due to the fact that savings have been increased by the process of repayment.

A second way in which retirement may affect specific prices is through the particular effect of indirect taxes levied for the purpose of retiring the debt. Since this is a matter of tax incidence, it will vary with the conditions of the country in question and the kind of tax used. Theories of the incidence of taxes will determine the interpretation of the facts. By some writers the distribution of the burden of repayment is thought to be the only important consideration. Although they may believe that an internal debt constitutes no burden upon a community as a whole, they think that the mode of distributing the burden of repayment is of considerable importance to society and to the individual. One writer states that this distribution is the chief consideration.[57] But this attitude possibly attributes an undue importance to the kind of taxation as against its amount. The effects of taxation upon the volume of production may be of greater importance.

[56] W. A. Brown in a series of four articles deals with some of the problems of debt retirement related to the money market. He points out definitely that debt retirement may not cause a net addition to capital funds and that if it does, it is probably due to the effects of taxation in increasing saving. *Cf. Annalist*, Aug. 20, Aug. 24, Aug. 31, Sept. 7, 1928.

[57] See Matsushita, *Economic Effects of Public Debts*, p. 155.

XIII. SUMMARY

In this chapter the way in which the retirement of public debts may affect the price level and change the burden of the debt has been discussed. It is widely believed that the retirement of debts sets up tendencies toward deflation. In reaching this conclusion the most important factors taken into account are the psychological effects of retirement, the degree of fixity of central bank reserve ratios, the relations existing between central and local bank credit, and the effects of taxation for debt retirement upon the volume of saving. Whether or not deflationary tendencies will be caused in any given country by retirement depends largely upon the operation of these factors in that country.

It was pointed out that some suggestions as to their operation may be gained by an examination of the conditions surrounding the origin of the debt and of the post-war history of central banking. In the United States the use of government bonds to borrow from the Federal Reserve banks, the concentration of debt holdings in the hands of banks, large corporations and wealthy individuals and the passage of the Glass-Steagall bill make it unlikely that any strong deflationary tendencies have operated or will operate in the immediate future as a result of debt retirement. In France and England, however, it is likely that the reduction of bank advances has had a deflationary effect. It may be said that deflationary tendencies will result from debt retirement to the extent to which that part of the government debt which serves effectively as a basis for central bank credit is reduced.

The monetary effects of changes in the debt burden were discussed from two angles: changes in the burden upon the non-debt holder, and changes in the burden of the various income classes as a whole. Contrary to a rather common opinion, the burden of debt upon non-debt holders is not always increased by falling prices, but only when these falling prices are a result of a reduction in the quantity of the purchasing medium.

The effects of debt retirement upon the money market may take the form of a fall in interest rates, a rise in the prices of some types of securities, and an increase in the kinds of securities used as collateral. The effects upon interest rates depend upon the kind of people the debt holders are, and the extent to which the money market is compartmental. A general decline in interest rates as a result of debt retirement would occur only if there was a net addition of investment funds. This would imply that the payment of debt may stimulate saving.

CHAPTER VI

Banking Effects of Debt Retirement

As stated in the last chapter, the public debt has long been closely associated with money. In the United States the banks have figured largely in this connection. The constitution was to a large extent an instrument designed to protect the interests of propertied classes. Financial difficulties arising out of the revolutionary and other wars had led to the issue of a paper money with much loss to creditors and monetary instability was thus a direct result of public debt and financial difficulty. Not only were money clauses inserted into the constitution to help eliminate these evils, but Hamilton advocated and secured the establishment of the United States Bank partly for that purpose. When in 1863 it was finally decided to reduce the numerous varieties of bank notes through the establishment of the national banking system, the new notes were based on public debt, a type of backing which had already been in use in New York state since 1838. In this bond-secured note system the increase in currency depended largely upon the increase in debt. It has been seen that much the same results followed from the methods used to finance the World War.

In this chapter we shall be concerned with the relations between the public debt and banking administration, which appear in four principal forms: the holding of government bonds for investment purposes, the use of bonds as collateral for loans, the use of bonds in the control of credit by central banks, and the service of banks as fiscal agents for the government. As the public debt is retired the character of these relations will be altered.

I. THE SERVICE OF THE BANKS AS FISCAL AGENTS FOR THE GOVERNMENT

The banks have long been considered as government fiscal agents. Hamilton's chief interest in the United States Bank was in connection with that purpose, and later Secretary Sherman regarded the national banks in that light. Certainly there is some basis for saying that among the most important services performed by the Federal Reserve banks thus far have been the fiscal ones. For the last fifteen years Treasury policy has considerably influenced American central banks, and it in turn has been influenced largely by considerations closely related to the public debt. These fiscal objects can possibly be more readily attained than certain others which were better regarded when the system was established, such as credit control and reduction of stock speculation. Strangely enough, to the extent that the banks have had any real success with the latter, it has been due to the use of the public debt. For the past twelve years an appreciable part of the work of the banks in the United States and abroad has consisted in serving as fiscal agents in the refunding and conversion of the debt. As the debt is retired, this work will decline in importance.

II. THE USE OF THE DEBT AS COLLATERAL FOR BANK LOANS AND IN BANK INVESTMENTS

In the preceding chapter it was noticed that government bonds have been frequently used during and since the war as collateral for loans and that the investment holdings of those bonds by local banks have greatly increased. As was pointed out, the main reason for these holdings and for their use as collateral was the increased ease of borrowing at the Federal Reserve banks, a possibility which was not properly dealt with by the framers of the act. But the bonds also constitute a safe form of investment and make a good appearance in a financial statement. The retirement of these bonds would probably cause an increase in the purchase of conservative local securities. There is already in the United States an increase in the amounts of local certificates held. It is probable that past custom will be followed and debt retirement will not lead to less conservative investment where there is a large amount of local bonds available, but to the extent that government bonds are not used, the collateral has deteriorated. The change from the use of government bonds has been much less in England, where government securities still serve to a considerable extent. In the years after the war the debt was used as collateral to a much greater degree than previously. It was estimated that five to twenty times as much collateral was used for loans as had been used before the war,[1] and there was no evidence given that the use of government collateral was declining. Its greater use in England might be explained by the relatively poor quality of private issues.

III. THE USE OF GOVERNMENT DEBT IN CREDIT CONTROL

The use of the government debt in credit control begins early in American history. The growth of industry and the inelasticity of bond-secured money had caused considerable problems of monetary adjustment during the existence of the national banking system. The independent treasury system, with its withdrawal of tax funds, added to these difficulties. In order to aid the banks in meeting the credit needs of the country, the Secretary of the Treasury replaced these funds whenever he thought the occasion demanded it, by redepositing government money in the banks and by occasional purchases of bonds. Thus during the depressions of 1853, 1873, 1884 and 1890 large purchases

[1] *Colwyn Report, Minutes of Evidence*, pp. 424-5.

were made.[2] Most of these were purchases of government bonds. Although this practice may have had the effect of increasing the government funds available for business needs, it had a very serious defect in that it reduced the amount of bonds available as a basis for note issue. The Treasury also engaged in the bad practice of paying interest on its securities in January and July, when the demands for money were usually at their lowest point.[3] It is evident, therefore, that even before there were central banks in the United States, government bonds were used as a means of expanding credit. The Treasury had exclusive control over these devices before the adoption of the present system. Long before the introduction of the Federal Reserve system we had at least the purchase of government securities as a means of controlling credit.

In the present banking system of the United States the government security plays a part in credit control through open market operations. Power has been granted the banks to deal in government securities. Congress, however, probably did not intend the power to be used as it is.[4] It was thought at the time that the banks should buy securities only occasionally and then for purposes of revenue. In 1914, however, there were only $60,000,000 of Panama Canal bonds that could be readily used for these purposes. The war made available a great supply of short-term securities. The reasons for this large floating debt are familiar. The securities were issued to anticipate the proceeds of the

[2] Chapman, *Fiscal Functions of the Federal Reserve Banks*, pp. 30 and 34.

[3] *Ibid.*, p. 38.

[4] Lawrence, *Stabilization of Prices*, p. 237. "The tax certificate did not constitute a part of government financing prior to 1917, a fact which in itself indicates that the framers of the Federal Reserve Act did not contemplate its use in effectuating a control of the volume and price of funds in the market."

Liberty loans and since 1922 have been issued for a like purpose in regard to the income tax receipts. Since 1917 the Federal Reserve banks have had a continuous supply of these certificates, their holdings advancing at times as high as $1,500,000,000. The purchase or sale of these instruments is of much significance in the control of credit. Government bonds have also had long use as means of investment and as collateral for loans. Senator Carter Glass, who was Chairman of the Senate sub-committee of the Committee on Banking and Currency in the 71st Congress, appointed to inquire into the administration of the national and Federal Reserve banking systems with respect to the use of their facilities for trading in securities, points out very clearly in the hearings of this committee that the Federal Reserve system had originally as " . . . its primary purpose if not its sole purpose " meeting the requirements of commerce and industry.[5] When the Federal Reserve Act was passed, the enormous increase in public debt was not envisioned nor was its use in the expansion of credit adequately realized.[6] The retirement of the debt will probably affect the supply of the instruments available for credit control.

(a) *The Use of Government Bonds in Central Bank Loans*

Of the four forms which the relations between the banks and the public debt may take, the use of government securities in credit control is probably the most significant. The subject has two main aspects: the use of bonds for collateral in central bank loans, and their use by the central bank to give effect to its discount policy. The use of bonds as collateral was treated in the last chapter from the standpoint of

[5] U. S. Senate, *Hearings* before a Sub-committee of the Committee on Banking and Currency, 71st Cong., 3rd Sess., S. Res. 71, pt. i, p. 50, Jan. 19-30, 1931.

[6] *Ibid.*, pp. 53 and 65.

its relationship to the price level. Of importance for credit control is the growing tendency toward a reduction in the use of government bonds as collateral for commercial borrowing and the use of government securities for central bank borrowing. The use of these bonds by the banks for central bank borrowing has been due partly to the greater yield of new industrial securities in the United States and to tax exemption. The latter privilege has led to a very considerable concentration of government bonds in the hands of wealthy men, banks and corporations. As a result commercial issues are performing in greater degree the collateral function in customers' loans. The figures given below indicate this tendency.

TABLE XVI

LOANS MADE ON SECURITIES BY APPROXIMATELY 700 REPORTING MEMBER BANKS

(in millions of dollars)

Year	Secured by U. S. Bonds	Secured by other Stocks and Bonds
1921	667	3,030
1922	331	3,424
1923	255	3,750
1924	206	4,142
1925	182	5,040
1926	154	5,447

This persistent tendency to use government bonds in central bank loans has led to serious consequences. It explains to a large extent the great concentration of the debt holdings in the banks. According to Professor Willis, in 1920

the (Federal Reserve banks) had close to $1,600,000,000 certificates either owned or carried as a basis of loans while the reporting member banks were owners of some $2,360,000,000 more bonds and certificates, a figure which meant for the country as a whole some six billions as a total. Loans on war obligations were $3,000,000,000 more, in all two-fifths of the volume of our outstanding bonds and certificates.

During this period some effort was made to drive government securities out of bank portfolios. This lasted through 1921.

But in 1922 under a new national administration a reactionary policy was introduced. . . . It was now sought to have the banks carry as much of the debt as possible; and as the Liberty obligations matured they were, instead of being funded into long-period securities and sold to investors, converted into short-term obligations and (then) sold to the banks.[7]

Beginning in 1925 there also developed a tendency toward low interest rates. This was ostensibly for the purpose of helping business, although no public statement was made to that effect. Professor Willis attributes the rise in stock transactions to this cause.[8] What is of most significance is the increase of member bank borrowings through the agency of their own notes backed by government securities. In August, 1928, member banks were indebted to the Federal Reserve banks to the amount of one billion dollars, of which 603 millions were secured by government bonds.[9] Such a method of borrowing is much more productive of inflationary tendencies than the use of bonds as collateral by the bank customer.

The Federal Reserve funds which the member banks obtained through the borrowing on government bonds were used to a considerable extent for loans to affiliated security

[7] "Who Caused the Stock Market Panic?" by H. Parker Willis, *North American Review*, February, 1930.

[8] Sales increased from 452,000,000 shares in 1925 to 920,000,000 in 1928.

[9] *Federal Reserve Bulletin*, Aug. 8, 1928.

companies and thus went indirectly into the stock market. Section 5200 of the National Banking Act, with many qualifications, prohibits loans to any one individual in excess of 10 per cent of the capital of a national bank. This would apparently limit the amounts that might be loaned in this way, but where the number of affiliates was increased the 10 per cent rule could be easily rendered ineffective, since the owners of the stock of these various affiliates might be largely the same persons. The number of affiliates may be as great as fifty. Comptroller General Pole, however, denied before the sub-committee referred to above that the amount loaned by national banks to these security companies was "inordinately large." He thought that only infrequently did loans to such affiliates amount to more than over a quarter of a bank's capital, but he did admit that there had often been a disproportionate amount of security loans.[10]

The concentration of bond holdings referred to by Professor Willis, and for which statistical evidence was given in Chapter V, reduces the availability of these bonds for customers' collateral loans. As Professor Brown has pointed out, most of the debt is now concentrated in the hands of banks and corporations. Thus it is seen that government bonds, because they are becoming increasingly concentrated in the hands of banks, are now much less available as a basis for customers' loans than just after the war, but much more of a basis for bank borrowing, and that tax exemption and desire for bank profit have led to the concentration of debt holdings. The result is probably less liquidity of bank assets and inflation in the stock market; and, most important, these conditions greatly increase the difficulties of credit control and indicate changes that must be made before that control can be made effective.

[10] U. S. Senate, *Hearings*, S. Res. 71, pp. 21 and 25.

(b) *Gold Imports and Credit Inflation*

Some writers, however, do not attribute inflation in the stock market solely to the type of collateral behind member banks' borrowings, but also to the great increase in the gold supply derived from Europe and the use of new business methods which reduce the need for commercial loans. Dr. A. C. Miller of the Federal Reserve Board says that the main basis for the credit expansion was the upward trend of the gold supply owing to imports from Europe.[11] The gold was deposited with the Federal Reserve banks and thus served as an increased reserve upon which new loans, in many cases for stock speculation, could be made. "The inflation which caused bad banking," says Dr. Miller, "came largely through gold imports and the open market operations of the Federal Reserve system."[12] Mr. J. H. Case may be cited as a spokesman for the theory that after 1920 corporations resorted to new financial methods which tended to increase the rise in stock prices. He claims that many corporations which found that they had borrowed too heavily through commercial loans in 1920 deliberately decided not to be caught again. They began to substitute issues of stock for commercial loans. The diminishing commercial loans caused the banks in their turn to increase their investments and to loan to customers who wanted to trade in stocks. The latter process was, however, carried too far.[13]

C. R. Noyes gives an admirable treatment of the theory that the increase in stock prices was partly based on the imports of gold. He says that from 1921 to 1929 the net addition of gold was approximately a billion dollars. The Federal Reserve banks attempted to "sterilize" this supply by substituting gold certificates for Federal Reserve notes in

[11] U. S. Senate, *Hearings*, S. Res. 71, p. 128.

[12] *Ibid.*, p. 149.

[13] *Ibid.*, p. 113.

accordance with a policy adopted in the summer of 1922. The process resulted in failure, because as the Federal Reserve notes were retired, an equal amount was added to the reserve accounts of members at the Federal Reserve banks. The result was a credit expansion due in part to the additions to the gold supply. From 1921 to 1929 the primary reserves, or the member banks' reserve accounts, expanded about 44 per cent, and the net demand deposits about 37 per cent. There was a still greater increase in time deposits.[14] This increase in credit did not increase commercial loans. In fact, during the early years of this period there was an actual decrease, which was recovered from only in the last few years of the period. About one-third, or 4,050 millions, out of a total of 11,589,000 millions of loans and investments, went into investments by the banks and were thus put directly into the security market. The greater part of the remaining loans and discounts were for securities and real estate.[15] It is thus seen that the new credit was partly due to gold imports, and that it was employed to buy securities because of the failure of the commercial demands to keep up with the demands for loans on securities.

The most obvious cause of the increase in credit in excess of the supply of gold was of course the use of government bonds as collateral for loans, as Willis has demonstrated, but as Noyes points out, this increase may have been partly due to the fact that needs formerly met through commercial loans may now be met by the sale of securities, or to the more rapid turnover of stock, the carrying of a smaller stock and the extension of less credit to customers. However, says Noyes, " To assume that this change in the character of bank credit has simply resulted in a more roundabout method of making

[14] *American Economic Review*, June, 1930; "Gold Inflation" by C. R. Noyes.

[15] *Ibid.*, pp. 183-5.

this credit available for commerce and industry would be to misread the facts. . . . It (credit) not only financed new flotations but it has enhanced old ones."[16] In the face of the fact that commodity prices rose only about 5 per cent during these years and, in some cases, actually showed a decline, an explanation of the disposition of these funds is needed. The stock market, which was the only field where prices rose considerably during this period, seems to answer this need. The new credit supply, according to both Willis and Noyes, was thus in excess of the demand to such an extent as to cause inflation in the stock market, commodity prices not being affected proportionately.

(c) *The Failure of the Use of Government Bonds to Give Effect to a Restrictive Central Bank Discount Policy*

Now although it is clear that the use of government bonds might cause an inflation in stock prices, it is not so clear why it did so, in spite of the employment of the much-vaunted open market operations. This difficulty is explained by the fact that member banks borrowed to offset the open market policy of the Federal Reserve banks. Attention has been called to this tendency by J. S. Lawrence.[17] It can be seen from the tables he presents that there was a roughly inverse movement between the bills discounted and the open market operations. Lawrence argues that the open market policy is ineffective as a basis of credit control since the holdings of government securities fluctuate widely and the deposits maintain an even upward trend.

Let us examine this point a moment. It seems clear that, as the sale of securities reduced the reserve accounts, the member banks did probably increase their borrowings. Thus it would be true that the process had not reduced their

[16] *Ibid.*, p. 186.

[17] Lawrence, *Stabilization of Prices*, pp. 270-90.

credit. On the other hand, when there was a purchase of securities credit would be increased. It is here that the theory discussed by Lawrence, of complete innocuousness of the open market policy, breaks down. The open market policy has, as Noyes points out, a one-way effect. This writer states that "the federal reserve system has expanded credit only a little when business was active and needed it and expanded it a great deal when business was dull and did not need it." He says also that " . . . radical expansions in open market credit have supplied the occasions and immediate causes and then an increase in gold or rediscounts or a decrease in note circulation have appeared in whole or in part to maintain the expansion when the open-market credit was removed." He even goes so far as to maintain that "the responsibility for practically the whole of the expansion of bank credit for this period rests with the open market operations of the federal reserve system." It would be nearer the truth to say that the increase in the gold and the one-way policy were jointly responsible. To a large extent the open market purchases may have increased credit in advance of the inevitable expansion from the increments of gold. They merely accelerated the upward tendency.[18]

Now it is apparent that government securities figure in this situation in the following ways. Without the ability to

[18] Dr. A. C. Miller expresses this point of view very clearly in his testimony before the Senate sub-committee mentioned above. He says that "...the Federal Reserve System has been a kind of alternating system as between open market operations and rediscount operations. It eases or inflates through the open market operations and then undertakes to firm or deflate (and usually fails) through the rediscount operation. That, in a nutshell, is the story of 1927 to 1929" (p. 128). He believed that the increased holdings by the Federal Reserve banks of United States securities in 1927 was the most costly error in American banking in the past seventy-five years (p. 134). "You have had too much inflation in the Federal Reserve system, and its favorite instrument is the open market purchase of Government securities" (p. 147).

borrow on government bonds the member banks would have been subject to at least some decreases in credit as the Federal Reserve bank sold bonds. Moreover, the large supply of these bonds allowed in bank portfolios served as a constant invitation to further borrowing. This was made easy by low rates of discount at the Federal Reserve banks. The government security is thus a factor in a secondary post-war inflation in the stock market just as it was the cause of such inflation in other markets during the war. But of greatest significance is the paradoxical situation that government bonds serve as the device for reducing credit and are at the same time one of the chief causes of the inflation it is sought to remove. It becomes absurd, therefore, in the United States to worry about the difficulties of credit control if the debt is retired, because with the system as it is now arranged bad credit conditions may be in large part due to these instruments. Furthermore, the government has not always been really eager to control credit. Nevertheless, Governor Strong, J. S. Lawrence and J. M. Keynes have all mentioned this difficulty with respect to credit control if the debt is retired.

(d) *The Effects of Debt Retirement Upon Credit Control*

The reduction of government securities for credit control with the retirement of the debt is not then a genuine problem for a number of reasons. First of all we have noted that, with the arrangements as they are, it is very doubtful if their use has any salutary effect. There are, however, a number of other considerations that preclude any pessimistic view about the effects of retirement.

In the first place one may raise the question as to whether it is after all a legitimate duty of the government to control credit. In their credit policies the Federal Reserve banks have paid little attention to price changes and have concentrated upon changes in commercial paper, the volume of trade, speculation, the status of agriculture and the effect of business changes upon the gold standard. These are broad objectives. Taken collectively they embrace almost the total field of business activity. It might readily be objected that it was not the purpose of Congress to set up the Federal Reserve Board as a " supreme economic council " even had it believed that such a measure was possible. We are not as yet committed to a centralized control over business. We can agree with Lawrence that " the central bank should be the servant rather than the master of the nation's business."

In the second place we have noted some of the reasons why the Federal Reserve banks, even with their full powers, could not hope for complete control of credit expansion if this were desired. Professor O. W. Sprague testified before a congressional committee holding a hearing on the Strong Amendment as follows: " I am very certain in my own mind that it is not possible to handle the ordinary oscillations in prices effectively by means of reserve bank operations." [19] He did not attribute the rise in prices in 1920 and in 1923 to policies of the Federal Reserve bank. It was concluded at the hearing (1) that it is impossible and dangerous to attempt to control prices within precise limits; (2) that the Federal Reserve banks have used their powers of control so far as they have them; (3) that in many price situations the Board would be powerless; and (4) that the gold standard would best promote price stability. The last named point is the culmination of opinion about a long line of stabilization schemes and represents the final conclusion of most thinkers on the subject at the present time. As we have seen in the preceding chapter, the ability of a nation to avoid inflation can be readily exaggerated. It is very doubtful, for instance, that Germany committed deliberate financial

[19] *Hearings*, H. R., 7895, pp. 125 and 408.

hari-kiri after the war, as some anti-German writers would have us believe.

The power of the banks to control credit is made doubtful further by the fact that there need be no functional relationship between the quantity of money in circulation and deposit credit in banks. According to Lawrence, "It is doubtful if such a functional relationship exists or in fact if any precise relation, valuable for the purposes of credit control, exists." [20]

A further difficulty was mentioned by Governor G. W. Norris of the Philadelphia Federal Reserve Bank in the hearings referred to above. He said that loans to customers were made prior to borrowing from the Federal Reserve banks. The latter, on the other hand, do not solicit borrowings or require payment. He declared that the open market operations constitute too small a part of the total operations to be capable of controlling credit strictly. The influence of the Federal Reserve banks was, according to Norris, confined largely to raising prices. It is possible therefore that people like J. R. Commons, W. T. Foster and J. M. Keynes greatly overestimate the efficacy of credit control, at least so far as it applies to present conditions in the United States.

If, however, the open market purchases are not satisfactory means of general credit control, it is still admitted by Governor Strong and others that they perform a useful function in emergencies such as occurred in the case of the run on Cuban banks on April 10, 1926, in the quarterly "mopping up" of funds due to the delay involved in the receipt of

[20] Lawrence, *Stabilization of Prices*, p. 76. In the hearings before the Senate Sub-committee mentioned above the views expressed by Professor Sprague were corroborated. Governor Harrison pointed out that the control of credit by raising the discount rate was ineffective in 1927. The Federal Reserve system lost $500,000,000 in gold in 1928, and raised the discount rate three times. As much as $400,000,000 of government bonds were sold, all to no avail. Dr. Miller said that open market operations had never brought a "noteworthy contraction of credit" (p. 155).

checks for the payment of income taxes, and in the seasonal variations in the demand for funds. The use and character of these operations are so well known that we need not go into them here. The exact amount necessary for this purpose is not known; Governor Strong believed that a supply of two billion dollars worth of bonds was ample.

Assuming, however, that the objects already sought are legitimate, and that the powers of the Federal Reserve banks are ample to accomplish them, the further objection arises that government securities are not absolutely necessary for or best suited to the accomplishment of these purposes. Among the weaknesses of these securities for use in credit control are the following. (1) Their supply is not related to credit needs but to fiscal needs. As was the case under the national banking system, an undue reliance upon them, if their supply became restricted, would reduce the elasticity of the currency. It is admitted by Governor Strong that in a sense the hoped-for elasticity through the system of rediscounting does not materialize. (2) The government bond does not constitute a satisfactory investment because of the few dates of maturity. It is thus concluded by Lawrence that although the certificates of indebtedness are better than government bonds for these purposes, the use of discounted export paper would be still better. There would be a steady succession of maturities and the supply would not depend upon the government budget. Tax warrants of municipalities and securities of state and local governments might conceivably be just as good if not better devices for these ends. It must be admitted, however, that the securities held by the banks consist largely of certificates of indebtedness with a variety of maturities.

The question arises as to the adequacy of the supply of these substitutes. The hope of an adequate American discount market has not been fulfilled up to the present time.

There is, however, reasonable hope for its greater development. With an increase in our foreign trade and the growth of American foreign banking and the increasing industrial importance of the United States, the growth of such a market is possible. If we do not build up a sufficiently large discount market, however, we can resort to state and local securities. Finally, the government is not under the absolute necessity of retiring all the floating debt. If, under certain conditions, it is necessary to the control of credit, we should run the risk and expense of its maintenance.

(e) *The Use of Government Securities in Credit Control in Germany and France*

It is interesting by way of comparison to note the European experience with the use of government securities for these purposes. The Bank of England has long used Consols, and Germany before the war used treasury bills and Imperial bonds. The experience of Germany shows a distinct parallel to that of the United States. In reading the report of the National Monetary Commission of 1908 one is reminded of present-day discussions. For example, some of the speakers considered the use of treasury bills indispensable for credit control. Dr. August Weber (at that time director of the Lobaner Bank) said,

> I consider that in a certain sense the Imperial treasury bills are a very desirable means of influencing the rate of private discount through their being put upon the house. If the rate of private discount is too far below the rate of discount at the Reichsbank, then putting the treasury bills upon the market is a means of bringing about a tightening of the rate of private discount.[21]

Adolf Wagner also said that " in the treasury bill the Reichsbank has a convenient means of obviating the great difference

[21] United States National Monetary Commission, *Report* 407, p. 1017.

between private bank discount and the Reichsbank discount when this difference reaches a certain point. . . ." [22] Dr. Jacob Riesser of the University of Berlin declared that "the Reichsbank in the discounting of such bills possesses about the only and in many ways a quite effective means of exerting an influence upon the determination of the private discount rate." [23] He felt that if the bills were retired the bank would be much crippled. Other speakers maintained that the existing supply of bills was insufficient for these purposes and one even went so far as to advocate the issue of treasury bills by the state when they were needed by the bank. (An aggregate of at least 150 million marks was needed.) [24]

One also finds in this report the current belief that the floating debt issued for these purposes may be too large. Thus Wagner objects to a large floating debt on this ground. "The thing is," says he, "that very unexpected events happen which may cause embarrassment as regards short-time bills." [25] It is also apparent that, as in the United States, the large size of the floating debt is due to the attempt of the Treasury to economize in interest payments. It is extremely interesting that at least two of these men imply that the issue of the treasury bill to banks gives rise to inflation. This is of course very à propos. Says Dr. Weber, " . . . in the issuing of these treasury bills the government takes no account of whether the time of doing so is convenient or not. It is often done at a time when the Reichsbank is already greatly overburdened with the requirements of business." [26] Further, he suggests that the bills be sold to the public or to foreign nations in order that inflation may be avoided. Dr. Wagner expressed much the same views.

[22] *Ibid.*, p. 1026.

[23] *Ibid.*, p. 1068.

[24] *Ibid.*, Evidence of Roland-Lucke, p. 1121.

[25] *Ibid.*, p. 1061.

[26] *Ibid.*, p. 1017.

In France prior to the World War the Bank of France participated very little in open market transactions and it has long been an accepted policy not to do so. Thus in answer to the question " Does the Bank of France sometimes purchase bills in the market? " M. Pallain, Governor of the Bank of France, when testifying before the National Monetary Commission, said, " No, never. Such measures would appear to us to be absolutely contrary to the mission of the Bank, which is to moderate as much as possible the conditions of credit." [27]

IV. SUMMARY

It was found in this chapter that the relations of the public debt to the banking system take four principal forms: the holding of government bonds by banks for investment purposes, the use of bonds as collateral in loans, their use in credit control, and the service of banks as government fiscal agents. United States government bonds have long been employed as instruments of credit control; they have been used in open market operations and they have served as collateral for member bank borrowings. Since the war these borrowings have resulted in a concentration of debt holdings in the hands of banks and in stock market inflation. This inflation cannot be attributed entirely to the type of collateral behind member bank borrowings; it was due indirectly to gold imports. The Federal Reserve banks did not effectively sterilize these imports of gold since the open market operations had only a one-way effect, this way leading to credit expansion. But the credit increase after the war cannot be wholly attributed to the increased supply of gold; it must be partly explained by the use of government bonds for the collateral of loans from the Federal Reserve banks.

[27] *Interviews on Banking and Currency Systems*, Senate Doc. No. 405, p. 217.

The reduction through debt retirement of the government bonds available for credit control is therefore not a serious problem. The use of these bonds for this purpose may not be salutary under some banking systems. Furthermore, it is doubtful whether credit can be controlled to any appreciable extent by their use. Although government bonds may perform useful functions in the case of temporary credit difficulties, they are probably not a satisfactory means of preventing large expansions of credit. Government bonds may not be necessary or best suited to meet even the temporary difficulties. The growth of adequate substitutes for the public debt to meet these temporary difficulties is also possible.

CHAPTER VII

International Effects of Debt Retirement

It has long been the practice of writers on public finance to classify debts as internal and external, the justification for this procedure lying in the different effects that result from each type. As with the other aspects of retirement, the conclusions reached with regard to the international effects will depend on one's theory as to what constitutes a debt burden.

I. THE RELATIVE BURDEN OF EXTERNAL AND INTERNAL DEBTS ON THE DEBTOR NATION

Most people who consider the international consequences of debt payment believe that the burden is greater in the case of foreign than in the case of domestic, or internal, debts. This goes back to the early theory that internal debts are not burdensome because they " merely " result in a transfer of capital within the country. Melon held to this idea, saying, " *Les dettes d'un État sont les dettes de la main droite à la main gauche, dont le corps ne se trouvera point affaibli.*" [1] Melon's theory is much nearer the truth when applied to debt retirement than when applied to debt conditions in general. The weakness of applying it in a general way was demonstrated by Leroy-Beaulieu, who pointed out that the proceeds of the internal debt might readily be squandered or used for unproductive purposes. He cites many cases of the misuse of borrowed funds. The greater plausibility of Melon's point

[1] *Cf.* Melon, " Essai politique ", chap. 23, p. 749 of *Économistes du 18 siècle*, cited by Bastable, *Public Finance*, 1st ed., p. 579. It is interesting to note that Voltaire also had this idea.

when applied to debt repayment shows itself in its acceptance in this regard by H. C. Adams. He said that "the payment of the principal of a debt tends neither to impoverish a nation nor to retard its material development. . . ." [2] This statement applied only to internal debts, as it was based upon the belief that their payment did not reduce the supply of capital. The same belief was held by J. S. Mill, who saw in payment merely a transfer of property within the nation. Later writers have carried this progression a step farther. They attribute some burden to the payment of internal debts but more burden to the payment of external debts. Thus we see that at first internal debts were considered burdenless, then only their repayment burdenless, and finally their payments only relatively burdenless.

This assertion of a difference between internal and external debts has been based on a number of grounds. The first of these is the loss of capital. This was implicit in the statements of Mill and Adams. It is also the chief basis of this view as expressed by the Colwyn Committee. In their report they state that "the service and redemption of the external debt is decidedly more onerous itself to the country as a whole than the service and redemption of the internal debt." [3] On the other hand the original borrowing is less onerous. Dr. Dalton, among English writers, holds this opinion. He has classified debt burdens as direct and indirect. The check to production which he thinks will result from the payment of external debts is considered to be an indirect burden.

A second ground relates to the time of debt payment. Thus in the Colwyn Report it was said that external debts are contracted during times of rising prices and repaid in the period of depression and low prices that usually follows a war. At these times the economic system is under unusual

[2] Adams, *Public Debts*, p. 243.

[3] *Colwyn Report*, p. 27.

strain because large numbers of workers must be reabsorbed; international trade is hampered by unstable currencies and multiplication of tariffs; and markets are generally disorganized. Furthermore it is maintained that while taxes during the war are levied upon industry when at full swing, the taxes to pay external debts fall upon industry without regard to whether it is flourishing or not. "The external debt," states the Colwyn Committee, "falls upon it (the country) year in and year out, the good years having to be taken with the bad." [4]

Another ground for maintaining that external debts involve a greater burden arises from the greater price instability created. In the case of an internal debt the effect of this is confined to domestic prices alone; moreover, to the extent that taxation for debt increases saving an increase of capital may occur. This increment is lost in the case of an external debt. It has also been objected that an external debt fails to create taxable securities and thus is more burdensome than an internal debt. According to this reasoning the retirement of the latter would be less burdensome than that of an external debt. But it may readily be objected that the nation's power to tax is not lessened by the reduction of certain paper evidences of its wealth. It is strange that the idea had apparently such currency. Furthermore it is claimed that there is a greater psychological burden resulting from the payment of external debts. The taxpayer comes to regard it as a tribute to a foreign power. It is well known that a great deal has been made of this argument in connection with the payment of the war debts to the United States. It is easy to exaggerate the point. The European debts to the United States have been treated as a moral issue. They would contribute an amount equal on the average to only a tenth of the income tax on the basis of the reduced terms of

[4] *Colwyn Report*, p. 29.

the Debt Funding Commission, yet the extent of the discussion on both sides of this question would indicate that the financial stakes were much larger at least so far as the United States is concerned, than those actually involved.

In addition Leroy-Beaulieu gives two other reasons for the greater burden of foreign debts. The first of these is the higher interest rates that may have to be paid and the second refers to the difficulties of transferring interest and principal. He says, "*Il ne s'agit pas seulement pour les premières* (*external debts*) *de recueillir la somme nécessaire; il faut encore transporter cette somme à l'étranger, ce qui est parfois un problème fort délicat.*"[5] This difficulty has aroused most interest in the case of reparations, but there seems to have been considerable interest in France in problems of this sort arising from the necessity of transmitting interest on railroad debts by Russia to France before the war.

Thus external debts may be considered more burdensome largely because of the capital lost, through the export of current output without return, and because of the conditions under which repayment occurs. It may be, therefore, that the more rapidly and easily these debts are removed, the better it will be for the country, since the burden is greater than in the case of other debts.

More definite conclusions are possible, however, and they relate to an argument much advanced in support of the cancellation of the war debts to the United States. This is the belief that their repayment would be harmful because it must be made in goods and this will cause a loss to those industries competing in export trade with the debtor countries. It is plain that this idea is at least an apparent direct contradiction of the previous arguments. It is harmful to repay the debt and also harmful to be paid. A clarification of this contradiction through a return to more remote matters is necessary.

[5] Leroy-Beaulieu, *Traité de la science des finances*, vol. ii, p. 644.

II. THE BURDEN OF EXTERNAL DEBTS ON THE CREDITOR NATION

In the above discussion the background of the belief that to pay debts is harmful to the debtor country was analyzed in part. Let us consider now the belief that payment harms the creditor. The usual argument is somewhat as follows. If the creditor is paid in any real sense he will in all probability be paid primarily in goods and services, as most debts in international trade are so paid. This will require the imports of the creditor nation to increase and the exports to decrease. To accomplish this the debtor country must outsell the creditor either in the domestic or in the foreign markets, and thus secure for itself a more favorable trade balance. The result that is claimed, therefore, is that the creditor country must take a loss in some of its industries in order to be paid.

In December, 1926, some forty-two Columbia University professors of economics, law, history and social science issued a "manifesto" in which one of the arguments advanced for cancellation of the war debts was substantially the same as this one. It was suggested that through adverse competition we might at least lose in export trade what we gain through debt payments. In addition, 116 Princeton professors concurred in these views. In April, 1926, Professor Taussig, in *Foreign Affairs,* had already pointed out the dangers of stimulating German competition by imposing upon her the payment of an annual $600,000,000 in reparations. Accepting this point of view, a recent brief book on the subject makes the following statement: "Here is a real reason why Americans should cancel the war debts. It is not novel; several people have called attention to it; but it happens to be a good reason, considerably better than any number of bad ones." And further, "The American people probably cannot afford to have these war debts paid in spite of the fact that the amount of the annual instalments is insignificant in comparison with their foreign trade or their estimated national income or their income tax." [6]

Obviously such inconsistency is unjustifiable. Either one or the other view is correct, or the truth lies between the two. The latter is the most probable. An examination of some of the factors involved in the payment of a foreign debt will enable us not only to settle this question but also to reach the more definite conclusions mentioned above.

III. THE RELATIONS OF THE METHODS OF PAYING FOREIGN DEBTS TO THE BURDEN OF EXTERNAL DEBT

(a) *Payments by Taxation and Export Surpluses*

As the English writer M. E. Robinson has pointed out, the payment of a foreign debt can be made (as in the case of an internal debt) through taxation or borrowing. Whichever method is used, the claims of citizens to the national dividend are reduced and the claims of outsiders increased. Assuming first of all that taxation is employed, the following steps will probably occur.

1. The debtor country accumulates a fiscal surplus within its own border.

2. This means that the spending power of the consumers is reduced and since production has not decreased this will cause a tendency toward falling prices.

3. This makes the debtor country a good nation to buy in and for this reason exports will be stimulated.

4. Consequently there will be a rising demand in foreign markets for exchange drawn in terms of the currency of the debtor country.

5. For these reasons it is possible for the debtor country to sell bills drawn on it and obtain bills on its creditor.[7]

[6] *Cf.* Dexter and Sedgwick, *The War Debts—An American View.*

[7] For a more detailed account of this analysis see B. M. Anderson,

Thus it is said that the result will be a reduction in purchases by the debtor from the creditor and an increase in exports to the creditor, provided a number of things are assumed: (1) that ordinary commercial methods of payment are used, (2) that world markets are reasonably open to movements of goods, (3) that both debtor and creditor are on the gold standard.[8] This conclusion rests upon still more remote considerations, however. The payment could conceivably be made in specie if the proper conditions were present. (By payment we mean here not necessarily remittance of commodities but the satisfaction of debt obligations regardless of consequences). There are also conditions under which the payment may be made by borrowing,[9] and when this fails inflation will be resorted to by the debtor country. It is clear therefore that one cannot stop with the customary analysis, regardless of what purposes are involved. It is surely the obvious and probably the normal thing that debts will be paid by export surpluses, but it is not an inevitable result. So far as it is true it can have certain important consequences that result from still other conditions than those mentioned thus far.

First of all some of the possible consequences will be considered. One of these is the possibility of competition by the debtor country with the creditor country in foreign trade. This may be extensive enough to injure severely those industries of the creditor country which are subject to such competition. It arises out of the fact that the attempt of the debtor to pay its debts will act somewhat as a bounty upon its

"Relation of International Debt Payments to Domestic Purchasing Power," Academy of Political Science, *Proceedings*, April, 1927, pp. 723-724.

[8] See Anderson, *op. cit.*

[9] The United States was "paid" entirely by its own foreign loans from 1918 to 1929.

exports. This increased foreign competition is a complaint frequently raised against the payment of a foreign debt. Robinson says, in referring to payment by an export surplus that " On the face of it this seems a desirable position, but at the present time some creditor countries seem to be suffering from considerable doubts as to whether they can afford to be paid." [10] Another similar result will be the probable reduction in imports by the debtor country, which also is likely to reduce the foreign trade of the creditor nation. Taking these two consequences together, it may be concluded that some disturbances in export industry may occur. There will, however, be a gain so far as the consumers are concerned owing to the cheaper products. When the capital and effort in the export industries of the creditor country are diverted to new uses there may be an increase in the total national dividend. In estimating the increase, however, account must not be lost of the expense of the disturbance involved in the receipt of payment. It can be seen from this that unless the payments are large and continue for a reasonable length of time the disturbance resulting from payment might be worse than the payment itself. Thus one condition for benefit is moderate and continued receipts.

It is not inevitable, however, that industry in the creditor country will be interfered with as directly as this. The directness of the effects will depend upon the types of exports the debtor is likely to increase. Where these exports are raw materials not produced in the creditor country, the result may just as conceivably be an increase in imports of these and no necessary decrease in exports by the creditor country. Also, the debt payment may merely stimulate an export to the creditor of goods not produced by it at all. In the former case, the importation might reduce the domestic production of raw materials. In case they were not so produced, but

[10] Robinson, *Public Finance*, p. 136.

were imported from other countries, there might result a depression in those industries that produced goods to obtain them. This latter result might also occur from the exportation of goods not produced by the creditor country.

In spite of all these dislocations, however, after readjustment takes place the creditor country will necessarily benefit from this mode of payment. Its evils for the creditor are not of a permanent variety. In the long run the creditor will benefit considerably if the payments are substantial and steady. The debtor, on the other hand, will lose and its payments, if made in this fashion, constitute a genuine burden which will tend to impoverish the nation. It must be remembered, however, that this need not result where the original debt was productive in character, for in that case both debtor and creditor may benefit. On the other hand, it is important to consider, as Robinson has pointed out, that the debtor country, if unduly impoverished or driven to political disorganization by the debt payment, may not be a customer of the creditor country in the future, and this loss of future trade advantages should be taken into account.

If there is then an actual burden upon the debtor country through payment by this method, the next question that suggests itself is the way this burden is distributed. Does it fall upon other industries in the country as in the case of a bounty? It is clear that in the case of those industries not subject to a bounty there is a double tax, one in the form of business depression and a second in the form of a tax to pay the bounty. In the case which we are considering other industries would not necessarily be depressed and it would be a matter solely of how the taxes to pay the foreign debts were levied. If they were levied equally according to net income the burden would be evenly borne. The fact that the payment of debt stimulated export industries would not cause them to escape a part or all of the debt burden. In the case of the country being paid those industries disorganized by the payment would bear a part of the burden. It would seem just to compensate them in some way if this were practicable, although it probably would not be so.

Another consideration that deserves attention is the relation of these changes to productive efficiency. It is clear that the payment of the debt increases the exports of the debtor nation, provided certain conditions mentioned above are present. These exports will presumably be those of the export industries producing most efficiently. To the extent, however, that exportation and export trade have been diverted from efficient channels by tariffs, bounties or other devices the payment of the debt may merely accentuate the inefficiency which is present. Furthermore the increase in exportation may be at the expense of what might be considered the most efficient arrangement, even if the existing condition is assumed to be efficient. This arises from the fact that any artificial stimulation may be unwise from the standpoint of efficiency, and the increase in exportation constitutes an artificial stimulation. However, little more can be said along these lines and no one can make any estimates as to the actual production effects in any given case because of the multiplicity of influences. It is probably true, nevertheless, that some inefficiency would result from this artificial stimulation and it would have to be added to the burden and subtracted from the benefits of payment.

All of the foregoing conclusions depend obviously upon the assumption that payment takes place in exports of goods and services. This mode of payment, although normal, may not be used. Much of the discussion about Germany's capacity to pay the reparations and the ability of the allies to pay their American debts assumes this mode of payment. According to Moulton this is the only *real* form of debt payment, that is, it is the only form beneficial to the creditor.

"Accordingly we must distinguish," says he, "between real and merely nominal payments—between actual transfers of wealth and merely bookkeeping operations."[11] "The total capacity of Germany to pay will be measured by the excess of her exports of goods and services rendered to foreigners over the imports of goods and the receipts of services from foreigners."[12] Not only is this considered as the only real but also as the only probable mode of German payment in the long run. Although the immediate mode of payment in the German case was borrowing, and the capacity to pay was the capacity to borrow, in the long run exports must accomplish the payment.[13]

(b) *Other Modes of Payment and Conditions Under Which They Will Be Used*

There are, therefore, other modes of payment, although these may be only temporary expedients. These are (1) gold, (2) paper money, (3) labor by debtor citizens in the creditor country, (4) transfer of title of property in the debtor country to the creditor, (5) delivery of foreign securities owned by the debtor country to the creditor country, and (6) borrowing. Moulton says that the last three are fallacious methods because they either postpone or avoid the transference of goods or real payment to the creditor country.[14]

To what extent, then, will these different methods be used? As was remarked several pages above, the use of different methods depends upon more remote considerations than have been raised thus far. To analyze these let us go back to our original reasoning as to the causes of payment in com-

[11] Moulton, *Germany's Capacity to Pay*, p. 68.

[12] *Ibid.*, p. 13.

[13] See Angell, *Recovery of Germany*, pp. 350-351.

[14] It is possible that the fifth method would not be "fallacious".

modities. Taxation created a fiscal surplus that could be used for payment. Both the withdrawal of purchasing power and the appreciation of domestic currency in terms of foreign exchange serve to stimulate exports. Such a stimulation implies an increase in production on the part of the debtor country. The ultimate basis of payment is therefore the increase in production. Hence the question of first importance is whether production can be increased in some export business. The increase will depend for the most part upon the ability of these industries to increase their capital. This may be done by greater saving on the part of the industry itself or by an increase in saving on the part of other industries through the agency of individual savings. Thus the capacity to pay foreign debts in commodities rests partly upon the possibility of increased savings and production. Moreover, Professor Angell is quite right in saying that among other things Germany's capacity to pay depends upon her progress in industrial technique.[15] But one must not lose sight of the fact that her capacity to reduce her standard of living through taxation, which is the negative side of the process, is also involved. Both of these things will be induced by the conditions artificially set up in debt payment. If payments are to be made in exports, one way this can be done is by a decrease of labor and capital in domestic industry and their increase in export industry, in order to increase the output of the latter. In that case the standard of living will be reduced by the amount of the debt payment. Thus saving will have been enforced upon the debtor by the price arrangements resulting from payment. The increase of interest rates arising out of this situation will, however, probably be the cause of still further saving supplied by the debtor nation itself, with the result of increased production and a return of the domestic standard of

[15] Angell, *Recovery of Germany*, p. 353.

living toward its former level. It will also serve to stimulate productive effort and industrial technique because of the higher reward offered for them.

To the extent, then, that the debtor nation is capable of increasing its production through increased savings and industrial effort it will be able to make payments in commodities and services. Moulton is only partly right, however, in assuming that an export surplus is necessary for the payment of the debt. The payment of the debt is also a cause of the export surplus. As far as Moulton's statement is true it is true because saving and production can be increased.

If, on the other hand, the debtor nation is not able to increase its savings sufficiently, payment will not be made through the exportation of goods, at least for the time being. The significance of the use of other methods of debt payment is related to the amounts of debt to be paid and the ability of the nation to accumulate capital. If the debt exceeds the ability of the nation to save there will be a resort to another method.

It can be seen from examining the above list of options that the most important are changes in the supply of money and changes in borrowing. In either form the method is resorted to because the depreciation of creditor money does not proceed rapidly enough to induce a surplus of exports. If this predicament is only temporary it can be overcome by the shipment of specie. If it is more lasting in character, borrowing will have to occur. In case of the use of specie, while the price level of the debtor country is being depressed by its shipment, not only are commodity payments postponed, but to the extent of the shipment they are obviated. Anything therefore that appreciates debtor money and depreciates creditor money reduces the amount of the debt to the extent of this price change. We have here naturally a parallel between national and individual debt burden. Here as with the individual an increase in prices which is due to monetary influences will decrease the debtors' burdens. It may be concluded that the debtor nation, by deflating its own currency or through an inflation of that of its creditor, can reduce its burden of debt. Where, however, there is a sufficiently large internal debt, it may not pay to increase internal burdens through deflation in order to decrease the burden externally. Yet if the falling price level in the debtor country does not retard saving or the accumulation of wealth and the unfortunate changes in the distribution of wealth resulting from the price change can be obviated in some way, the nation may be better off because of the lessening of the external burden. Granted these provisos, the deflation rather than the devaluation of European currencies after the war, wherever it was possible, had something to commend it. Certainly payment in commodities could not be as readily escaped by any other economic device.

In case gold cannot be shipped or the domestic price level cannot be further depressed, the last resort is some method involving borrowing. Borrowing represents the supplying of savings and capital accumulation by some other country because the rise of domestic interest rates does not call forth enough saving from the debtor nation itself. This constitutes, so far as the debtor's actual payment in commodities is concerned, a tiding-over process until the accumulation of capital by the debtor nation itself can be stimulated up to the point of meeting the requirements of the debt. It is probable that a part of Germany's reliance upon borrowing in the payment of her debts arises from this inability to build up capital rapidly enough. Particularly is this likely because of her reparations paid in kind. "As her foreign properties and her mercantile marine are now to be taken from her," said Keynes in 1920, " and as her foreign banking and other miscellaneous sources of revenue from abroad have been largely destroyed, it appears that on the pre-war basis of exports and imports, Germany, so far from having a surplus wherewith to make a foreign payment would be not nearly self supporting."[16] Borrowing here, as in domestic borrowing during a war, merely constitutes a postponement of actual payment by the citizens of the debtor nations. Borrowing in this case, however, is only indirectly connected with the payment of debt and because of that fact can be in the long run more readily repudiated by the borrowers. If it is not repudiated an actual payment will have to take place eventually. It is probably true that the possibility of eventual repudiation of the borrowings of Germany from individuals in order to meet reparations has prompted the United States Treasury Department to state at various times that it favors loans to Germany but that the federal government is not the proper agency to make them. If these reparations were directly owed to the United States, it would mean that the Treasury favored, in the event of repudiation by German business failure, the payment of Germany's debt to the whole people of the United States by a part of the people. The government should not be embarrassed, even at this cost.

(c) *Conclusion With Regard to Debt Burden*

We have stated that the conclusions reached about the burden of external debts some pages back depended upon the assumption that they were paid in commodities or services. It is apparent that (1) they will not be paid in goods if the accumulation of capital is too rapidly entrenched upon, and (2) that it may be said that the necessity of payment is just as much a cause of an export surplus as that the export surplus is a cause of payment. In other words, given reasonably favorable conditions, a nation with a debt to pay will eventually develop an export surplus whether it has it in the beginning or not. The case of Germany and the persistency

[16] Keynes, *Economic Consequences of the Peace*, p. 189.

of a growing export surplus in the face of the depression of 1930-31 is some evidence in substantiation of this view.

It has been claimed in the past, however, that some nations (Germany being taken as the example) are virtually incapable of developing an export surplus. From 1919 to 1923 Germany had no surplus. There was really a deficit to the amount of ten billion gold marks. The fact that her imports were of coal and raw materials made some people pessimistic about payment because it was believed that she had to increase imports in order to increase exports. This would not have been such a problem had it been possible to build up the service and invisible items. This potential difficulty was noted by Keynes and Moulton and more recently by Professor Angell who says, " . . . all these service items taken together are as yet a comparatively small factor in the general aggregate of Germany's international transactions. The principal share in overcoming the international payment deficit must almost certainly be borne by the commodity balance of trade." [17] The conclusion, however, which is coming to be accepted is expressed further on in his book by Professor Angell, that these difficulties are only temporary and that there is no inevitability about the impediments to an export surplus. Speaking of Germany, Professor Angell says, " Taking the foreign trade situation as a whole, it can thus be stated with a good deal of assurance that commodity exports will expand steadily relative to imports." [18] These difficulties, then, will merely retard the processes mentioned above.

IV. PSYCHOLOGICAL CONSEQUENCES OF EXTERNAL DEBTS

Two more points remain to be considered: the psychological consequences of external debts, and the effects of payment upon the balance of payments. In regard to the

[17] Angell, *Recovery of Germany*, p. 351.

[18] *Ibid.*, p. 355.

former, several arguments have been made to the effect that the consequences of external debts are good, several to the effect that they are bad. It is said that the payment of an external debt develops a sense of tribute in the debtor nation. Thus Keynes says, " A debtor does not love its creditor and it is fruitless to expect feelings of good will from France, Italy, and Russia towards this country or America, if their future development is stifled for many years to come by the annual tribute they must pay us." [19] Much was made of this feeling by the American professors in their protest against the foreign debt settlements. It is interesting to note that the Colwyn Committee scarcely mentioned this possibility in their discussion of external debts and one witness actually stated that he believed there would be very little effect of this kind.

Another reason for ill-will mentioned by Keynes is the constant attempts at evasion of payment. This, he thought, would cause financial instability for many years to come. The debts would also result in financial instability everywhere, arising partly from the numerous entanglements and interrelations of debts.

Arguments on the other side of the question are given by Dexter and Sedgwick. They do not believe that great war debts have ever been or are likely ever to be a cause of war. On the contrary they see some reasons to believe that war debts will prevent or reduce the possibility of war. " So long as the debts of the last war are felt by those who are drifting toward another, there may be some reason to hope that people who have to pay them will compel their statesmen to avoid war. . . . The generations who pay will have that much incentive to keep peace." Furthermore they believed that " If the United States cancel their claims it will furnish a precedent that debts incurred for future wars need not be paid

[19] Keynes, *Economic Consequences of the Peace*, p. 278.

either, and that if the United States can be drawn in, they can be used to pay for those wars. That seems a little like putting a premium on war." [20] It would seem that any attempt to reconcile these various points of view would be virtually futile. The final conclusion of the Colwyn Committee on this point is of considerable interest. They said, "We do not think the external debt exerts any very strong psychological effect. Large and burdensome as it is, it seems to be overshadowed in the popular imagination by the much larger, but in other ways less burdensome internal debt." [21]

V. THE EFFECTS OF THE PAYMENT OF EXTERNAL DEBTS UPON THE BALANCE OF PAYMENTS

In regard to the effects of debt payment upon the balance of international payments it is obvious that there will be a tendency toward an increase in commodity exports and an increase of invisible items. Germany's balance was adverse for twenty years, from 1894 to 1913. The unfavorable balance rose as high as 1,933,000,000 marks in 1909. This was made up by interest on investments, shipping and inland transport charges and banking and insurance earnings. Interest on foreign loans varied annually from 600 to 800 million marks. In 1930 there was a favorable balance of trade. Thus we can agree with Dr. Anderson that " . . . the mere fact of debt payments through the creating and transferring of a fiscal surplus via the exchange markets from a debtor to a creditor country leads to increased exports and diminished imports in the debtor country and to increased imports and diminished exports in the creditor country." [22]

[20] Dexter and Sedgwick, *op. cit.*, pp. 104-5.

[21] *Colwyn Report*, p. 98.

[22] Anderson, "Relation of International Debt Payments to Domestic Purchasing Power," Academy of Political Science *Proceedings*, April, 1927, p. 722 *et seq.*

Not only, however, does it change the amount of the total balance but it changes the relative importance of different items in the general balance. Dr. Anderson has carried this analysis further to the point of estimating the extent of the increase. He says that " . . . the payment of international debts reduces domestic purchasing power by an amount equal to the payment of the debtor country and increases domestic purchasing power by the same amount in the creditor country." [23] He qualifies this statement, however, by the following one. " The amount received by the creditor country will be less than the amount paid by the debtor country to the extent that the exchange rate of the debtor country is depressed toward the lower gold point." [24]

VI. SUMMARY

It may be concluded then, contrary to Dexter and Sedgwick, that the payment of an external debt is burdensome only to the debtor nation, provided that it is made in commodities and services. It will usually be paid in this way by export surpluses induced by the mere attempt to pay the debt. It will be paid by other methods temporarily or permanently when a sufficiently large export surplus for some reason cannot be built up. This may be due to the requirement of larger debt payments than the nation can readily build up through the accumulation of capital from savings, or it may be due to the peculiar nature of the debtor's industries, which do not lend themselves readily to the building up of an export surplus. The burden of foreign debt payment arises out of the degree to which this payment prevents or fails to stimulate the accumulation of capital which would ordinarily have taken place. The ease of debt payment and the degree to which methods other than goods payment are used depend upon the effects of payment upon the accumulation of capital.

[23] *Ibid.*, p. 722.

[24] *Ibid.*, p. 726.

CHAPTER VIII

Effects Upon Distribution

The most important effects of public debt retirement are those upon the production and distribution of wealth. A great deal has been written on this subject, most of which is based upon certain chosen assumptions. There is insufficient breadth in the choice of these assumptions; in particular the writers have failed to relate their theories to monetary changes. The purpose of this chapter is to analyze the most important theories that have been developed and the assumptions that lie back of them.

Sir Walter Layton has wisely pointed out in his testimony before the Colwyn Committee that one must have an answer to five questions, if the effects of retirement on production and distribution are to be properly understood. The questions are: who are the taxpayers; who are the interest receivers; what use would the taxpayers have made of the money; what use have the interest receivers made of it; and what waste was involved in the process of collection? The answers to these questions are obviously very difficult to obtain and the student must rely chiefly upon psychological assumptions to support his opinions. The cause of the difficulty, it was pointed out, is that the data are largely estimates.

I. The Nature of the Distribution of Debt Holdings

Let us turn first to the facts about the distribution of debt holdings. It is clear that a decided change has occurred in the character of the distribution of the debt since its original issue, a change in the direction of greater concentration. In the beginning there was more equality of holdings, partly because special attempts were made to bring this about. In 1917, the Secretary of the Treasury in the United States declared that a man who bought a bond as a patriot stepped out of that role when he sold it on the market.[1] Protests were also made against the exchange of bonds for merchandise. The exchange of government bonds for other bonds was criticized and federal "blue sky" legislation was urged. Option in the purchase of bonds when loans were oversubscribed was given in many cases to the subscribers of small amounts. In England and France similar methods were used.

In spite of these efforts, a great deal of concentration has developed. The debt in England and the United States is chiefly held by banks, insurance companies, railways and local government units. It is also held in considerable amounts by wealthy individuals, particularly where, as in the United States, there is a chance of obtaining tax exemption by such holdings. One-third of the floating debt of England is held by banks, according to J. B. Pease.[2] This concentration is true of the debt holdings of many countries at the present time and seems to be a natural feature of any post-war period.

The causes of the concentration are not hard to find. They consist of the numerous concessions granted the bond holders in order to strengthen the public credit—tax exemption, legal tender privileges and concessions of a banking or credit nature.

Tax exemption is generally considered a failure as a means of accomplishing the purposes for which it is used. The

[1] *Annual Report of the Secretary of the Treasury*, 1917, p. 3.

[2] *Colwyn Report, Minutes of Evidence*, p. 324, par. 4492.

reduced interest that the government pays on tax-exempt bonds does not compensate for the loss of the taxes, particularly such taxes as would be collected under a system of progressive taxation. It has not been sufficiently pointed out, however, that tax exemption involves the still further defect of promoting the concentration of debt holdings. W. A. Brown believes that this concentration has gone so far in the United States as to eliminate the small investor from the market for government bonds. Because he does not have to pay a surtax, the small investor does not find it profitable to hold government bonds. Wealthy men are willing to loan at a lower rate of interest because of the advantages they obtain from tax exemption. This fact has a tendency to keep the interest rates for exempt bonds down. Brown believes that in addition to tax exemption there are three important reasons for concentration in the hands of corporations and banks. These are (1) purchase by banks to secure government deposits against which no reserves need be held; (2) purchase by banks to provide secondary reserves and to get at the funds of the Federal Reserve banks; (3) purchase by corporations in order to maintain a strong cash position and to employ funds in anticipation of large periodic payments. The statistics of income of the United States Bureau of Internal Revenue indicate that there is a very considerable amount of concentration of the debt in the hands of the higher income classes. (See Table XVII.)

It is obvious that in spite of some reaction since the war taxes have become heavier upon the richer groups. It may be said that in the post-war as compared with the pre-war period progressive taxation has increased, but it has not been carried to the point where the wealthy groups who hold most of the debt pay back to themselves not only all of the debt service but also their proportionate share of the government

TABLE XVII

INCOME FROM GOVERNMENT BONDS NOT EXEMPT FROM TAXATION

(In thousands of dollars)

Net income classes	1924	1925	1929
$10,000 under 11,000	$907	$779	$1,503
11,000 " 12,000	858	720	1,409
12,000 " 13,000	728	730	1,224
13,000 " 14,000	706	620	1,249
14,000 " 15,000	761	675	968
15,000 " 20,000	2,894	2,670	4,890
20,000 " 25,000	2,534	2,420	3,644
25,000 " 30,000	2,373	1,794	2,877
30,000 " 40,000	3,319	2,800	2,538
40,000 " 50,000	2,461	1,970	2,176
50,000 " 60,000	1,750	1,460	1,527
60,000 " 70,000	1,555	1,055	1,153
70,000 " 80,000	1,113	897	917
80,000 " 90,000	824	668	732
90,000 " 100,000	632	742	2,510
100,000 " 150,000	1,686	1,857	1,189
150,000 " 200,000	1,267	1,018	785
200,000 " 250,000	611	447	641
250,000 " 300,000	393	219	827
300,000 " 400,000	445	412	472
400,000 " 500,000	245	730	780
500,000 " 750,000	640	323	349
750,000 " 1,000,000	258	208	290
1,000,000 " 1,500,000	327	150	514
1,500,000 " 2,000,000	6	16	152
2,000,000 " 3,000,000	179	2	268
3,000,000 " 4,000,000	6	144	208
4,000,000 " 5,000,000	....	....	623
5,000,000 or over	163	125	
Total	29,645	25,651	40,184

Source: United States Bureau of Internal Revenue—Statistics of Income.

expenses in taxes. In England the amounts paid in income taxes roughly balance the debt service.[4]

When one turns to the third and fourth questions, refer-

[4] Pigou, *Public Finance*; also, *Reports of Secretary of the Treasury of the United States.*

ring to the use that tax payers would have made of their tax money and the use to which the interest receivers would put it, the task of obtaining any definite evidence becomes an almost impossible one. Outside of statistics on the growth of savings deposits, the increase of state and local bonds, and the expansions of security issues, in the United States there is apparently nothing. We thus fall back upon reasoning from assumptions. Those which underlie conclusions about the social effects of debt retirement will be first considered.

II. THE THEORY THAT THE DEBT MAINTAINS AN UNPRODUCTIVE CLASS

Probably the oldest theory about the social effects of the public debt is the theory that its existence maintains an unproductive class. One of the earliest writers to advance this theory was J. R. McCulloch.[25] Closely related to this belief is the one given as an argument against the removal of the Civil War debt: that the debt holders, though unproductive, were deserving people, such as widows and orphans. The retirement of the debt would leave them without a proper means of investment. H. C. Adams, by showing that the debt was held to a very large extent by banks and insurance companies, was one of the first to correct this false impression.[6] In England the same belief that the debt maintained an unproductive class was expressed by Cobbett, who said that he could tell the number of fund holders by the number of new houses erected from time to time.

The most important objection to this old theory is that the public debt is held for a variety of reasons. The degree to which concentration has resulted from the concessions mentioned above indicates this. Moreover, it is probable

[5] McCulloch, *Select Tracts*, p. 291.

[6] Adams, H. C., *Public Debts*, p. 46.

that if there was no government debt, those desiring to live solely on their capital would find a sufficient amount of satisfactory commercial securities. It must not be supposed, however, that since this old theory in its original form can be so easily discredited that it contains no elements of truth. The recent history of public debts shows that the evil of the situation is not merely fictitious. But it arises not from the existence of debt holders who wish to live upon their income without further labor, but from the fact that most large national debts are unproductive, or "dead weight," as the English say. There would be no objection to living on the proceeds of productive investments. The question arises, therefore, as to whether criticism should not be directed against the state for allowing unproductive expenditures rather than against the individual for taking advantage of opportunities to invest in government bonds. Such a criticism would be valid even if the debt were held largely by inactive groups. There is no more reason for objecting to the public debt as a source of capital income than for objection to any other source. The real fault lies in its lack of productiveness.

It is not true, however, that the national debts do support a distinctly idle class at the present time. Pigou, after a careful examination of available debt statistics, was impressed by the comparatively small proportion of the debt held by people who might be called "drones".[7] In summarizing his conclusions the majority report of the Colwyn Committee stated that the contention that the debt maintained an inactive class seemed questionable. According to Layton's analysis, as well as Pigou's, the average debt holder was far from inactive. Although the debt might have some influence in increasing the number and importance of *rentiers,* this was doubted, as the heavy taxation and the fall in the

[7] *Colwyn Report, Minutes of Evidence,* vol. i, p. 184.

value of money were considered to be influences tending to decrease their number.[8] Thus it cannot be claimed that the debt will increase production by reducing this form of idleness.

III. THE THEORY THAT THE DEBT INCREASES THE INEQUALITY OF WEALTH

Not only is it believed that the public debt maintains an unproductive class, but also that the payment of the debt interest causes social discontent, arising out of the transfer of wealth through the debt service from the poorer to the richer classes. As Davenport has expressed it, it arises from the "mortgage of the masses to the classes." Pethick-Lawrence, for instance, speaks of the laboring classes as having a legitimate grievance in the payment of debt interest because such payment increases the inequality of wealth.

(a) *Two Ways in Which an Increase in the Inequality of Wealth May Appear*

There are two ways in which this may come about. In the first place, the debt holders, who are an essentially wealthy group, may not pay in taxes as much as they receive in interest and in government services. As mentioned above, the payment in debt service roughly balances the amount of income tax, at any rate, in England and exceeds it in the United States, whereas the debt service should be considerably less than the total net taxes paid if the payment of the debt came from the non-debt holders. Secondly, the large debt payments may be an effective check upon expenditures for social services. A group of men representing the Cooperative Congress testified before the Colwyn Committee that high taxes in England to pay the debt service would reduce the funds available for social services,[9] and a representative of

[8] *Colwyn Report*, p. 102.

[9] *Colwyn Report, Minutes of Evidence*, p. 311.

the Trades Union Congress said that this was by far the most important burden caused by the public debt.[10] Thus not only would the monetary income of the less wealthy be reduced by taxes, but the free income received from the state would be reduced. It is questionable whether the national debt actually does reduce social services. This is, however, a very common belief. Dr. Dalton, for instance, includes reduction of social expenditure as one of the indirect burdens of the debt.[11] The logical basis for this belief is not that the budget is large due to the public debt. After all, the transfer of debt service and repayment funds has only an indirect effect upon the real income of the nation. Yet those who argue that the debt service reduces the capacity for social expenditures do not usually take account of the fact that this capacity depends largely upon the amount of real income. To a large extent the process is merely one of transferring rights to income. Superficially, therefore, it seems that debt payment will not reduce the capacity of the government to pay for social services. Nevertheless the Colwyn Committee concluded that social services would be reduced, owing to the fact that the greater proportion of taxes to total income caused by the debt makes their levy more difficult. The arguments involved and their relation to the theory of debt burden and debt criteria will be discussed more fully at a later point.

In his brief volume on public finance, Dalton relates the above point in a suggestive manner to the whole body of tax criteria by applying a criterion of maximum benefit to the problems of public debts. This criterion is the counterpart of the more familiar criterion of minimum sacrifice. The policy of the National Minimum applies the second criterion, but the first (he thinks) is not attainable, at any rate while

[10] *Ibid.*, p. 228.

[11] Dalton, *Public Finance*, p. 190.

" large public debts remain, and considerations of production limit the height at which national minimum standards can be set." [12] Although there may be weaknesses in this criterion of maximum benefit, it extends to their logical conclusion certain ideas that have arisen in public finance owing to the existence of inequality of wealth and the use of orthodox value theory. Its application to the problems of debt payment seems to the writer particularly pertinent. It might be added that Dr. Dalton's treatment of public debts has the further merit of giving proper attention in general to distribution effects. In his testimony before the Colwyn Committee, he definitely stated that he considered the latter no less important than production effects.

It is thus possible that because debt holdings are concentrated in the hands of the wealthier classes and the payment of taxes is not nearly so concentrated, the inequality of wealth may be increased by the payment of interest. The payment of the debt service should from the standpoint of just distribution be effected through the use of highly progressive taxes. This argument may have limited value but there are, of course, many other considerations. The way in which wealth is distributed has its effect upon the volume of production, and it is through altering the distribution of wealth that debt payment may have its chief effects upon production. There is some evidence that the arrangement most suitable to distribution objectives may be unsuited to those of production; Pigou, for instance, believes that taxes should be regressive if production is the object; progressive in the case of distribution objectives.[13]

[12] *Ibid.*, p. 169.

[13] *Colwyn Report, Minutes of Evidence*, p. 44.

(b) *Conditions Under Which the Inequality of Wealth May Not Be Increased*

One must be cautious, however, in assuming that the inequality of wealth will be increased by the payment of the debt service, not only because there is little accurate knowledge of how the debt is distributed and what the incidence of the tax system is, but because under certain circumstances the inequality of wealth may not be increased at all even if the entire debt service is borne by non-debt holders. Even when the debt service is only partly borne by the debt holders, the distribution of wealth may actually be equalized. It is characteristic of the superficiality of thought concerning public debts that the tendency toward inequality is invariably assumed, although this is not justified if the bonds have been purchased out of capital or savings and are repaid without the accumulation of capital. There is here, as in every other aspect of the subject touched thus far, a close relationship between the burden of the debt and inflation. If there is no inflation, war loans would merely cause certain existing goods or a part of the accumulation of them to be transferred to the government and employed by it in the prosecution of war. Presumably those making the loans would be of the wealthier classes. They would be deprived by the loans of real wealth and rights to real wealth would be substituted. Nominally they would be as wealthy as before. Actually, however, to the extent that they could not purchase as much with their rights owing to the fall in the value of money, which in its turn is due to the check put upon production by the unproductive war use of capital, they would not be as wealthy as before. Now, if no attempt is made in repayment to obtain the funds from actual accumulation of savings, with the result of a rise in the value of money to its pre-war level, the holder will be permanently worse off. To pay the debt service from taxes levied upon him would make his condition still worse. It is obvious, therefore, that in such a case the country could have nothing to fear in regard to the distribution of wealth from either the payment of interest or the repayment of the debt. Unless prices are returned to the original level or no taxes are levied upon the bond holder for his own debt service, the payment process would actually have an equalizing tendency, assuming, of course, that the wealthy hold most of the debt.

These possibilities have been recognized by several students of the subject, but not with a degree of definiteness that suggests complete understanding. D. H. Macgregor, for instance, made the following statement before the Colwyn Committee: "The distribution of wealth is not made more unequal by the fact that fund holders may receive more interest on the debt than they pay in taxation on account of it. This means that they hold more public securities than in proportion to their taxable capacity, and to that extent less of other securities." [14] W. L. Hichens, a member of the Colwyn Committee, declared that the payment of interest on any kind of securities would have the same effect. It would thus be an objection to any kind of income in the form of interest or profits, and would constitute an argument not against the public debt but against the capitalist system.[15] Sir Alan Anderson was of the same opinion. He did not think it was reasonable to allow the payment of interest on commercial debts and at the same time oppose or prevent the payment of interest on the public debt.[16] Pethick-Lawrence, however, comes nearer to the point in question when he states that the war was paid for too much from loans and that this caused inflation. Thus, through the processes of inflation, the wealthier bond holders escaped the tax burdens that

[14] *Colwyn Report, Minutes of Evidence*, p. 426, par. 37.

[15] *Colwyn Report, Minutes of Evidence*, p. 398.

[16] *Ibid.*, p. 398 and par. 5405.

should more properly have been borne by them. The payment of debt interest perpetuates this unjust condition and passes an undue proportion of the national dividend to the bond holders. This, he concludes, is an important reason for the retirement of the debt as rapidly as possible and thus becomes a part of the argument for the capital levy. There is much to be said for this point of view; an insufficient emphasis, however, is placed upon the original injustice of inflation. If taxes had been levied, falling upon the poorer groups in the form of indirect taxes on consumption goods, the burden would have also been increased, although it must be granted that because the holdings of the wealthy would not be government bonds, the problem of remedy would be much more difficult and would have to be solved through progressive taxation. Had the government resorted to the issue of paper money, however, it is possible that no increase in inequality of distribution would have resulted. Thus it is apparent that the problem is not so much that of the use of inflation versus taxation—the issue raised by Pethick-Lawrence—but a problem of the kinds of inflation or taxation employed and the circumstances attending their use. Pethick-Lawrence has, however, performed a useful service in pointing out that the respective use of taxation or inflation is important for the problem, and that one must go back to the methods by which the debt originated to learn how the retirement will affect the distribution of wealth.

IV. ANALYSIS OF THE THEORY THAT THE DEBT INCREASES THE INEQUALITY OF WEALTH

(a) *The Influence of the Conditions Under Which the Debt Originated*

Although no exactly similar situations may be found, it is useful for purposes of analysis to examine a number of hypothetical situations, describing the origin and repayment of the debt in each. A case where the loan is made and repaid entirely from the accumulation of wealth or savings, with the result that there is no increase in the quantity of purchasing medium, will be examined first. In such a situation the person who lends to the government merely transfers his actual wealth, or rather his claims to such wealth, the government giving in exchange for the wealth claims upon the general wealth. Two consequences are evident, assuming that government expenditures of the proceeds of the loan are unproductive: first, the supply of money or its equivalent does not change; second, the quantity of goods entering into exchange is somewhat reduced in the beginning and will be still more reduced later on. If one accepts a quantity theory of money, prices are likely to rise. They are likely to rise in a degree related to the proportion of the unproductive debt to the total wealth. To the extent that prices rise due to the unproductive use of the debt proceeds the rise will constitute a tax upon the entire country in proportion to the wealth of each person. This is the way unproductive expenditures would exert their influence upon distribution. The interesting point to note, however, is that if the tax is to be of this weight, the nominal income of every person would have to remain the same after the redistributing process of taxation to pay the debt service is completed.

The nominal income of the debt holder is likely to remain the same since his loan consists in this case of the transfer of rights to real property for identical rights to money income from the government, not necessarily based on any given real property. The nominal income of the non-debt holder is, however, likely to rise, and superficially it would appear that more of the burden is shifted to the debt holder. This is, however, not likely, since taxes upon the non-debt holder will be raised, thus reducing his nominal income to the former level. (The taxes referred to are, of course, for the debt service.) If, however, in this case taxes are levied likewise upon the debt holder for his own service, the burden will not be according to the amount of nominal income and a tendency toward equality of distribution will have been artificially created. Thus if the debt holder is taxed for the payment of his own service, his burden would be more than proportional to the total public burden, and, where incomes are fixed, as are those derived from the public debt, the income receiver would be taxed most heavily.

From a superficial analysis of these relationships it might be concluded that to tax a debt holder at all for his own debt service in such a case would reduce his income in comparison to the general social income and would tend to exert an equalizing influence upon the concentration of wealth if that debt holder were wealthy. Such a general conclusion however, does not necessarily follow. It would be true only if the debt holder were wealthy and also derived all or most of his income from the debt service. It is based also on the supposition that the debt arose in the way described above and this is not necessarily true. Those holding the debt hold other forms of securities, the income from which is not fixed or derived from the government.

A more reasonable conclusion would be that in such a hypothetical case no tendency toward inequality of wealth would be promoted if the taxation for the debt service were in proportion to income from a " fixed source." Neither an increase in the progression of taxes nor undue haste in the retirement of the debt because of the fear that it was increasing the inequality of wealth would be warranted. However, the analysis does show that in the case of fixed incomes, whether derived from the government through the debt service or not, there is possibly an undue burden of taxation. It might be that for those who failed to loan money to the government in times of need this burden is justifiable; for those who had done so it would not be.

One is not justified, however, in assuming that a large public debt which has any economic significance ever comes entirely out of public savings. On the contrary, the transfer of wealth is usually effected through an increase in purchasing power, or inflation. The question arises, therefore, as to what the effects of the debt service would be in case the original funds were obtained through the increase of purchasing medium. The consequences in such a case would depend largely upon the measures used to increase the medium. Let us consider first the direct issue of paper money by the banks to the government or, what is substantially the same thing, the issue of paper money by the government. If such methods are used the results may be different from those mentioned above. There will, however, be some similarities to the first case. There will be a rise of prices which will tend to place a tax upon all the citizens in proportion to their wealth in terms of money. There will in this case be no difference from the first case discussed except that prices and taxes would rise much higher. These facts by themselves would not cause the rich to benefit at the expense of the poor. There would be, of course, no debt service unless taxation to accumulate funds to deflate may be called such.

The increase in bank credit based on government bonds, a most important measure in war finance, differs from the case of increased issue of paper money in that it usually results in an increase of fixed incomes which are subject to gain or loss in real purchasing power with changes in prices. Thus, instead of the rise in prices taxing all merely according to their wealth, the non-debt holders, regardless of their wealth, would be exceptionally burdened. Although prices would rise, the debt holders would have had their money incomes especially raised, for though the money incomes of non-debt holders would rise, they would not rise nearly as much as those of the debt holders. For example, if the rise in prices were proportional to the rise in money incomes, and the amount of increase in the money was ten per cent, this ten per cent being held by ten per cent of the population, then this ten per cent of the population would have their money incomes approximately doubled, whereas the incomes of other citizens would have risen only ten per cent. In such a case taxation should be in proportion to the wealth *including the amount of public debt held.* If taxation took account of the increase in money income of all the tax payers it is difficult to see how an increase in the burden of debt would come to the poorer classes. In the above case the taxes upon the debt holders would increase one hundred per cent, whereas those upon the other tax payers would increase only ten per cent. Such an adjustment in taxes would not necessarily occur in practice, however, and the increase in inequality would not be nearly as great if, as is frequently the case, the price level was increased more than proportionately to the debt.

(b) *The Influence of Taxation for the Payment of the Debt Service Upon Production and Saving*

This discussion has hitherto neglected the dynamic factor of the effect of taxes for the payment of the debt service upon production and saving. Would the periodic levying of taxes for the debt, if it stimulated production, result in a different condition in the debt burdens than if it checked or left unaffected the trend of production? Let us assume first that savings have been stimulated by taxation for the debt service in the above mentioned cases. In the first case, where the debt originated with the increase in savings or the transfer of purchasing medium, the situation would not be altered by the effects of taxation upon savings. It is true that those with fixed incomes, such as the interest on government bonds, would gain from a fall in the price level but probably not any more than any other group.[17]

In the second case mentioned, namely, where the proceeds for the war are obtained by an issue of paper money, there would also be no effect resulting from the stimulation of saving. It is when one turns to the third case, or that where borrowing by individuals from banks and the use of bank credit have been resorted to, that the results of the taxation for the debt service become problematic. But where the money incomes of the debt holders were originally increased, the increase in savings and the consequent fall in prices will only apparently raise the incomes of these debt holders. Confusion results here from the fact that originally there was an undue burden of debt. The rise in the real incomes of the debt holders will be no greater than the similar rise for other income receivers. Fairness in such a situation, as in other cases, will require progressive taxation, but that progression need not be affected by changes in the price level if they result from accumulation of savings. On the contrary, however, if a fall in prices occurs because of actual deflation and not because of the increase of goods, the burden of the debt will have been increased by this situation and more progression should be introduced than that justified by the amount of the debt held. The point of greatest importance is that the increased burden is not caused by price changes alone, but by the circumstances under which the debt is incurred. Although the original inequality remains and the maintenance of the debt in this case increases the concentration of wealth, this concentration is unaffected by certain kinds of price changes. It is pertinent to mention here the interesting analysis given this problem by Pigou. According to Pigou there is likely to be a burden upon the poor

[17] For the explanation of this position the reader is referred to the discussion of this subject in Chapter V.

arising out of the fact that taxation upon the wealthy is not as large as the debt service they receive. As he points out, there is no close correspondence of taxes on any individual to the amount of his debt holdings, although in recent years, through the use of progressive taxation, a somewhat closer correspondence has resulted. Thus he says that in actual practice,

> loans are generally voluntary and large subscribers have good reason to hope that the interest on their holdings will exceed the contribution in taxes which they will have to make to provide this interest, for experience has never yet revealed a tax system graduated for increasing incomes anything like as steeply as loan subscriptions are likely to be graduated, at all events when the loan required is large.[18]

For these reasons Pigou holds that persons with money to lend will think themselves better off if war is financed by loans instead of taxes. It should be apparent, however, from the preceding discussion in this chapter that Professor Pigou's conception that fair treatment results only when the borrower pays back in taxes what he receives in loan interest is too simple for the needs of the problem. Changes in prices and changes in the causes of these price changes must be taken into account if conclusions more nearly approximating reality are to be obtained.

Let us turn now to the supposition that saving or production are not stimulated by the payment of the debt service. In the first case, where savings were the source of the original proceeds, there would be no increase in burden upon the poor or upon non-debt holders if prices remained constant or rose. On the contrary, in so far as the debt is a fixed income the real income of the debt holder would fall neither more nor less than that of other groups. The same conclu-

[18] Pigou, *Political Economy of War*, p. 77.

sion would follow in the second case, where the debt is in the form of an increased supply of paper money, and in the third case, where the increase of bank credit was the source of government proceeds.

V. SUMMARY

It may be concluded, therefore, that the answer to the question of whether or not the payment of the debt service would continue or increase the inequality of wealth depends upon a great variety of circumstances, among which are the distribution of debt holdings, the changes in the price level, the causes of these changes, and especially the conditions surrounding the origination of the debt. It is fair to say that the current conclusions about the effect of the payment of debt service in most cases are not considerably altered by the foregoing discussion. It is usually true that the debt originates through the inflation of bank credit. It may be true also that the effect of taxation for the payment of the service is to stimulate production and saving. Under these circumstances, as we have indicated, the increased burden upon the poorer classes owing to the debt is perpetuated. This increased burden, however, arises essentially from the methods employed to finance the war and not from changes in the price level, as is frequently supposed. It is not made heavier by changes of the price level caused by the conditions of increasing production that we have mentioned above. Falling prices due to deflation are the exception. If deflation is very extensive the war burden will be considerably increased. Under certain circumstances, therefore, it is quite apparent that some measure such as progressive taxation to offset the increased burden caused by the price change would be justifiable. It may thus be concluded that, although there is some truth in the belief that the payment of the debt service increases the inequality of wealth, it is also true that in certain hypothetical cases it might not have such an effect. To the extent that these hypothetical conditions are present the tendency toward inequality will not be as strong as is generally supposed. In addition it is apparent that the effects of price changes are not as simple as is sometimes thought. Finally, most writers are now agreed that the debt does not maintain an unproductive class.

The repayment of a debt is therefore not rendered imperative by the fact that its service necessarily promotes the inequality of wealth. This tendency depends on a variety of circumstances, some related to the conditions that originated the debt, others to the consequences of paying the service. Repayment of principal is merely an increase of the service. The process would thus merely capitalize the inequality present in some cases of interest payment; it would not eliminate it. Here is a fatal error in reasoning on the part of those who recognize that a debt promotes inequality. Escape from these difficulties involves the use of a well devised system of repayment and care as to the conditions surrounding the origination of the debt. Suggestions for the remedy of these evils will be given in a later chapter.

CHAPTER IX

Effects Upon Production

Both the origination of a debt and its repayment involve changes in the distribution of wealth. So obvious is this fact that in the theory of public debts attention has been unduly concentrated upon it to the exclusion of any changes in the production of wealth consequent upon the changes in distribution.[1] The problem is much more than one of the distribution of wealth. It is apparent in the whole field of economic theory that more emphasis must be placed upon effects of distribution upon production. The next logical step in this study should be, therefore, the consideration of the production effects of debt retirement as they arise from the changes in distribution resulting from retirement.

I. THE REDIRECTION OF INVESTMENT FUNDS AS A CONSEQUENCE OF THE DEBT SERVICE

The payment of the debt service may involve a redirection of investment and the funds taken in debt service may not necessarily return again to their source. The effect of the debt service upon investment may relate to domestic or foreign enterprises. In regard to investment in domestic enterprises it has been asserted that the payment of the service discriminates against small businesses in favor of large ones. Sir Felix Schuster, for instance, in his testimony before the Colwyn Committee stated that the payment of the debt involved a redirection of investment and that the funds taken in debt service would not necessarily return again to

[1] See, e. g., Matsushita, *op. cit.*, p. 155.

their source. Instead these funds might flow into new business, giving rise to an undesirable amount of friction. It was pointed out in the discussion that followed his remarks that this friction might be greater in times of depression. Sir Felix thought that reinvestment funds would flow into large businesses as against small businesses. This belief arose out of the feeling that small firms could not get loans from banks as easily as large ones. In support of Sir Felix's contention it should be recognized that there is little doubt that corporations of large size and wide reputation find greater ease in marketing their securities and obtaining capital than small ones. Much discussion over this point took place before the Colwyn Committee. Professor Cannan, for instance, opposed the views of Sir Felix. He believed that money taken from small businesses outside of the larger financial centers would gradually spread back to these concerns, in that an excessive demand for investment in the larger, more important concerns would lower interest rates and cause some investors to seek the more profitable investment of their funds in the smaller concerns. Sir Josiah Stamp was, however, of the same opinion as Sir Felix. It was his belief that funds taken in taxes from small but efficient textile mills, such as exist in Yorkshire and Leicestershire, would not be reinvested in them.

Closely associated with this idea that the small business will be discriminated against is the notion that capital is more likely to be used effectively if left in a business than if a process of reinvestment is introduced, causing the friction of transferring funds and possibly leading to an increase in the control of capital by inexperienced persons. R. S. Wright, representing the National Union of Manufacturers, made the statement that everyone desires " . . . to develop the resources of the country and the man or men or firms who leave capital in the business for that purpose are serving the country better than the man who takes it out." [2] Much the same opinion was expressed by J. W. Clark and Felix J. Blackmore, representing the National Chamber of Commerce, who said that " . . . money left in industry and trade possesses increasing and ever growing possibilities, but extracted for the state these qualities are diminished and even lost altogether." [3]

Much discussion has also taken place over the possibility that the payment of the debt may increase conservative investments as over against hazardous ones. In the Colwyn Report and elsewhere there is no consensus of opinion that the payment of a debt tends either to reduce or increase conservative investment. Reginald McKenna was of the opinion that it would increase the tendency to take risks.[4] He said that the increase in taxes would cause this because of a desire to compensate by a higher speculative return for the loss through the taxes. Layton also believed that more risky investments would be induced. In conflict with these opinions we find J. M. Keynes maintaining that the effect of debt payment is to divert investments largely into the gilt-edged money market. He did not hold that all of it would go there, but he believed that there is a presumption that conservative securities please the debt holder and that therefore he will seek a similar form of investment.

Professor Seligman is of the opinion that such problems cannot be decided readily without reference to the kind of taxes used. Thus he states that, among the other indirect effects, the income tax may reduce investment in venturesome types of industry. In explanation he says,

The continual growth of a country's prosperity depends largely

[2] *Colwyn Report, Minutes of Evidence*, p. 94.

[3] The same opinion was held by R. G. Glenday of the Federation of British Industries. *Ibid.*, p. 350, par. 51.

[4] *Ibid.*, p. 350, par. 51.

upon the readiness of the able and the venturesome to start new enterprises and to take the risks of the unknown. Where the hazard is great the profits must be correspondingly great; for in the long run in new and untried fields the profits of some are likely to be overbalanced by the losses of others. If the government, however, demands too large a percentage of these anticipated profits the individual may prefer not to subject himself to the risk and may decide to be content with a smaller but surer return.

Whether or not taxes will give rise to such consequences depends according to Seligman upon a variety of circumstances, among them being the use to which the debt is put.[5]

The analysis given by these men shows clearly what influences are at work. They are the loss of income, the investment preferences of the debt holders, and the discrimination of taxation against some forms of investments. It might be added that the distribution of the debt is of great importance. If the debt were held by persons also holding speculative investments, discrimination against this form of income by income or excess profits taxes would not result. It is because such distribution of investments is not common that discrimination probably does result. The preference for conservative investments on the part of the debt holder indicated by this fact gives some value to Keynes' contention that the reinvestment will tend to be conservative. It is also likely, as he believes, that although originally the debt may be more evenly distributed as between conservative or non-conservative investors, it tends to fall with time into conservative hands. Moreover, the holding of parts of it by less conservative investors does not preclude its reinvestment in a conservative manner. The idea expressed by McKenna is erroneous in that it supposes a loss to the country from the payment of a domestic debt which does not necessarily follow.

[5] Seligman, *Studies in Public Finance*, pp. 78-79.

On the whole, therefore, it seems most reasonable to conclude that if a debt is repaid it will have a conservative effect upon investment.

As to effects on foreign investments, most of those appearing before the Colwyn Committee were of the opinion that high taxes decrease the investment of money in England. Sir Felix Schuster stated that " . . . a heavy income tax would deter investment by foreigners in England." [6] This he thought was particularly true where the investments had a fixed rate of interest.[7] Professor Pigou was also of the opinion that this tendency could be presumed.[8] A. M. Samuel said that foreign investments by British citizens have increased and that this is due to high domestic taxation.[9] But another witness, James Walker, a Scottish banker, believed that the actual effect of taxation for the payment of the debt was not very great because of the presence of so many other factors. Lowes Dickinson also concurred in this view. It seems reasonable to conclude that although a tendency in the direction of driving capital out of the country would be present, it would probably be made unimportant in a country such as England by a multitude of other influences. Another qualifying circumstance in the case of Great Britain is the fact that British residents are taxed on their income whether derived from foreign or domestic investments. The result of this, according to the final report of the Colwyn Committee, is to preclude the possibility of investment in foreign countries to escape the tax, except through emigration.[10]

[6] *Colwyn Report, Minutes of Evidence*, p. 10.

[7] *Ibid.*, p. 13.

[8] *Ibid.*, p. 41.

[9] *Ibid.*, p. 75.

[10] *Colwyn Report*, p. 407.

II. ECONOMIC DISLOCATION AS A RESULT OF THE SIZE OF THE DEBT SERVICE

Besides the effects of the debt service upon the form of investment, the service causes difficulty because of the mere transfer of funds it involves. Because of the unevenness of debt holdings and the burden of taxes to pay the debt, there results inevitably a certain amount of economic dislocation. This dislocation would increase with an increase in the proportion of national income taken in taxes for this purpose. Too frequent and too large demands might require an undue amount of readjustment. This idea, expressed by several British writers, is closely akin to some such conception as taxable capacity, but it involves something quite different, since it relates to funds not spent by the state. The " capacity " concept frequently refers to the relation of taxation to the standard of living and the degree to which the standard of living can withstand the burden of taxation. In regard to the payment of the debt service the standard of living is presumably not directly affected. The collection of taxes, however, involves the conversion of assets into a liquid state. Strain of a different sort is involved in the maintenance of liquidity necessitated by high taxes. Thus although Dalton does not believe that the idea of taxable capacity is significant he nevertheless was forced to admit that his testimony before the Colwyn Committee had implied a limit beyond which taxes could not be raised in any one year. He did not specify how this limit could be determined nor did he give any indication of why it was ever reached in the case of taxation for the payment of an internal debt.[11] McKenna indicated in his testimony that he had much the same idea. He said that the height to which taxes could be raised was limited by custom. The sign of the limit having been passed

[11] *Colwyn Report, Minutes of Evidence*, p. 39.

was the tendency of people to borrow to pay taxes (1926). Although custom may be involved, the liquidity required for taxation and the increased difficulty of maintaining it is probably more important.

Closely associated with this point is the belief that debt payment should vary with the degree of prosperity of a country. This idea is expressed by Pigou and Bowley and will be discussed more fully at a later point. It is sufficient to point out here that the idea is also related to a conception of taxable capacity. Where the taxation is for the debt service the question of maintaining liquidity is involved. In a period of depression the dislocation involved in the maintenance of liquidity sufficient to meet the current debt charges would be greater than in times of prosperity because the liquid or tax portion would be greater in proportion to the total assets.

III. THE DEPRESSIVE PSYCHOLOGICAL EFFECT OF THE DEBT SERVICE

In addition to the effects upon investment and the dislocation caused by the transfer of funds, it has been claimed that the raising of taxes to pay the debt has a depressive effect upon business from a psychological standpoint. It is also believed that to the extent that prices are depressed by the process of payment the result will be depressive. Thus the theory that taxes for the payment of debt are depressive is based upon two claims. The first is that the mere height of the taxes will have this consequence; the second is that taxes cause falling prices which in their turn are depressive. The first belief is closely associated with the points previously discussed in this chapter. For instance, R. H. Brand said in his testimony before the Colwyn Committee that " . . . the most serious result of heavy taxation is that it tends to discourage initiative and enterprise." His explanation for the more conservative trend of business was the higher level of taxes.[12] Another witness said that the great evil arising out of the national debt is that it doubles the amount of taxes that must be raised annually and the very height of these has a depressive psychological effect.[13] We noted above Reginald McKenna's notion that taxes greater than is customary constitute a burden which is implicitly psychological. Stamp refers to the psychological depression induced by falling prices. In making this point, however, he was thinking particularly of the severe deflation that might follow from the capital levy.[14] The belief that falling prices cause business depression is sufficiently well known to require no further comment. Although it has been criticized, there is a possibility that falling prices may have an adverse effect and to the extent that debt payment does cause falling prices it may likewise tend to depress business.

Another interesting psychological approach to this problem of the effects of debt retirement upon production is given by Dalton. In his treatment of the effects of taxation upon production he stresses the influence of the elasticity of the desire for income. Where this desire is relatively inelastic an increase in taxes would have little effect upon production; if there is elasticity, the opposite would be true. The use of the concept depends, therefore, on our knowledge of the real nature of the desire for income. The use of the concept is also limited by its indefiniteness. Some writers have stated that the desire for income in general is unlimited and it may be assumed that in Dalton's terminology this would be expressed by saying that the desire for income is absolutely inelastic.[15] In attempting to get some information about the

[12] *Colwyn Report, Minutes of Evidence*, p. 105.

[13] *Ibid.*, p. 331. Evidence of P. D. Leake.

[14] *Contemporary Review*, January, 1924, p. 26.

[15] R. T. Ely, *Outlines of Economics*, 5th ed., p. 160.

desire for income one finds, as Dalton points out, that "the psychology of the business world remains something of a mystery though it occupies a central position in some economists' theories of the causes of trade cycles."[16] More light is needed on this subject but it is difficult to see how it can be readily obtained. There is a wide diversity of opinion. For instance, Lord Leverhulme in England takes the extreme position that every raising of the rate at which the income tax is levied has been followed by increased efforts, successfully made, to increase the income out of which to pay the increased tax.[17] This assumes what Dalton would call an absolute inelasticity in the desire for income. In the evidence given before the Colwyn Committee, F. W. Hirst expressed much the same opinion. He qualified his statement, however, by introducing the influence of the height of taxation. Lord Bradbury also believed that enterprise would not be deterred. He said in part, ". . . people are actuated by an idea of conventional rate of profits—what they think is the proper rate of profit." If this conventional rate is not obtained the result will be additional effort to obtain it. In the end the opinion of the Colwyn Committee was that

> the trader of reasonably good ability and enterprise will, we think, in the normal case be impelled by an Income Tax at a high or fairly high rate to increase his efforts: we have stressed his need of all the savings he can make and we think that the tax will as a rule exert quite a powerful driving force.[18]

Somewhat in contradiction to this point they state that high taxes will nevertheless not have the tonic effects of good business prospects. Excessive taxation, it was thought,

[16] Dalton, *Public Finance*, p. 108.

[17] *Ibid.*, p. 107.

[18] *Colwyn Report*, p. 159, par. 424.

would have just the opposite effect and heavy taxation throughout Europe was thought to be a cause of industrial depression. However, since there are no reliable facts or a sufficient sample of opinions one cannot do much more than conclude that there is some elasticity to the desire for income and that high taxes may have a slightly depressive effect. The use of the concept is made especially difficult because of the fact that taxes may be productively employed or may involve, as in debt payment, merely a transfer of income.

IV. THE EFFECTS OF CHANGES IN THE DISTRIBUTION OF WEALTH UPON PRODUCTION

Besides effects upon investment, industrial adjustment and the incentive to produce, the payment of the debt service may cause general changes in the distribution of wealth which may affect production. For instance, J. A. Hobson is of the opinion that if the payment of the debt reduces the inequality of wealth the buying power of the great mass of poor consumers will be increased. This he believes would aid industry by promoting a more satisfactory adjustment of demand to supply. If Hobson had carried his reasoning further in this direction his theory of unemployment would have led him to believe that the repayment of the debt was one way of reducing unemployment. Professor Seligman has also pointed out the fact that taxation has an important effect upon demand for commodities. He says that a heavy tax on income may affect not only the capacity to save and to produce but the ability to spend; and in the latter case it may substantially reduce the consuming powers of the community or the demand for commodities.[19] It should be apparent, however, that very little that is certain can be said along these lines.

[19] Seligman, *Studies in Public Finance*, pp. 85-90.

V. THE EFFECTS OF PARTICULAR TAXES UPON PRODUCTION

Much attention has been given in the literature of public finance to the effects of particular taxes. A great deal of this knowledge applies to taxation for the debt service If the capital levy is adopted for the removal of a large part of the debt it will greatly accentuate these effects. As it is, taxes are higher in many countries than they might be, as a result of the debt service, intensifying to a slight extent the effects of various kinds of taxes. Since the nature of these has been thoroughly considered elsewhere there is no point in repeating the theories here.[20] However, a few comments on the effects of taxes in England are worthy of notice.

(a) *Indirect Taxes*

In regard to indirect taxes the following remarks were made before the Colwyn Committee. Stamp taxes, according to Sir Felix Schuster, have a slight effect in preventing the formation of new companies. Cannan, for instance, in his criticism of the use of the English duty on the conveyance of land said that " . . . everything which makes it more expensive to transfer property must tend to keep it in the hands of people who really ought to get rid of it." [21] The Law Society and the National Gas Council both pointed out in their testimony that new or reconstituted companies were discriminated against. Sir Felix Schuster also pointed out in regard to the duty on the transfer of stocks and shares that it obstructed investment in the class of securities subject to the tax.[22] It was believed by other witnesses that this form of duty was unfair. In addition both the Association of British Chambers of Commerce and the Law Society held

[20] *Ibid.*, pp. 85-90; see also Seligman, *Incidence of Taxation*; Brown, *Economics of Taxation.*

[21] *Colwyn Report*, p. 201.

[22] *Colwyn Report, Minutes of Evidence*, pars. 13 and 68.

that the duty on companies' share capital was too high and reduced the number of company registrations.[23] Numerous witnesses, including Sir Felix Schuster, Mr. A. M. Samuel and Mr. Beaumont Pease were of the opinion that if the duty on checks were reduced the amount of payments through checks would greatly increase. The final conclusion of the Committee was, however, that these duties were chiefly a source of irritation. There was little interest in either the business effects or the revenue obtained.

The testimony of the witnesses, however, was that taxation of this sort has been shifted by affecting the supply of the objects offered for sale. It is usually supposed that these taxes are shifted, and it is important to have this evidence in favor of a popular belief. However, the degree of shifting is of most significance and this depends on the height of the tax, the character of the business and the elasticity of the demand.[24] It is evident that the testimony of the Colwyn Committee throws a little more light upon the operation of these factors.

The Colwyn Committee concluded that excise taxes are likewise shifted, that the amount passed on to the consumer is roughly equal to the amount of the duty, and that to the extent that they fall upon wages, wages will tend to rise in an equal amount. It was also their opinion that, "The tendency of indirect taxation is, in general, to cause not only dislocation when first imposed or varied, but a continuing diversion of trade from the course it would otherwise pursue. . . ." The regressive character of these duties is clearly pointed out in the report and it was finally concluded that through both the unproductive expenditure of the proceeds of these taxes and the dislocation of industry resulting from their collection, the rise in the standard of living, particularly

[23] *Ibid.*, pars. 69-70.

[24] Seligman, *Incidence of Taxation*, 4th ed., p. 379.

of the poorer classes, had been slightly retarded. The duty on whiskey, it was thought, diverted consumption to tea, and the duties on both tea and whiskey apparently left money available for other commodities. It was also believed that in so far as the excise duties involved a transfer of income from the less wealthy to the more wealthy saving was promoted.[25]

(b) *Direct Taxes*

In regard to direct taxes, the chief concern is with those on income and inheritance. Since the effects upon saving of the income and other direct taxes are in most respects rather general they will be considered later in this chapter, where these more general effects are discussed. Some specific considerations have been brought out by various writers, however; Dr. Dalton, for instance, is of the opinion that the income tax especially reduces saving because it falls upon the marginal saver.[26] In this respect it is unlike taxes upon windfalls and on monopolies, which he believes do not affect the marginal saver. Furthermore, he believes that a tax upon commodities will not usually reduce the desire to work and save as much as a tax on income, although it will have some effect because of the fact that a given amount of income has yielded little reward.[27] The effect of the income tax is most severe because it is levied directly upon the margin above consumption. It is thus apparent that the income tax in Dalton's estimation is harder on savings because it affects the rewards of saving more directly.

Professor Pigou considers the income tax especially depressive. To him, " . . . the income tax is really a differential against saving." [28] This is due to the fact that spent

[25] *Colwyn Report*, pp. 211-232.

[26] Dalton, *op. cit.*, p. 42.

[27] *Ibid.*, pp. 88-90.

[28] *Colwyn Report, Minutes of Evidence*, p. 50.

income is only once taxed whereas the saved income is taxed a second time. He believes that his point is limited in its importance by the facts that (1) the savings might yield no income to be taxed a second time, and (2) the tax on the income of savings might not be as heavy as the tax upon savings themselves.[29] A number of other factors, such as the elasticity of the desire for income, are probably of more importance and will be discussed later.

Besides affecting the desire to save, the income tax may affect the volume of production from which savings are to be made. The income tax, along with other direct taxes, may occasion less friction as a result of its collection and thus have a less harmful effect upon production than indirect taxes. This fact might to some extent counteract the supposed harmful effects upon saving mentioned above, as was recognized by D. H. Macgregor, who testified that ". . . when both forms of taxation are thought desirable, the direct tax causes less loss of real income through the arrangement of expenditure, but a point is reached where the obtrusiveness has a greater effect on saving than an extra cost imposed on commodities, especially since it is mainly paid by the classes of people who save." [30]

In the final conclusions of the Colwyn Committee the following assertions were made: (1) that if the income tax through its supposed depressive effect upon savings reduced production, prices would rise; (2) that in so far as the income tax has had any effect in reducing consumption, at least luxurious consumption has not been affected; and (3) that the income tax has apparently not affected savings in the form of corporate reserves. They believed that it had little influence upon enterprise. It may, however, have resulted in a slight transfer of business to beginners in the professions

[29] Pigou, *Public Finance*, pp. 136-138.

[30] *Colwyn Report, Minutes of Evidence*, p. 425, par. 32.

and in ordinary enterprise a tendency toward conservative as against speculative enterprise. On the whole, however, they concluded that " . . . wider causes than taxation . . . and particularly the dislocation of old export markets must be held mainly responsible for the lack of buoyancy. Relatively, income taxation has not been a factor of high importance." [31]

Certain special effects have been attributed to the inheritance tax. On this subject there is much diversity of opinion in the Colwyn Report. Sir Felix Schuster, for instance, described the tax as a " very injurious form of the Capital Levy." [32] Lord Hunsdon said that it seemed to him to have " almost every defect that a tax can possess." Many economists, however, rendered their allegiance to the tax. On the whole it may be concluded that there is little difference between the use of this tax for debt payment and its other uses and that it serves as a good supplement to the income tax in so far as its equity is concerned.[33]

The Colwyn Committee in its final report stated that since saving is greater on the part of the wealthy, the inheritance tax, in equalizing the distribution of wealth, has to that extent a bad effect upon saving, but that the tax could not have any effect upon saving prior to its payment.[34] These effects of the tax were attributed to changed ownership and management of capital and to the retardation of the growth of new capital.[35] The effects of the tax were also classified as effects

[31] *Ibid.*, p. 169.

[32] *Ibid.*, par. 12.

[33] Some interesting difficulties were indicated by the witnesses before the Colwyn Committee. Among these were difficulties arising (1) from fluctuations in the value of securities, (2) from the varying frequency of deaths, and (3) from an indefinite variation in the history of estates. (See *Colwyn Report*, pp. 179-82.) The first of these should be of interest in the light of the recent history of American securities.

[34] *Colwyn Report*, p. 190, par. 519.

[35] *Colwyn Report*, p. 189.

upon physical production and psychological effects. In the case of the first of these the Colwyn Committee referred to the damaging effects upon enterprise of the inheritance tax because of the uneconomic changes it causes in the control of capital. Since the transfer involved in the case of the inheritance tax is greater than that in the case of the income tax the deleterious physical effects were thought to be greater.

As to the psychological effects of the tax, they are at least not more injurious to saving than those of the income tax. Pigou, for instance, thought that the effects were less injurious " in that the people are probably not discouraged from saving by thinking of death duties as they are from thinking of income tax on unearned income." He also believes that people tend to compensate for the inheritance tax by increased saving.[36] His final conclusion is that inheritance taxes have little effect either way, the deleterious effect of the lump sum feature being compensated for by the above considerations, and that taxes on inheritance are not inferior to taxes on income in these respects. He states that, " It will not make much difference to saving or to anything else whether one or the other is chosen." [37]

Dalton goes further, however, maintaining that inheritance taxes are less discouraging to work and saving than income taxes and stressing one of the above factors. In explanation he says that " . . . the prospects of heavy death duties will stimulate those who are waiting for a windfall of inherited wealth to work harder and to save more than they otherwise would do." Furthermore, Macgregor pointed out in discussing the motives that lead to saving that death duties " . . . missed these motives," and therefore did not reduce saving.[38]

[36] Pigou, *Public Finance*, p. 165.

[37] *Ibid.*, p. 165.

[38] *Colwyn Report, Minutes of Evidence*, par. 24.

On the other hand Sir Felix Schuster thought that death duties were a more important deterrent to saving than the income tax. He thought that a distinct loss of capital resulted from death duties and that a reduction of income follows. When asked whether he preferred an income tax to a death duty he said that he decidedly did. "Death Duties indefinitely hanging over a man who does not know how he will have to provide for them and what his children will do drive people out of business and drive them out of the country and drive them to adopt measures which none of us approve of." [39] These opinions assume that capital disappears when it is broken up into a number of holdings and this does not of course necessarily follow. There is, however, some basis for the belief that book value is not necessarily the value realized upon liquidation. Although this may be true, there is no reason to suppose that in the payment of inheritance taxes, particularly for the purpose of debt retirement, there results any serious amount of business liquidation. In so far as it may be caused by these taxes, it is not unreasonable to suppose that the values may be largely reestablished by the subsequent business reorganization of the capital assets. It has been realized by economists for some time that inheritance taxes and capital levies do not necessarily destroy any value. Yet among the most current lay objections remains the one that they are destructive taxes upon capital.

The final conclusions to be drawn are that the physical effects of the inheritance tax upon saving and enterprise may be somewhat greater than similar effects of the income tax. The psychological effects may be negligible. Taking the physical and the psychological effects together the Colwyn Committee concluded that the Estate Duty was " . . . distinctly more damaging to saving than the Income Tax,"

[39] *Ibid.*, p. 21.

although they did not wish to suggest that the difference was great.[40]

In attempting to answer these questions some very interesting statistics were provided for the Committee by the Board of Inland Revenue. 373 estates were examined and it was found that in only 0.8 per cent did the Estate Duty entrench upon the trade assets of the tax payers. It was agreed that in spite of the high rates existing at that time the estate duty did not appear to be a factor tending toward the disintegration of business.[41]

VI. GENERAL EFFECTS OF TAXATION FOR THE DEBT SERVICE UPON PRODUCTION AND SAVING

In the preceding discussion the specific effects of taxation for the debt service have been treated. Underlying these considerations are certain general ones concerning the effects of taxation upon production. This has been and still is a very live subject. The assumptions supporting any particular belief in regard to these effects may be among the most fundamental ideas affecting one's theories of taxation. Hence it is very important to analyze these assumptions, not alone for the solution of problems arising from debt retirement but for broader problems as well. It is upon the exact way that taxation affects saving that much of the retirement theory is based. As Foxwell has pointed out, in war finance "The real problem concerns the economic conditions which lie behind the Chancellor's figures of account; viz: the balance of national production and consumption." [42]

At the outset one finds a wide diversity of opinion as to the effects of taxation on savings. Some writers still believe that any form of taxation diminishes saving; others that it

[40] *Colwyn Report*, p. 198.

[41] *Ibid.*, p. 185.

[42] Foxwell, *Papers on Current Finance*, p. 27.

decreases saving only after it reaches a certain level; still others attempt to determine this level. Most writers agree that taxation at a certain level reduces saving. Those who believe that taxation reduces saving usually hold that it does so by reducing the interest paid, i. e. the reward for saving. For example, H. G. Brown thinks that taxes on income reduce the rate of interest and thus the amount of saving. Although he admits that lower interest may induce some people to save more, he believes that these people are in the minority and thus a rise in taxes will for all practical purposes reduce saving.[43] Dalton, it was seen, had much the same opinion as a result of his concept of the elasticity of the demand for income. As will be shown below, Marshall took a similar position.

Such men as Pigou, Bonar Law, and Hartley Withers have different views. To them a fall in the rate of interest operates to decrease saving only after a certain point is reached. Thus Pigou says that " . . . even though the income raised by taxation were all simply transferred within the country, being neither handed over to foreigners nor yet spent by the government in the production of goods and services, nevertheless, high rates of taxation would discourage work and saving and so check national productivity." [44] He believes that through high taxation future generations may be made to suffer, owing to the check placed upon the accumulation of capital, even though this taxation is for debt purposes.[45] On the other hand, one finds that Pigou does believe a moderate amount of taxation increases savings.[46] This opinion was persisted in, in spite of his belief that the income tax acted as a differential against saving. Sir Josiah

[43] Brown, *Economics of Taxation*, pp. 184-186.

[44] Pigou, *Political Economy of War*, p. 194.

[45] *Ibid.*, p. 79.

[46] *Colwyn Report, Minutes of Evidence*, p. 50.

Stamp takes the same position even more definitely. For example, he says, " It may well be that as the consumption level is reduced by taxation, some temperaments will be tenacious of the old standard of comfort, and work harder than before to maintain the consumption level; in this case taxation will make total production greater than before. Similarly the desire to save may be quite discouraged by the low net yield after bearing a tax and no attempt to save is then made. Then capital is less and production does not grow as it might—he may even dissipate the savings already made." [47] Withers and Bonar Law have expressed similar opinions, but less definitely. The former says that " a levy on capital which would certainly check the incentive to save . . . would dry up the springs of that supply of capital which is absolutely essential to the increase of the nation's productive power." [48] This belief was held in spite of the conflicting one that taxation is superior to borrowing in that it promotes saving. The extreme position of debt payment as an influence toward capital increase is held by Cannan. He says that " . . . against taxation for replacement of National Debt the objection that high taxation reduces saving has no validity at all. . . ." [49]

The diversity of opinion expressed above requires a return to more fundamental matters in order to arrive at definite conclusions. These fundamentals are the factors that influence the desire and the ability to work and save. Only through analysis of these is one able to arrive at a theory of the effects on production and from thence at a theory of debt burden. To accomplish this let us examine the origin and nature of the theories about these matters.

The general effects of taxation were considered by very

[47] Stamp, *Wealth and Taxable Capacity*, pp. 115-116.

[48] Withers, *War-time Financial Problems*, p. 75.

[49] *Colwyn Report, Minutes of Evidence*, p. 60.

early writers. Originally it was believed that all taxation is a necessary evil, that it does not increase production and that it has no compensating advantages. The rise of democracy, however, led to a better opinion of taxation and there was a tendency even to appraise it too highly. Bastiat, writing his *Sophismes économiques,* found it necessary to attack a number of rather optimistic beliefs about taxes.[50] Hume was one of the first to call attention to the belief that taxes tend to increase production, or as he expressed it, " . . . every new tax creates a new ability in the subject to bear it and . . . each increase of public burdens . . . increases proportionately the industry of the people." Hume subscribed to this belief only when "it [taxation] is kept within bounds." [51] It was based on the fact that physical obstacles sometimes increase effort. The same result was supposed to follow in the wake of artificial obstacles. McCulloch revealed that he had much the same belief when he ascribed the increase in the wealth of the country after the Napoleonic wars to the increased production induced by high taxes. He says that " . . . it is undoubtedly true that the desire to maintain and improve their condition stimulates most men to endeavor to discharge the burden of additional taxes by increased industry and economy without allowing them to encroach on their means of subsistence or their fortunes. The operation of this principle has been strikingly evinced in the financial history of this country since the commencement of the American war." At a later point he says in criticism of Smith, who believed that the burdens of war restricted the growth of capital, " Smith forgot that an increase of taxation has the same influence over nations that an increase of

[50] Bastiat, *Oeuvres,* vol. v, pp. 344-345. Cited in Bastable, *op. cit.,* p. 269.

[51] Hume, " Essays on Taxes," in *Essays Moral, Political and Literary,* vol. iii, p. 356.

their families or their unavoidable expenses has over individuals." However, "Had taxation been very oppressive, it would not have had this effect." According to McCulloch, "Man is not influenced solely by hope, he is also influenced powerfully by fear," but "To render an increase of taxation productive of greater exertion, economy, and invention, it should be slow and gradual, and it should never be so great as to make people believe that it cannot be countervailed by a moderate increase in industry and economy." [52]

Ricardo in his chapter on taxes accepted a position somewhat similar to that of McCulloch. He did not think that taxes necessarily impair the supply of capital. He writes, ". . . notwithstanding the immense expenditure of the English Government during the last twenty years, there can be little doubt but that the increased production of the people has more than compensated for it." He was of the opinion, however, that "there are no taxes which have not a tendency to lessen the power to accumulate." By this he meant that if the taxes had not been levied the power to accumulate would have been greater, not that the total accumulation was smaller. He admits that taxes would stimulate effort and saving. Furthermore it was his belief that "It should be the policy of the governments to encourage a disposition to do this in the people, and never to lay such taxes as will inevitably fall on capital; since, by so doing, they impair the funds for the maintenance of labour, and thereby diminish the future production of the country." [53] Not only does he imply that accumulation may be stimulated by taxation but that there is some tax level at which accumulation is greatest and after which it declines. But, what is most important of all, he states that when this level has been reached taxes will be falling upon capital. This point is very similar to

[52] McCulloch, *Taxation and Funding*, pp. 7-10.

[53] Ricardo, *Principles of Economics*, p. 96.

some opinions expressed by A. M. Samuel and R. G. Glenday of England and will be taken up more thoroughly later.

J. S. Mill seems to have adopted a similar view. Like McCulloch he believed that obstacles set up by taxation might increase invention and consequently production. He even goes so far as to say that taxation may in some cases stimulate profits more than the amount of the tax.[54] Mill, however, cites no example as McCulloch had done.[55]

Bastable attacks the views of both Mill and McCulloch on two grounds. First, he states that their beliefs would imply that the wealth of a nation could be indefinitely increased by taxation. Secondly, he says that natural obstacles do not always increase the output. Economic development is not greatest among those who have the greatest obstacles; a case in point is that of the Eskimos. He believes that the analogy between natural and artificial obstacles is unsound and concludes that

> . . . any compensating effect of taxation in increasing production is extremely doubtful, and is at best so small, and occurs in so few cases as not to form an element worthy of entering into the rational calculations of the financier. The raising of compulsory revenue means so much less to the tax-payer and to the community, for which the only return obtained is the benefit resulting from the efficient execution of state functions. Any doctrine that removes attention from this cardinal fact is erroneous in principle and may lead to serious practical evils.[56]

Thus it can be seen that among the more prominent early writers on public finance, Ricardo, Mill and McCulloch be-

[54] Mill, *Principles of Economics*, bk. v, chap. vii, par. 3.

[55] The case of the Scottish distillers, who, because of a tax upon the contents of vessels, had improved them so as to run the contents off in three minutes, whereas formerly it had taken a week. See McCulloch, *op. cit.*, pp. 151-152.

[56] Bastable, *Public Finance*, 1st ed., p. 265.

lieved that there might be some indirect benefits from taxation, whereas Bastiat and, in more recent times, Bastable thought an undue emphasis had been laid upon these benefits. The chief weakness of the whole analysis was that it had too little basis in fact. McCulloch alone cited any concrete evidence to substantiate his beliefs. The others may have had certain examples in mind but they failed to cite them. Even from the standpoint of *a priori* reasoning their opinions, although suggestive, had not a sufficiently broad foundation.

The writings of older economists bring out the significant fact that they had made about as much progress with the effects of taxation upon the ability and the desire to work and save as more recent writers. The opinions of Ricardo and Stamp are strikingly similar. It is also apparent that the chief attention was from the first directed toward the effects of taxation upon the accumulation of capital. Not many of these men, however, have been clear or consistent in their use of the term capital. This is of course not strange, but it becomes at once the one most important obstacle in thinking about this whole subject. It is therefore necessary to take some position as to the meaning of this term before entering into the subsequent discussion that so much involves its use.

The word capital has been used with many different meanings, which fall roughly into two types. One is monetary; capital is regarded as an investment fund from which income is derived. The other is physical. Capital is considered to be a stock of goods directed toward the production of other goods. These two meanings have been confused from the times of Cotgrave, in the seventeenth century, to the present. The confusion arises from the concept of value, and as long as this concept is retained in economics the difficulty is inevitable. No one has ever satisfactorily bridged the gap between physical goods and their monetary claims, and the paradoxical aspects of value have never been completely explained. In view of these facts anyone who defines capital according to either one of the above concepts is open to criticism. This is, however, what will be done here. In the subsequent discussion capital is used in the sense of physical goods and concrete abilities applied to the production of additional goods. Saving is the accumulation of capital so defined. Since the standard of living is of the utmost importance and it in turn is to a large extent a supply of concrete things, capital should here be defined in terms of concrete things.

VII. THE SOURCES OF THE TAXES FOR DEBT SERVICE AND THE ABILITY TO SAVE

Turning now to the question mentioned above, viz., the effects of taxation on the ability to save, it can be said that these effects depend upon the incidence of the taxes and the sources of the savings. Let us consider the latter. If a government raises additional taxes the funds may be obtained through (1) reduced consumption, (2) a reduction in saving, or (3) an increase in production. At the outset it can be seen that taxation, although it may reduce the ability to save, need not do so in the sense of reducing the absolute amount of the goods that may be devoted to production and thus saved. In the narrow meaning of Ricardo, any tax must necessarily reduce the ability to save. This fact is not, however, especially significant. The effect of taxation on the supply of goods available for saving is much more so. Let us consider this.

In case taxes come from the first source or from goods that would otherwise be devoted to consumption it is obvious that the ability to save would not be affected. Derivation of taxes from this source depends upon the types of taxes used and upon the extent to which taxation affects the desire to save of those upon whom it falls. The Colwyn Committee, after studying this problem for some time, concluded in reference to taxation for the English debt service that

It is probable that a high proportion of the tax is paid out of money that would otherwise be spent on consumption. To this extent it does not reduce savings. Moreover, so far as the tax is applied in payment of debt interest to persons in a better position to save it may be presumed that the effect upon the aggregate actual savings is actually beneficial.[57]

The second source of taxation mentioned above was savings. Some economists believe that taxes come to a large extent from savings. This is the result especially attributed to taxes levied upon income directly, as was seen in the preceding discussion. The reasons for the belief that taxes are derived to a large extent from this source seem to be based in some instances on the concept of a fund or margin set aside for saving. The existence of such a fund, which would resemble the historic wages fund, is suggested by Dalton. He says,

The ability to save is reduced by all taxes on those who have any margin out of which saving is possible. The only taxes therefore which do not to some extent reduce the ability to save are those which fall exclusively on people who are so poor that they have no such margin. It is evident that taxes on the rich, though defensible on other grounds, reduce ability to save to a specially marked degree.[58]

The ability to save, in the way it is here used by Dalton and which is roughly similar to the use given it by Ricardo, either implies such a fund or it is an ambiguous and insignificant notion. In what does the ability consist? If taxes fall on those persons who have means above the level of sub-

[57] *Colwyn Report*, p. 136.

[58] Dalton, *op. cit.*, p. 83.

sistence they may be derived from consumption. In such a case the "ability to save" has not been reduced, assuming that if taxes had not been levied the amount of consumption would have been larger by the amount of the taxes anyway. If all this conception means is merely that since taxes fall upon persons with more income than mere subsistence they reduce the ability to save it is true, but there is no significance in the point. The ability to save is essentially a matter of how taxation affects attitudes toward saving and the volume of saving and production. Assuming that those who vigorously state that the margin of saving is reduced by taxes believe that they have really offered some reasonable objection to taxation, they must have some conception of a savings fund; viz., that saving and consumption are in a fixed relation and proportion to each other.

This idea of a fund might postulate that savings cannot increase without a decrease in consumption and vice versa. It would assume that the volume of production would not usually be affected by taxation. Nor would the proportion of income the tax payer would save be affected. In fact, Sir Felix Schuster openly carries the argument to this extreme point of assuming that consumption goods and goods to be saved comprise a common fund in which one profits at the other's expense, and that taxes always cause savings to suffer.

Although it may be true that taxes are derived from savings to some extent, this fact does not necessarily arise from the existence of a margin for saving or a savings fund. It is unreasonable to say that taxes reduce the ability to save except in so far as they affect the desire to save, the habits of saving, and the quantity of production. Since the effect of taxation upon the ability to save reduces itself mainly to the effects of taxation upon the quantity of production and the decision or desire to save, let us consider these in their turn.

The first of these two points has been dealt with to a considerable extent elsewhere, but its relation to the effects of taxation upon saving has not been sufficiently stressed. It was demonstrated that the payment of taxes affects production largely through the changes in investment that result. Keynes and Dalton see in the payment of the debt service the direction of funds into conservative channels. Bailie James Walker and Joseph F. Duncan, representing Scottish banks, even went so far as to testify before the Colwyn Committee that the only effects of debt payment consist in the redirection of investment funds. It is true therefore that in so far as this redirection reduces production, the ability to save is thereby diminished. Whether or not production is actually reduced or its trend lowered by the redirection of investment cannot be determined in any general way. Although the effects may be clear in any specific situation no generalization can be made.[59]

Besides the redirection of investment funds the tax collection processes resulting from the payment of the debt may have other effects upon production. These may be psychological. For instance, the payment of a debt usually improves the credit of the government. This improvement in credit is likely to spread beyond its original source, giving rise to increased general business confidence. It is possible that anything that increases the credit of the government is likely to be a source of optimism that will spread to some extent. If the payment of the debt is too rapid, however, taxes may have to be so high that the good effects of the debt payment will be completely offset by the bad effects of the

[59] Some witnesses before the Colwyn Committee believed that no capital is destroyed by the processes of repayment and the effects depend entirely upon the mode of expending the taxes levied. Bowley in particular was of this opinion. See *Colwyn Report, Minutes of Evidence*, pp. 317 and 272.

taxes.[60] It is thus apparent that the debt payment process affects production through the changes it causes in investment and in business confidence. In these two ways it affects the ability to save.

VIII. THE EFFECTS OF THE DEBT SERVICE UPON THE DESIRE TO SAVE

(a) *The Theory that a Certain Level of Taxes Reduces the Desire to Save*

Turning now to the effects upon the desire to save, two facts stand out. The solution of the problem involves the theory of interest and this in its turn is based upon many of the assumptions supporting the theory of value. The writer believes that no theory of value, as well as no theory of interest, is entirely satisfactory. Especially is this true of neo-classical value theory, which although it is subject to much criticism when treated as an entity, still passes muster to a considerable degree as the basic theory underlying the incidence and effects of taxation. To go further than the writers cited above into the problems of the effects of taxation on saving, a reexamination of interest and value theory relating to this problem must be undertaken. In the preceding discussion the problem has been reduced mainly to the effects of taxation upon the desire to save. Some writers think the desire to save is greatly reduced; others that it is not much diminished, depending upon the height of taxation. The solution of the problem requires a more detailed analysis of how the various writers arrived, through value and interest theory, at their respective beliefs.

Among those who believe that taxation reduces the desire to save, probably Dalton gives the most definite exposition. He asserts definitely that taxes on income reduce the desire

[60] See testimony of Sir A. Lowes Dickinson. *Colwyn Report, Minutes of Evidence*, p. 246.

to save. The degree to which this will occur depends upon the elasticity of the demand for income. Although it may be that the demand of some persons is completely inelastic, as Lord Leverhulme believed, Dalton thinks that for most persons it is elastic.[61] In the testimony given before the Colwyn Committee, Hobson has taken a similar though less unqualified position. Taxation indirectly reduces saving because the interest rate is decreased. He says, " Let us take the case of interest. Supposing people are living upon interest derived from businesses which are engaged in free competition, and where the conditions are such that profits are kept down to a minimum. Any attempt to tax that income will be an attempt to reduce the income that I shall receive from my saving and will on the whole prevent me from saving as much. I admit of course that the whole question of the incentive of saving is an elaborate one and there are people that hold that the fall in the rate of interest will not cause any interference with the quantity of saving. But I do not hold that view." [62] Keynes in his testimony was of the same opinion, and said that since the income tax falls upon funds which would accumulate at compound interest and in which no question of personal expenditure could enter, " it is especially deterrent to saving." [63] Reginald McKenna, a former British chancellor of the exchequer, took a more cautious position. He said, " Taxation to meet the interest on National Debt may, like taxation for any other purpose, diminish the incentive to save and thus reduce the supply of capital. . . .[64] It is obvious that if taxation is carried to extremes there may be no saving at all." [65] It appears that

[61] Dalton, *op. cit.*, pp. 42, 83, 90.

[62] *Colwyn Report, Minutes of Evidence*, p. 124, par. 1569.

[63] *Ibid.*, p. 277.

[64] *Ibid.*, p. 132.

[65] *Ibid.*, p. 143.

at the time of the Colwyn Report the theory that taxes reduce savings was rather widespread in England, since the body of accountants mentioned above testified without qualification that taxation reduces the will to save. The British Trades Union Congress also took an extreme position on this point.[66]

In America a number of economists and business men have the same views. For example, Professor Seligman, although he has never completely covered the problem in his writings, indicates at various points that taxation upon income has some effect in reducing the incentive to save. Thus he says that Walker contended that a fatal weakness of the property tax is its adverse effects upon saving. "This criticism seems to be questionable for the same objection would attach to any tax based upon income just as far as income exceeds expenditures." [67]

E. B. Tredwen of the London Chamber of Commerce, Hugh Bell and P. D. Leake all declared that taxation might reduce the rewards of effort to such an extent as to prevent them from doing business,[68] and, as was shown above, H. G. Brown believed that taxation reduced the desire to save by decreasing the interest incentive.[69]

It appears that those who believe that taxation reduces the desire to save also believe that saving is motivated by pecuniary incentives and that interest is determined by the point where marginal incentive balances the marginal cost of waiting. They also believe that income taxes hit the margin. Brown, Dalton and Pigou give a marginal analysis. It is difficult to conceive of any other explanation, if it is thought that saving may not be deterred by taxation up to a certain

[66] *Ibid.*, p. 237.

[67] Seligman, *Essays on Taxation*, p. 59.

[68] *Colwyn Report, Minutes of Evidence*, pp. 337, 518, 604.

[69] Brown, *op. cit.*, p. 184.

point. Theories of this sort are based upon three assumptions, in the examination of which we will go some distance toward explaining the effects of taxation upon the desire to save and also the nature of interest itself. If taxation reduces the desire to save, questions of how much and in what ways are most important. The assumptions are (1) that the marginal saver determines the interest rate, (2) that taxes hit the marginal saver, and (3) that the law of supply operates in the manner postulated by classical writers.

(b) *The Assumption that the Marginal Saver is Affected by Taxation for the Debt Service*

The first two will be considered jointly. These assumptions are founded on a theory of interest involving the concept of marginal cost. In the effort to prove the theory that taxation decreases the desire to save the latter concept is usually employed. The determination of price by marginal cost is by no means granted in the general theory of prices. In the accounting of businesses, costs are much more definite than the psychological costs suggested by marginalism.

The influence of the marginal cost upon price arises frequently in attempts to solve taxation problems and particularly problems relating to the incidence of taxation. At the time of the Colwyn Report the problem of the effects of income taxes upon prices was rediscussed. It was clearly shown that this problem depends upon general theories of prices for its solution. Members of the committee took Marshall's concept of the representative firm for that of marginal cost. This was a fatal error, since Marshall's modal concept was essentially devised, in the writer's opinion, to avoid the difficulties of the marginal concept. Robertson clearly disclosed the differences between these two ideas. Since the representative firm represents a great number of producers the income tax might readily fall upon them, thus causing a rise in price. This rise would come about, as Hobson had stated in a memorandum to the Colwyn Committee, through the decrease of the supply factors in the equation of exchange.[70] Robertson believed that this would not be permanent inasmuch as business men would in the long run become accustomed to supplying goods at a lower profit and would therefore increase their output to the former amounts, thus decreasing prices to their previous level.[71] Seligman, Stamp, Coates and others base their opinions that the tax will not be shifted on the theory that it does not touch the " marginal " producer.[72] At a later date this theory was defended from the attacks of Robertson by T. R. Snavely, who maintained that the representative firm was not shown to exist by the war studies of Taussig, which indicated no tendency of costs to cluster about a mode, and that the marginal concept should be retained, but in the form enunciated by Bullock. The latter he quotes as saying that " it is not the average cost or the cost to the representative firm but the marginal cost of production that is decisive in fixing the normal value of all commodities." [73]

It thus appears that the solution of these problems, of which the effects of taxation upon savings is but one, involves a controversial theory of prices. It is unfortunate that the theoretical structure of taxation leans so heavily upon a foundation that some of the most advanced theorists consider weak. In regard to the problem at hand it is clear that since marginal cost may not determine prices in general it may not determine interest in particular and taxes levied indiscriminately upon income need not reduce savings simply because their indiscriminate levy reduces the income of the alleged marginal saver.

[70] *Colwyn Report, Minutes of Evidence*, pp. 126-127.

[71] *Economic Journal*, Dec., 1927, pp. 579-581.

[72] *Ibid.*, pp. 566-567.

[73] *Quarterly Journal of Economics*, Aug., 1927, pp. 641-668.

It must not be supposed, however, that marginal price has no contribution to make. The contribution of the marginal concept is the idea of sensitivity of output to price. This is plausible, because even such writers as Bullock would admit that the highest cost is not necessarily the marginal cost. Thus in most price situations some producers would be paying higher than marginal costs. Marginal costs are thus sensitive costs. Marginal savers would be sensitive savers, those who had the highest cost of those who were sensitive. The conception assumes a supply curve of saving with variations according to cost up to the highest sensitive cost, or marginal one.

If the marginal concept were valid in price theory, a further difficulty inheres in the location in the mental field of the marginal costs of waiting. This would be so difficult as to make it virtually impossible to tell whether a given tax had hit it or not. In the face of this obstacle much of the discussion based on the supposition that the margin is touched is of little value.

(c) *The Role of the Law of Supply*

The third assumption mentioned above was that the law of supply operates in the traditional manner. The analysis of this assumption is pertinent since, although a marginal theory of interest may not be acceptable, it can still be maintained that there is some distinct relationship between the quantity of funds saved and the interest paid. If the amount of saving does not depend upon the rate of interest or the reward, then it cannot be claimed that taxation has bad effects. The problem of the effect of taxation on the desire to save is essentially that of the validity of the law of supply.

The belief in the direct variation of supply and reward goes back to classical economics and suffers from its attachment to certain more fundamental beliefs which are open to question. One of these is that incentive or reward operates in determining the amount of saving offered in the market. Another is that, granted the primary influence of incentive, its influence is such as always to produce direct variation of supply and reward. Subsidiary to the first point is still another, viz., that saving is rationalistic behavior.

That rationalistic behavior based on incentive would subscribe to the law of supply is by no means obvious to men who have studied this problem in a broad way. Andrew Carnegie, for example, believed that inheritance taxation would increase saving, for " . . . to the class whose ambition is to leave great fortunes and be talked about after death, it will be even more attractive and indeed a somewhat nobler ambition to have enormous sums paid over to the state from their fortunes." [74] Andrew W. Mellon is, however, of just the opposite opinion.[75]

Gonner and Cassel, who, using a psychological analysis, have perhaps given this whole subject its most thorough examination, come to a relatively neutral position in regard to the operation of the law of supply. They start from a reexamination of the motives that promote saving.

Cassel in his analysis finds two major classes of motives, (1) those involved in saving for future needs, (2) those for mere accumulation.[76] Gonner recognized two similar classes but describes them as saving (1) not to be worse off, and (2) to be better off.[77] The first one of these he subdivides into

[74] Carnegie, *Problems of the Day*, p. 5; D. H. Macgregor has a similar opinion. He says, "The progression of Death Duties may intensify the motives to save in order to meet them"; see *Colwyn Report, Minutes of Evidence*, p. 424.

[75] Mellon, *Taxation: the People's Business*, p. 110.

[76] Cassel, *Nature and Necessity of Interest*, p. 145.

[77] Gonner, *Interest and Saving*, chap. i.

(a) saving to provide for contingent loss of income and (b) saving for maintenance of present income at some future date.

Both Cassel and Gonner maintain that the functioning of these motives varies with income and age. Cassel believes that the first motive is more characteristic of saving by the middle class. Thus he states that it is unreasonable to expect that the middle class will save for more than the maintenance of their existing income or the education of the young. Taxation upon them, however, will tend to increase their saving. In their case taxes cut into the standard of living that can be maintained in the future, and increased saving will occur to prevent this cutting from being excessive. On the other hand the large capitalist whose living standard is not likely to be tapped by taxes will make no efforts to reduce his consumption in compensation for the taxes. Thus Cassel believes that the effect of taxes upon saving varies according to the degree to which people save for set amounts, such as saving for retirement or accidental loss of income. With people who save for these purposes taxation may actually increase the amount of saving. For those who save due to the second motive, taxation reduces saving except in so far as a fixed future standard is visualized.

Gonner's conclusions are especially significant, since they are similar in many ways to Cassel's. Gonner also believes that saving as a result of the first motive is little affected by reduced interest. So long as a given standard of life is desired, lower interest may stimulate saving. Thus he says, "Minor differences have little or no effect, it is only when the difference is such as to involve a change from one grade of life to another that the nature of the provision required in the case of these emergencies undergoes an important change." [78] He believes that lower interest may actually

[78] *Ibid.*, p. 10.

increase saving where the motive is to be better off. "Here indeed the general principle would seem to be that a rise in income would be followed by a fall in desire and a fall in income by an augmentation in the extent to which saving is stimulated, since fresh increments of enjoyment diminish in their utility as the area of desire already satisfied enlarges."[79] He qualifies this, however, by saying that if the desire is to attain a higher rank in society or if the complete satisfaction anticipated, as in the case of saving for retirement, cannot be realized, the effects may be the opposite. Thus both Cassel and Gonner think saving is affected by reduced interest only by conscious appreciation of the way this reduction impedes the realization of certain fixed standards or income aims. They both clearly demonstrate that saving is governed by no one motive, varies with age, time and place and may be increased as well as decreased by smaller interest. Cassel says that the rate of interest "has had no very considerable effect on the actual accumulation of capital. In a broad sense it may be said that capital is just as willingly supplied at three per cent as at six."[80] He visualizes no considerable fall in the interest rate in the future and would not regard such a fall as a serious obstacle to the accumulation of capital if it did occur, so long as the minimum of two to three per cent was provided.

Gonner believes that the determination to save is growing on account of the greater uncertainty and decreased "sanguinity" about the future. In most cases a "make weight" of interest is necessary where saving takes place for greater luxury. Thus although in some cases there is a cost of waiting he concludes that, "Whether such differences are in particular instances sufficient to counteract the gradual discount of distance depends on the case in question and is a

[79] *Ibid.*, p. 11.

[80] Cassel, *Nature and Necessity of Interest*, p. 155.

matter of detail." [81] Also, "Interest . . . does not stand in uniform relation to saving as an act . . . It is neither an invariable nor a constant motive." [82] He believes that a great amount of interest may be unnecessary. One idea especially coloring his theory is that "future wants . . . are more fixed in given figures than that of the present." [83] This strengthens the tendency to save more as interest falls. No one rate of interest is necessary to elicit a given supply of saving and interest is considered as by no means the only incentive for saving. In determining the exact way a reduction of interest will affect saving the most important procedure is to determine what shares of distribution are affected by it. However, Gonner as well as Cassel is convinced that a minimum rate of interest is necessary.

These opinions, as was indicated above, are in sharp contrast to those of Alfred Marshall, who states that human nature being what it is "we are justified in speaking of the interest on capital as a reward for the sacrifice involved in the waiting for the enjoyment of material resources because few people would save without reward; just as we speak of wages as the reward for labour because few people would work hard without reward." [84] Notwithstanding the authority of Marshall, no end of writers who criticize the psychological approach to the interest problem could be quoted against him. Those men who, like Gonner and Cassel, have given interest special study and who treat it with minimum bias and maximum eclecticism take a neutral stand. The difficulties encountered by the "psychological school" in winning a place in economic theory have been so great as to discount theories based on such psychology.[85]

[81] Gonner, *op. cit.*, p. 48.

[82] *Ibid.*, p. 55. [83] *Ibid.*, p. 74.

[84] Marshall, *Principles of Economics*, p. 232.

[85] See Brown, G., "Capital Valuation and the 'Psychological' School,"

Some economists have expressed the conclusions of the preceding pages more precisely in terms of the elasticity of the demand for income. Dalton, Robertson and Robbins prefer this form of expression. It is more accurate since, as Robbins points out, the question is not one of the amount of utility of the income and effort but of an elastic ratio of income to effort. Thus Pigou says that " Since income is taken away from tax-payers the marginal utility of money to them is raised but the marginal utility of work to them is unchanged. Hence unless they are somewhat impeded they will increase the amount of work done." [86] Robbins rightly demonstrates through unit and integral demand curves that the truth of Pigou's carelessly phrased statement depends upon the presence of an elasticity of the demand for income which is less than one.

However, not only is it doubtful that saving incentives operate in such a way as to validate the law of supply, but these incentives may not be nearly so significant as certain other influences. D. H. Robertson believes that the variation of supply with income frequently does not take place through incentive at all, " but along the route of an alteration in the magnitude of the sources from which the factor in question is supplied." [87] Thus a rise in interest rates would increase saving not because of a greater reward for it but because of a greater amount of income with which to save. He says that " The real objection to heavy taxation is less that it diminishes the inducements to save than that it entrenches upon the sources of saving." Incentive is for

American Economic Review, Sept., 1929; Davenport, H. J., " Interest Theory and Theories," *American Economic Review*, 1927, p. 636; writings of D. H. Robertson, A. C. Pigou, F. H. Knight and others.

[86] Pigou, *Public Finance*, pp. 83-84, cited by Robbins in *Economica*, June, 1930.

[87] Robertson, " Economic Incentive," *Economica*, October, 1921.

Robertson a minor influence, the sources of saving being most important. The supply of labor, for example, increases not because of the increased incentive of higher wages but because of their effects upon death, marriage, and fertility rates. He is, however, inclined to believe in the operation of the law of supply, with qualifications.

(d) *Monetary and Institutional Factors Affecting the Desire to Save*

This raises the question of the rationality of saving, in the classical sense of motivation by pecuniary incentives. In the first place the volume of saving depends upon the shares of income possessed by the saver and this is in part affected by monetary changes. Compulsory saving through changes in the supply of money and credit that occur in the boom periods of business cycles is sometimes postulated. These effects are at best obscure but there can be little doubt of their great significance. One of the arguments most commonly used against inflation is its destructive effect upon saving habits. Thus the volume of saving may be determined by changes in distribution and some economists attribute great importance to such influences.[88]

Not only is the saver at the mercy of the monetary system and its effects upon distribution, but the operation of his incentives is further obscured by the system of corporate organization. W. I. King found that business enterprises were normally responsible for about forty per cent of the entire savings of the country. Apropos of the above point he estimated that their savings increased during prosperity and decreased during depression.[89] The increased dictation

[88] See Robertson, D. H., *Banking Policy and the Price Level* and Bickerdike, C. F., "Saving and the Monetary System," *Economic Journal*, Sept., 1925, p. 366.

[89] King, W. I., "The Net Volume of Saving in the United States," *Journal of the American Statistical Assn.*, December, 1922, p. 470.

of saving by business enterprises and corporations in England was noted by Sir Josiah Stamp. Speaking of the operation of individual motives in saving he says that they " operate over a diminishing part of the field; they are also stronger over a short period and of diminishing effect over a long period of time. In other words, communal saving via company reserves not subject to the individual volition for saving against spending and via the repayment of debt through funds derived from taxation and via large capital efforts (housing, etc.) partly financed through taxation is an increasing proportion of the total." [90] It is therefore apparent that saving as behavior is becoming more impersonal and institutional. The operation of incentive in the traditional way is less evident. It would be very difficult to prove that lower interest necessarily causes a decline in the amount of saving done by business enterprises. In the United States a comparative analysis of the interest rates and the amount of capital accumulation shows an upward trend of the latter, while interest rates fluctuate widely without any movement that may be considered a trend. They have been since the beginning of the twentieth century, which was a period of phenomenal saving, on a much lower level than at many other periods of our history. Although this is not conclusive, it does show that no substantiation of the classical law of supply can be found in such statistics as are available.[91]

It thus appears that saving has become to a great extent institutional and habitual. Marshall has given especial emphasis to this fact in spite of his final conclusions. Thus he says, " The accumulation of wealth is governed by a great variety of causes; by custom, by habits of self control and realizing the future, and above all by the power of family

[90] Stamp, " Inheritance as an Economic Factor," *Economic Journal*, Sept., 1926, p. 373.

[91] Edie, L. D., *Economics*, pp. 276-285.

affection."[92] This may be inconsistent with his final conclusion that interest is the reward for saving and has to be paid in the great majority of cases. Liberal interpretation in view of the above quotation might enable one to classify him with Cassel in the belief that some minimum interest must be paid.

(e) *The Significance of the Saver's Income Class*

To the extent that saving is habitual, rationalistic reward-seeking behavior does not operate. Saving must vary then according to the income class of the saver and according to certain special attitudes he may have about saving and particular forms of investment. In regard to income classes and their saving habits a great deal has been written. The consensus of opinion expressed by those testifying before the Colwyn Committee was that the rich and middle classes had better saving habits than the poor and saved a greater proportion of their income. Thus Dalton says that a heavily graduated tax will cut into the earnings of the people who do the most saving and this will occur to an extent greater than the amount of the graduation.[93] D. H. Macgregor concurred in this opinion.[94] Lord Hunsdon said,

> The intention and effect of disproportionate taxation of the rich is to provide the poorer classes with means for greater expenditure with the result that the expenditure of the country increases and savings diminish; for it is the rich who in proportion to their incomes are the saving class and the poor who are the spending class.[95]

Pigou has similar opinions. He says that "as between persons of unequal incomes, since there can be no question

[92] Marshall, *Principles of Economics*, p. 236.

[93] Dalton, *Principles of Public Finance*, pp. 88-90.

[94] *Colwyn Report, Minutes of Evidence*, par. 5746.

[95] *Colwyn Report, Minutes of Evidence*, p. 148.

that the rich save more, not merely absolutely but proportionately also than the poor people, to exempt savings from income tax and do nothing else would involve a distributional evil of giving a substantial bounty to the rich." [96] The conclusions of the Colwyn Committee were that the income tax has greater adverse effects on saving at the top of the income scale than at the middle ranges. They felt that the tax might very definitely decrease the savings of the wealthy.[97] Seligman in the United States holds similar views. He thinks that if the payment of a debt results in increasing the holdings of the lesser income classes, these may invest a smaller proportion of their income and capital accumulation will therefore be reduced. If, however, large corporations hold a large part of the debt, an increase in the amounts "plowed back" into business may result.[98] Rightly or not there is scarcely anyone who believes that the saving habits of the poor are better than those of the rich. If this can be accepted, taxation bearing more heavily upon the rich is likely to reduce the supply of saving.[99]

(f) *The Influence of Certain Attitudes Toward Saving and the Standard of Living*

Not only do the habits of saving vary according to the income classes of the savers, but they vary with certain attitudes held in regard to saving. One of these attitudes may

[96] Pigou, *Public Finance*, p. 139.

[97] *Colwyn Report*, p. 136.

[98] See Seligman, *Studies in Public Finance*.

[99] According to H. G. Brown the desire to save varies with its marginal cost, and thus graduated taxes up to a certain point do not reduce the desire to save. He says, "Yet all things considered, it seems a not unreasonable conclusion that a graduated tax on incomes from capital probably tends to discourage saving less than would a proportional tax levied at a high enough rate to yield an equal total revenue." *Economic Effects of Taxation*, p. 198.

be described as regard for the principal. Where a saver is interested in keeping a certain amount of principal intact or in accumulating a certain principal he is very little affected by the reward or interest he gets from it. The writer has known men who like to feel that they have a certain amount of money invested, and the ability to realize so much if needs arise looms much larger in their estimation than thoughts of the income derived from it. This fact was clearly brought out in the testimony before the Colwyn Committee. Thus Cannan pointed out that the payment of the debt was more conducive to saving than the payment of interest because in the case of interest it is less likely to be saved, since it is looked upon not as "capital" but as income.[100] Pigou makes the same point. He says that if ten people pay one hundred pounds in order to pay one thousand pounds to a debt holder, the latter would not be likely to regard it as income and thus would tend to save it.[101] At a later point in the report Cannan expresses himself as follows:

> But against taxation for repayment of National Debt the objection that high taxation reduces saving has no validity at all. The boot is on the other leg. Not a penny paid to the holders of the debt in redemption of the debt or the purchase of stock for cancellation will be regarded by them as anything but a part of their capital requiring reinvestment, while those taxed are sure to reduce their consumption to some extent so that the amount saved on balance must be greater unless the cost and inconvenience of collecting the extra taxation is greater than the reduction of consumption on the part of the tax-payers, which is not likely to be the case if the amount collected is kept within limits.[102]

Thus it is seen that where there is a desire to maintain a

[100] *Colwyn Report, Minutes of Evidence*, p. 99.

[101] *Ibid.*, p. 52.

[102] *Ibid.*, p. 60.

certain principal, reduced interest may have little effect. In the case of debt payment the regard for the principal insures the reinvestment of retired funds. This may make the repayment of debt conducive to saving.

But regard for the principal may be a part of the tendency to save for the fixed income aims mentioned by Gonner. Throughout the testimony of the Colwyn Committee there are indications of this point. Pigou, for example, says that "If there is a high tax and a man has less income, that tends to make him work harder, but on the other hand he knows that each unit of effort he makes gives him a less amount of money and those two things have to be balanced and unless you know the facts, which we do not know, you cannot balance them in that particular case." [103] In its final conclusions the Colwyn Committee pointed out that men continue to save in spite of taxes because they want to accumulate given amounts. It was shown by insurance statistics that people in the middle ranges of income invest chiefly for the purpose of security. An income tax placed upon them would thus not decrease the incentive to save. It may be, however, that there is an essential difference between the "regard for the principal" and saving such as the above.

Closely related to the attitudes about principal and amounts to be saved are the attitudes about the standard of living. Layton believed that the desire to increase the standard of living caused a reduction in saving. It is possible that in England, where a great struggle to get back to pre-war living conditions has been carried on, taxation may not reduce consumption. In the long run, however, the desire to improve the standard of living is usually accompanied by an increased desire to save. Thus the effect of the tax system upon estimates of and motives related to the standard of living will determine to a considerable extent the effects of taxation.

[103] *Ibid.*, p. 50.

Gonner touched upon this point when he described the way aspirations to change one's income class alter the effects of reduced interest upon saving.

(g) *The Anticipation of Taxes*

Still another psychological factor in the situation is the degree to which taxation is anticipated. Especial credit for bringing out this point is probably due to Pigou,[104] although others have expressed the same idea. J. B. Pease, for example, in his testimony before the Colwyn Committee stated that the anticipation of future taxes reduced the incentive to save.[105] Dalton also points out that inheritance taxes may have less effect upon saving than income taxes in that the anticipation of an immediate tax upon income will more heavily reduce saving than the remote possibility of an inheritance tax.[106] Effects of taxation upon saving will thus vary according to the degree to which they are anticipated and according to the changes taxes effect in the mental attitude with regard to anticipation.

It is also true that taxpayers have certain attitudes about the amount of the taxes paid. Pigou gave much weight to the effect of high taxes upon attitudes about saving. Thus he intimates that after taxes reach a certain amount they enter into the taxpayer's estimates of the proportion of income to effort and thus affect saving. In the discussion of his point that income taxes are a differential against saving he admitted that most people do not realize the way it is operating and therefore do not act much upon it. He believed that English taxes in 1926 were so high, however, as to be appreciated and that their anticipation reduced saving. The fact that a part of these taxes went for the internal re-

104 See Pigou, *Political Economy of War*, p. 79.

105 *Colwyn Committee, Minutes of Evidence*, p. 317.

106 Dalton, *op. cit.*, p. 91.

tirement of the debt he did not think altered matters.[107] Balancing the influences tending both to increase and decrease saving, he thought that taxes were high enough to make the latter influences the strongest. D. H. Macgregor's opinions were very similar. He stated that a "high rate" of taxation diminishes the will to save. Taxes of certain amounts therefore might have no effect because the taxpayer becomes accustomed to them or does not appreciate them.[108]

Hartley Withers apparently has much the same opinion when he says that if we " . . . penalize the Rentier too severely we shall discourage his future creation; the present race of earners, if they see that those who are living on past savings are shorn too close, will be deterred from saving. . . ."[109]

It is also apparent that where little or no effort is involved in earning an income the attitude of the taxpayer toward the payment of taxes upon it is different from that where the tax is upon "earned" income. The former taxes, owing to the different attitude toward the income from which they are taken, may have little effect upon the amount saved. It is partly for this reason that taxes on unearned income have grown in popularity.

IX. SUMMARY

These opinions are quite significant in that they tend to round out the picture of the influence of incentive. With their addition the role of incentive can be more readily coordinated with that of habit and institution.

Some very definite conclusions may then be stated with regard to the effects upon saving. In the first place, the

[107] *Colwyn Report*, p. 436.

[108] *Colwyn Report, Minutes of Evidence*, pars. 5759-5768.

[109] Withers, H., *War-time Financial Problems*, p. 214.

effects of taxation for debt retirement are by no means general in their determination and depend very definitely upon specific conditions. The determination of the effects in any given case cannot be readily derived from a set of general principles. This does not mean, however, that in the solution of any particular problem attention can be confined to matters very immediately related to it. Social, political and psychological as well as economic aspects must be considered. In other words, although generalization should be avoided, synthesis is quite desirable. Furthermore these problems are much broader than problems of the effects of particular taxes. Yet some writers on public finance see the effects of debt retirement largely as the effects of given taxes.[110] Such an approach is objectionable since it usually implies the application of a given set of tax theories to the problem and this impedes the social synthesis so much to be desired. This is especially true where the tax theories are based upon orthodox and psychological theories of value. The journey taken at the present time by those who wish to determine the effects of taxation is first to theories of incidence based on orthodox value and thence to theories of effects similarly grounded. It is the writer's belief that since the investigators do not start in the right direction they can hardly arrive at the true destination.

The effects of taxation for any purpose depend upon habits and institutions as well as reasoned incentive. Where the approach is through a supposedly universal value theory the former are either neglected or inadequately treated. This seems so likely to be the result of the value-theory approach that one is tempted to warn against it. Since habits and institutions are most important they should be treated most extensively. Two channels that their treatment may take have been indicated in the foregoing analysis: (1) through

[110] See Matsushita, *op. cit.*, p. 155.

the effects of taxes upon the habitual and institutional sources of savings; (2) through their effects upon specific institutions and attitudes and the reciprocal effect of these upon attitudes in regard to saving. Thus in the first case one should concentrate upon the tax effects relating to institutions that supply savings, viz., the sources of saving. In this chapter the sources have been discussed under the title of the ability to save. The second case relates to effects of the tax upon the motives that influence savings and to the institutions which affect these motives. It relates to the attitudes about saving, which are to a large extent determined by social conditions. Among these are the regard for the principal, attitudes about the standard of living in its relation to saving, and attitudes about saving for fixed amounts. Knowledge of the effects of taxation upon saving depends therefore in large measure upon a thorough study of the attitudes and institutions affecting saving behavior.

The influence of incentive must not, however, be overlooked. It has been clearly shown that the older value theory based upon the assumptions of incentive, rationalistic behavior, and the concept of the margin is very weak. It is unsafe to build the structure of tax effects upon such a foundation. But it cannot be said that there is no reason and incentive connected with the saving process. It must be agreed with Cassel and Gonner that some minimum incentive in the form of interest is required. To some extent the supply of saving is sensitive to the factor of monetary reward. Attention should be concentrated upon the causes of this sensitivity, of which a minimum degree cannot be questioned. Pigou, Macgregor, Stamp and others tried to explain this sensitivity on the ground of the amount of taxes and interest. This harmonizes with the belief of Cassel that the supply of saving will be decreased if the interest rate falls far enough, but that there is a wide margin of insensitivity. At a later point it will be shown how the crossing of this margin can be detected. Before this happens, other things being equal, taxes will have no deleterious effects.

To sum up, the determination of the effects of taxation upon saving in a specific situation requires a synthetic analysis of the way institutions, habits and attitudes related to saving are affected by taxation and the degree to which taxes make the saver sensitive to a loss of the interest incentive. It cannot be definitely shown that taxation will decrease the amount of saving and there is considerable plausibility in the belief that it will increase it. Certainly so long as taxation does not unduly reduce the efficiency of production, leaves the habits and institutions affecting saving unchanged, and is insufficient to discourage those who are motivated by the variations in the rate of interest, there is every reason to suppose that it will not decrease but increase saving. Particularly is this likely when the use of the proceeds is for debt retirement, since these proceeds are not devoted to expenditure but are usually replaced in the form of capital. Where a debt is originated for unproductive reasons, such as war, the repayment of it, so long as it stimulates saving, is likely to replace savings squandered in the course of the war. This presents an usual spectacle of a country through voluntary organized effort replacing the void in its capital equipment. It is interesting to note that a theory similar to this was advanced by Bastable in 1892.[111]

[111] He says, " So far as loans are derived from capital their repayment by taxes levied out of revenue is a restoration of the wealth previously abstracted from the work of production to its earlier and more economic use.—The redemption of debt is thus a mode of increasing the amount of national capital, unless on the hardly possible assumption that the whole amount of taxation raised for the purpose is drawn from capital or in the case of a foreign loan." *Public Finance*, 1892 ed., p. 613.

CHAPTER X

Theory of Debt Burdens

The preceding treatment of the history and theory of debt retirement was undertaken mainly for the purpose of elucidating the nature of debt burdens. It is only when a clear picture of such burdens is visualized that a satisfactory theory of retirement can be constructed. A little thought reveals the fact that all past theories of retirement depend upon conceptions of burden which for the most part have been too narrow in their scope. This narrowness has been shown by the undue emphasis put upon some one of the variety of elements in debt burden mentioned in the foregoing chapters. The construction of burden theory requires some summary of these miscellaneous elements at this point.

I. THE CATEGORIES OF DEBT BURDENS

The elements fall into nine categories. The first may be termed *transfer burdens,* the burdens of collecting sufficient taxes to pay the debt service. Some would give this form of burden an important place. Thus Mrs. Barbara Wootten believes that, " . . . if the debt is burdensome the burden must consist either in the friction involved in collecting funds by taxation to meet the debt service or in the fact that when the interest is paid off the funds are less advantageously used by the debt-holder than they would have been by the tax payer."[1] On the other hand there are those who ignore this form of burden altogether, and they generally believe that a very large proportion of war expenses can be met by taxation.[2] Most writers, however, are willing to concede this

[1] *Colwyn Report, Minutes of Evidence,* p. 65.

[2] Withers, H., *War-time Financial Problems,* p. 53.

type of burden a fairly important place. Three ideas are usually associated with this conception: (1) that the payments reduce the amounts that can be spent on social services; (2) that collection of the debt service is expensive; (3) that the process of collection causes industrial friction. It is reasonable to suppose that in so far as high taxation for debt payment reduces the power of the state to spend money for social services it does so through the fact that there is a limit to the ability of a state to raise taxes and not because of an expenditure of real income in debt payment. Thus one witness before the Colwyn Committee expressed the point as follows: "The immediate obstacle to increased social expenditures is the difficulty in raising the necessary taxes."[3] The two other aspects of transfer burdens are self evident. Suffice it to say that in the last analysis transfer burdens consist mainly in the scarcity of liquid assets resulting from the debt-payment process. There are also involved the technical limitations of the tax system itself, however. If income taxes rates, for example, are too high, the tax administration breaks down. As pointed out in Chapter V, debts originate out of these difficulties of liquidity and may even be said to consist fundamentally of the increased exchange media developed to meet these needs. Debts might be cancelled by an increase in purchasing medium and this would be the most rapid form of removal. They should not be removed in this way for reasons obvious to the reader. The important fact is, however, that any debt service by increasing the amount of taxation increases the problem of getting liquid assets, the very problem which probably gives rise to the debt in the beginning. After a war, since nations are sometimes not disposed to a further increase of their exchange medium, the problem may not be met in this way.

[3] *Colwyn Report, Minutes of Evidence*, p. 359. Evidence of A. M. Samuel.

In meeting it through restricted social expenditures concrete burdens result.

Another category of burden mentioned by various economists is *burden from undesirable redirection of industry due to taxation for the debt service.* Since the various forms of these burdens have been adequately discussed elsewhere [4] and are closely related to those in the last-mentioned category, they need not be further discussed here.

A third category, which was seen to be closely related to the foregoing, is *the burden of false government economy arising from the large size of the debt service.* In regard to the first category it should be pointed out that there are other factors causing the reduction of desirable social expenditures than the mere difficulty of raising taxes in the face of a large debt service. Concentration of attention on the absolute amounts of the service increases the demand for governmental retrenchments to an extent greater than would be dictated by the difficulty of raising funds. Economy becomes a popular national policy and is followed blindly in some cases for the sake of political advantages.

The fourth category and the one most considered by writers on this subject is that of *savings burdens.* In Chapter IX it was pointed out that the effects of the debt service upon savings must be given primary importance in determining policies of debt retirement. A good many of the men cited on this point assume that saving may be retarded by very high taxation. A review of the theories of value underlying such an assumption did not indicate the level at which deleterious effects would begin; it did, however, show the way in which such effects would come about.[5] In view of the multiplicity of influences the latter information is more important. Such

[4] See Chapter IX.

[5] See the opinions of Brown, Pigou, Withers, Law and Dalton, cited in Chapter IX, pp. 245-247.

burdens, which according to Pigou are among the most important of those relating to internal debts, do not arise with the moderate taxation for debt retirement that is usually levied. On the contrary there is some basis for belief in Bastable's theory of the effects of debt retirement.

The fifth category is that of *psychological burdens.* They consist of psychological depression resulting from falling prices or other changes due to the payment of the debt service and the pain of the effort and saving necessary to pay the debt. They are to a considerable degree a result of distributional changes and proportions of income to debt payments. Professor Seligman has found that subjective war burdens may be shifted to the future.

A sixth category comprises the *distributional burdens.* This form of burden consists largely in the tendency toward inequality of wealth assumed to result from the payment of the debt service. It is thought to come about through a failure of taxation upon debt holders, who are the wealthier classes, to equal the interest paid to them. Pigou, who has made the most of this point, says that " . . . large subscribers [to loans] have good reason to hope that the interest on their holdings will exceed the contribution in taxes which they will have to make to provide this interest; for experience has never yet revealed a tax system graduated for increasing incomes anything like as steeply as loans are likely to be graduated, at all events when the loan required is large." [6] Dalton and many others are of the same opinion.[7]

It has been pointed out that these burdens come about largely through price changes and are by no means as simple as has been assumed. Their exact character (as was shown in Chapter VIII) depends upon (a) monetary changes before and after the war and (b) the effects of the repayment

[6] Pigou, *Political Economy of War*, p. 77.

[7] Dalton, *Principles of Public Finance*, p. 192.

process, as well as (c) the distribution of the debt among income groups. The most important fact to remember, however, is the influence of monetary changes.

Pigou and others have linked these distributional changes to changes in saving and production. It was seen that in so far as the wealthy are more apt to save, a distribution favorable to them might result in increased savings. Thus Pigou saw a conflict between saving and distribution objectives in debt payment. So much emphasis has been placed upon these distribution changes that many persons have assumed them to be the only real burdens of internal debt. Closely associated with the idea that after the war the burden which was originally concentrated on the bond holders, who are identified with the wealthy, is spread over other people, or in other words that the inequality of wealth is increased, is the idea that the burden is spread over time. This refers to the original lump payment of the loan and the subsequent repayment in small portions.

A seventh category is *burdens arising from monetary and interest changes*. The general fall in prices has long been cited as an important source of burden. In Chapter V it was pointed out that the debt may become more burdensome owing to a fall in prices, but only under those circumstances where the fall is due to a contraction of purchasing media. To understand burdens of this nature requires a survey of the conditions surrounding the origination of the debt. They are in large measure distributional burdens viewed from the monetary angle. They may have production aspects in so far as falling prices affect business enterprise adversely. Where the form of the debt affects the banks the unfortunate results mentioned in Chapter VI may be considered as burdens. The payment of the debt may also affect particular prices and interest rates. These effects may prove burdensome to certain types of business enterprise.

An eighth concept of burden consists of ***burden arising from the unwise expenditure of debt proceeds.*** Since the days of Bastable, the idea that taxation is necessarily an evil has been discarded and attention has been shifted to the nature of public expenditures. Thus in the field of public credit debts have come to be judged in the light of their productivity. Most debts can now be imagined to have a productive character, if ever so remote, but burden is sensed where the product is too far away or too small.

A final category might be termed ***burdens arising from uncertainty.*** Large debts have been declared " burdensome " because they make difficult and uncertain the raising of large amounts for future contingencies such as wars, catastrophes, and large social expenditures. The variation of the actual burden with the price level was cited by R. G. Glenday as an example of uncertainty that should not affect public credit. Where also the size of a public debt is such that the debt service can be collected only with the greatest difficulty, deficits may be incurred with any new need. The mere possibility of such an occurrence decreases public credit and constitutes a kind of burden. Uncertainty arises also when the debt is largely unfunded and conversions are constantly imminent.

It is thus seen that the various aspects of debt burden fall roughly into these nine categories: (1) transfer burdens, (2) burdens from industrial change, (3) savings burdens, (4) psychological burdens, (5) burdens from the nature of public expenditures, (6) distributional burdens, (7) monetary burdens, (8) burdens from unwise government economy, (9) burdens from uncertainty. According as one or the other has been emphasized the customary debt classifications have been devised. Thus that of external and internal debts refers to the first three; that of funded and unfunded to the ninth; that of productive and unproductive to the fifth; that of forced and voluntary to the fourth; and that of subjective and objective also to the fourth.

In the preceding pages the nature and causes of these burdens were discussed mainly in regard to specific conditions. It cannot too often be repeated that any rational plan of debt retirement depends upon such analysis. It is also true that certain general aspects of debt burden arise from this study and, though it is not proposed to set up here any one theory of burden, there are certain notions common to all forms that should be treated. The exposition of these notions is indispensable to the formation of any general plan of debt retirement and to a complete understanding of the nature and causes of any specific form of burden.

II. FOUR GENERAL CONCEPTIONS BASIC TO THE THEORY OF DEBT BURDENS

The first notion is that there is a distinct difference between the burden of debt and the burden of war. Although this distinction has been recognized by many economists in their treatment of the various burden categories mentioned above, they show a constant confusion between the more fundamental war and debt categories. Misunderstanding of the distinctions between the latter seems to the writer an important source of general confusion in thinking about debt burdens. This confusion has no respect for ability and knowledge. It arises especially when economists analyse subjective burdens. The following quotation from Professor Hunter illustrates the ease with which one becomes confused. He says: " It is very probable that a tax may stimulate production but its burden is felt none the less in (the) increased use of energy which the payment of the tax has called forth." [8] Thus the subjective effort accompanying the production stimulated by the payment of the debt is considered a debt burden.

[8] Hunter, *Public Finance*, p. 130.

At a later point it will be shown that a certain part of it, perhaps all of it, should be classified as a war burden. Knowledge that the burden arises after the war and that it is not similar to the subjective burdens of war that are shifted has led Professor Hunter to classify it with the debt burdens. Had he not been dealing with subjective burdens, and had he accepted a different conception of debt burdens, he would not have made this mistake. As the nature of debt burdens is developed in the chapter the cause of this confusion between war and debt burdens will be clarified.

The confusion also inheres in the well-known belief that only the subjective war burdens may be shifted to the future. The Colwyn Committee, in summarizing the nature of war burdens, says: "The War, except in so far as the money was raised abroad, had clearly to be paid for immediately and the burden on the community as a whole could not be thrown on future generations." [9] When one knows in addition that capital and bodily efficiency have been impaired by the war, the subjective or objective effort of improving these conditions must be implicitly regarded as debt burdens. The difference between such people and Professor Hunter is that the latter is more consistent and thorough in his thought on this point. He is not content to leave it merely to implication. If one recognizes as R. H. Brand does [10] that some objective war burdens may be shifted to the future, and at the same time, however, omits any discussion of such subjective burdens as are mentioned by Hunter, he shows a fundamental confusion between war and debt burdens. He does not know what to do with the subjective burdens of the post-war increase in production.

This confusion, however, does not show itself solely in the treatment of subjective burdens. It appears also in the

[9] *Colwyn Report*, p. 27.

[10] Brand, R. H., *War and National Finance*, pp. 94-105.

contrast of burdens arising from production and distribution. If as some writers assume the burdens of debt are wholly distributional in character, then the burden of any increase in saving that results from the methods of taxation employed for the debt service must be either omitted from consideration or attributed to the war. But still more important, the lack of clarity as to the difference between war and debt burdens leads to the confused conceptions of relative distribution burdens and absolute production burdens. To such people the burden of the war is the loss of a given quantity of raw materials, capital, and man power; the debt burden is the increase of the wealth of the rich not absolutely but relatively to the poorer classes. The depressive effect of the debt service upon saving is considered to be a reduction in the "amount" of saving. This amount of saving is left unrelated to any other economic factor. If the differences between war and debt burdens were properly understood, production burdens would not be considered so totally different in character from the distribution burdens. The similarity between these two forms will be somewhat clarified as we proceed.

A second fundamental notion is that of the existence of both individual and national burdens and the distinction between them must be kept clearly in mind. These types transcend the production and distribution burdens, although at first glance they seem not to do so owing to the influence of distribution upon production. In fact some people estimate this influence so highly as to believe all national burdens are caused by changes in distribution.[11] A failure to recognize the existence of national burdens arising from internal debt leads to many omissions. For example, we saw above that

[11] See opinions of A. L. Dickinson, *Colwyn Report, Minutes of Evidence*, pp. 246-247; Pigou in his final conclusions virtually reaches this point.

the treatment of the effects of debts on social expenditures by the state, when undertaken with the assumption that there are not national burdens, leads one to ignore the savings and transfer categories which are really among the most important national burdens. It causes an excessive regard for distribution at the expense of production considerations.

Third, it may be said that all burdens are reduced in the final analysis to two: real and psychological burdens. But the psychological burdens, although they may be most fundamental, should not be given much place in the theory of debt burdens because of our inability to deal with them concretely. Attention should therefore be concentrated upon physical changes. The debt and war burdens relate to less raw materials, less machines and less men. More particularly they relate to proportions of physical things and the changes in them. Thus a burden is not a given amount of physical things but the proportion of some of them to others and the changes in these proportions over time.

The fourth important notion then is that burdens are relative. This fact has been recognized for a long time. For instance, Leroy-Beaulieu saw that the burden of debt is reduced by the development of national wealth.[12] This point was echoed in Bastable, who also included several dynamic considerations in his estimation of debt burdens.[13] In more modern works, such as that of Shirras, one finds this point thoroughly realized, with the result that many dynamic elements are taken into account.[14] In spite of this fact, however, it is not clearly understood that debt burdens are relative. If it were, the very process of estimation would not be taken so seriously. The confusion of war with debt burdens would be less, and debt burdens would be viewed

[12] Leroy-Beaulieu, *Traité de la science des finances*, vol. ii, pp. 446-447.

[13] Bastable, *Public Finance*, p. 554, 1st edition.

[14] Shirras, *Public Finance*, p. 411.

rather as changing proportions of economic factors—not as deductions of absolute amounts of wealth. To estimate a burden in money assumes that it is a certain amount. Such estimates have been made of the burden of the World War; they have also been made of public debts arising from the war. Some of the weaknesses of the use of price indices as deflators in these estimates were pointed out elsewhere.[15] In both types of estimates dynamics have been considered. Yet the belief that burden varies with altered proportions does not clearly indicate to these men that it relates to the proportions and not to any absolute sum of money.

If burdens concern the relations of economic factors they must arise when the proportion of some factor decreases so as to cause an inferior combination. This conception resembles that of the Law of Proportionality. Thus, if war decreases the supply of capital the inferior proportion of capital to man power is a burden. It may be objected that there is little value in such a conception owing to the obscurity of the "most desirable proportions." These exist as between a great number of factors and cannot be readily isolated. But the problem of their determination is probably not nearly so difficult as it seems. Some of the most simple and fundamental proportions may be recognized at once. The broadest and most fundamental of these exist between capital, labor, natural resources, and industrial technique. With little study the excessive loss of capital can usually be recognized. In regard to some particular forms of capital such as railway rolling stock an inefficient proportion can also be detected. Yet another objection is that burden may result not from a disproportionate but from a general loss of factors. Thus men as well as capital may be lost. A general loss of factors is seldom even approximated, however. But granting this approximation, time must be admitted as an

[15] See Chapter V.

element in production if not as a causal factor, and such a situation constitutes a disproportion of production to time. Progress is set back a number of years. Therefore it is safe to say that the burden of war arises usually from the alteration in the existing factors of and elements in production and that it consists in this alteration. This one statement therefore takes account of both time and proportions. It should enable us to make our conception of burdens homogeneous and to coordinate the progress in theory up to this point.

Such a theory places the emphasis upon " desirable relations " and therefore requires a more thorough analysis of these in their connections with debts than has yet been given them. It cannot be said that merely because one factor of production is increasing it has a desirable proportion to the other economic factors. Thus, apropos of past progress in debt theory, it is not enough to say that the debt service must not check the accumulation of capital. Also it cannot be assumed that the debt service by increasing the inequality of wealth is necessarily at fault. However, it is clear that the analysis of these relations presents many difficulties and that they are constantly changing. If it were necessary to determine specifically what they are we could not hope to get very far. But only a general notion of them seems to be needed and this we are trying to formulate.

Several writers on public debts have thrown considerable light upon the nature of desirable relations of savings to other factors. Bastable, as was stated in Chapter IX, believed that the debt service stimulates savings and accumulates an amount of capital roughly equaling that destroyed during the war.[16] Henri Adam, who may have been influenced by Bastable, takes this possible tendency as a criterion of satisfactory debt retirement. He says, " *La prati-*

[16] See Chapter IX, p. 277.

que par l'État de l'amortissement est la perception progressive d'une somme égale aux capitaux empruntées. Cette perception n'est possible que dans la mésure où la richesse nationale permet de surlever l'impôt. L'amortissement offre donc ce caractère de ne pouvoir être pratique qu'à un moment où il n'est pas immédiatement nécessaire."[17] A satisfactory retirement, according to Adam, would be one replacing the lost war capital. This is an absolute criterion, a fact which is an immediate presumption against it. Also the exact amounts of capital lost during a war and created by debt retirement are so much affected by a variety of monetary influences that their estimation is extremely difficult. As a useful *pratique* it affords little promise.

In the way of dynamic criteria there is little help. Many writers state that the debt service should not retard the accumulation of capital. Cucheval-Clarigny, whom Adam quotes, has this point of view. He says, "*Il y a comme il arrive toujours en politique une question de mésure. Une Nation a le devoir de ne pas rêjeter sur l'avenir les charges qui incombent au présent; toutefois le but serait depassé et l'avenir lui-meme compromis si des charges trop lourdes et trop multipliées avaient pour conséquence de paralyser l'activité nationale et de tarir les sources de la richesse publique.*"[18] A number of other economists have taken this same position. Among them are Seligman, Pigou and Hartley Withers.[19] Still others, such as Stamp and Fred Hall, have proposed to estimate the amount of savings needed and to use this as a criterion of retirement.[20] Many others believe that taxation

[17] Adam, Henri, *L'Amortissement de la dette publique*, p. 83.

[18] Cucheval-Clarigny, *Essai sur l'amortissement*, 1886, p. 153. Quoted from Adam.

[19] Seligman, *Essays in Taxation*, p. 744; Pigou, *Political Economy of War*, p. 79; Withers, *War-time Financial Problems*, p. 75.

[20] Stamp, *Wealth and Taxable Capacity*, pp. 134-135.

should not take more than savings and the criterion thus cited is a vague one of accumulating savings. Where there is an attempt to estimate the amounts needed, as with Stamp, pre-war consumption and production and half of pre-war savings are assumed. A group of accountants appearing before the Colwyn Committee attempted to determine the amount of saving that should be allowed and in doing so estimated the needs due to growing population, capital depreciation, new undertakings, and improved living standards.[21] In their treatment they came the nearest of anyone to presenting practical criteria. However, the majority of the Committee thought it still too impractical. They said that they were ". . . forced to the conclusion that there is no formula by which one may determine the rate at which debt payment should proceed." [22] The Committee were unsatisfied as to the relations the accountants set up and could see no prospect of success in this direction. All that these people have accomplished is to emphasize the existence of a trend of savings which if retarded by debt taxation indicates the presence of burden. But the criterion of trend has many possibilities. It has already been applied to the field of public credit in a concrete way.[23] Its potentialities are, however, more theoretical than practical. When it is combined with the work of Adam and Bastable greater insight is gained.

In both the trend-of-saving and the replacement-of-war-capital criteria there is an assumption of normality. It is also assumed that normality is good. Burden results from unfortunate dynamics. In war the trend which indicates the proportion of capital growth is altered. A reversion occurs to a former level. This is to a large extent the burden of

[21] See *Colwyn Report, Minutes of Evidence*, p. 243.

[22] *Colwyn Report*, p. 339.

[23] See Paul Studenski, *Public Borrowing*.

war. The concept of trend has contributed the idea of the altered proportion of the rate of growth; that of amount, the idea of reversion to the previous level of growth. The first is similar to reduced interest, the second to reduced principal. Of these the second has only specious reality. The real change is in the proportions of the rates of change. Thus the idea of an absolute loss of capital would indicate a reduced absolute amount of capital but in the last analysis it is the reduced rate of accumulation that has any reality as a burden.

When one applies this reasoning to debt burdens rather than to war burdens, what conception results? Since war burden arises due to alterations of the normal, which is interpreted as good proportions between rates of change, consistency would require a similar form for debt burdens. But there is a distinction between the debt and war burdens originating in the history and conditions that are considered normal. If, for instance, the theory suggested by Bastable be granted, then an accelerated growth of capital would be normal while the debt service was being paid. Thus debt burden would arise not when taxation merely checked the rate of capital accumulation, but when it retarded the accelerated capital accumulation that normally should accompany the debt service. To illustrate this point let us return to the criticism of Professor Hunter's remarks made above. If Professor Hunter had accepted this theory of debt burden he would not be interested in subjective costs and he would also not regard the replacement of war capital as a burden. On the contrary the absence of the accelerated growth would be a burden. Likewise, those recognizing debt burdens through the decreased accumulation of capital would be still more exacting in estimating burdens of this sort. They would not make the mistake of considering production burdens absolute and distribution burdens relative. Moreover, a case may be made for the increasing inequality of wealth after the war not being a burden, or for greater inequality being perpetuated by the payment of the debt.[24] The one most important thing that may be said about any form of burden is that not only does its incidence depend upon value but the value process gives birth to the very concept of burden itself.

At this point it may be well to return for a moment to the nine burden categories mentioned earlier in the chapter and show how the preceding discussion relates to them. The rate of capital accumulation may not be accelerated because the payment of the debt service causes a scarcity of liquid funds, production may be diverted into less profitable channels, optimism and the application of human effort reduced, unwise government expenditures or undue restriction of desirable expenditures made, uncertainty arise and altered savings habits occur. This gives rise to national debt burdens. Individual burdens may arise from all of these changes as well as from an increase in the inequality of the distribution of wealth through monetary or other causes.

III. CERTAIN CURRENT BELIEFS REVIEWED IN THE LIGHT OF THE THEORY OF DEBT BURDENS

Viewed from this angle a number of current beliefs take on a different meaning. First let us consider the contrasting classifications of productive and unproductive debts. This old distinction is related of course to the use of the proceeds of loans. The preceding discussion should show the reader that the confusion between war and debt burdens may be much increased by the use of these terms in their old meanings. The term unproductive debt assumes that burden has resulted from the use of the funds. Concentration on these burdens and the confused linking of the term debt with the

[24] See Chapter VIII.

burdens of expenditure is likely to lead to unsound reasoning. It would therefore be better to use these terms to designate debt rather than expenditure burdens. Those debts, therefore, whose service proves burdensome in the sense used in the above paragraphs might be called unproductive.

The burden theory just developed should lead one to question some current notions about the differences between external and internal debts. External debts have usually been asssumed more burdensome than internal debts. This greater burden does not arise from the loss of capital, a most common belief. Many writers make this mistake. For example, Dalton says of external debts, " During any given period the direct money burden is measured by the sum of money payments . . . to external creditors, while the direct real burden is measured by the loss of economic welfare, which these money payments involve, to members of the debtor community." [25] The burden really arises as with internal debts, from the effects upon saving, transfer difficulties and changes in the distribution of wealth. If a nation were incapable of accelerating its saving processes there would be a debt burden. There is, however, a distinct difference in that the difficulties of transfer are greater. A check on the accumulation of capital is more likely to arise from this source. Another difference arises out of the fact that the burden is more perceptible in the case of external debts. By this, however, it is not meant that capital can be seen leaving the country, but that if saving cannot be increased enough to pay the debt, i.e. if debt burdens develop, they immediately become obvious through defaulting. This is well illustrated by the reparations difficulties.

These burden conceptions also affect the meaning of debt payment. From a national standpoint it is not easy to

[25] Dalton, *Principles of Public Finance*, p. 189.

understand what payment means. As stated at an earlier point, the public debt is really a monetary instrument. It has long been associated with money. It might almost be termed a form of credit money. It is a process of exchange. Like most other money processes it involves a matching of goods and credits. It is unhealthy when this is not properly accomplished. A public debt is similar to private debt in that it is not really paid unless through a supply of goods. For example, the objections to rapidly rising prices are framed in the terms that the creditor does not receive in goods the values that he loaned. According to this reasoning no national debt is really paid unless in the paying process the loss of the capital occasioned through the debt is replaced. Any economic obstruction to this end may be termed a debt burden. From this angle debt burdens become monetary deficiencies. They are weaknesses in the exchange medium. This point has been approached by all those who oppose taxation for the debt service in excess of annual savings, and consider such taxation capital confiscation. They do not usually relate it to the nature of debt burdens, to which it is so closely allied. A. M. Samuel, a prominent English manufacturer, has given the clearest expression to this notion about debt payment. He makes a very desirable distinction between cancellation and debt payment. The latter occurs only when debt payments are made out of savings. He seems to recognize the close relation between debt payments and the monetary system, since he points out that if payments are made through the transfer of capital, deflation will result. Although this is good reasoning, it has certain defects. Inflation rather than deflation may actually be the cause of the "cancellation." In fact, falling prices, at any rate, are likely to result from the payment of debt in his sense. In so far as the payment process leaves the saving processes unaccelerated, cancellation may result. Payment therefore takes place only when the rate of capital growth is accelerated, and it is only in such a way that the health of the monetary system is restored. Otherwise there is no "payment" and capital is "confiscated."

As was shown in Chapter VIII, the way in which individuals may be repaid depends upon the way the debt originated as well as the effects of the debt service on the volume of savings. Thus the original conditions surrounding a loan become of great importance from the standpoint of individual burdens. The reader may wonder why this is true from the individual point of view and not from that of the nation. A little thought shows that the nation always meets a war burden through capital and savings. Individuals in loaning to the government may not entirely do so. From the standpoint of the distribution of wealth the incidence of borrowing is of great importance; for some purposes it is just as important as the incidence of taxation. With the advent of large war debts some study of this matter becomes of importance. At first glance it seems to differ in its causation from the incidence of taxation, having come about through general rather than specific price changes. Since general price changes are made up of a variety of changes, the intricacy of this incidence may be as great as that of other forms of incidence. Its study is indispensable to any thorough treatment of the inequality of wealth after a long period of war. In addition it suggests that in some of the discussions of taxes versus loans a few important considerations have been omitted.

It was hoped at the beginning of this study that some light might be thrown on the problem of choice between taxes and loans in public finance. The problem is essentially one of the nature and incidence of burdens. It is the writer's belief that the previous analysis throws some light on the arguments that have been raised on both sides of the question of loans versus taxes. On the whole, loans come out with an improved standing. This conclusion is arrived at through the examination of some of the arguments raised against the use of loans.

One common argument against war loans is that taxes would increase savings to a greater extent during the war.[26] It is generally admitted that even in countries that make a great effort to increase savings during a war a great increase is not possible. Perhaps Great Britain and the United States have been as successful in this respect as might have been expected. Against these difficulties one may set the fact that a moderate replacement policy may actually stimulate the accumulation of capital by an increased rate of savings after the war. The argument against loans, that they do not increase savings during war, therefore is somewhat weakened by our conception of debt burdens.

Another argument against loans is that the burden of the war is increased by the payment of the interest. If this fallacious point has not been sufficiently shattered, the foregoing chapters should do it. There can be no burden apart from the production, transfer and distribution burdens already treated. A point closely related to this is that a large debt requires the payment of excessive interest, thus increasing the burden. Since the credit of the government in such countries as Great Britain and the United States has up to the present time been essentially that of the nation and this in turn has varied with economic conditions, it can be argued that a large debt will not increase the interest paid unless taxation seriously burdens the nation. Where the debt is well funded, and taxes are not too high because of the large size of the debt, its size would not be a burden.

[26] For exposition of these arguments, see Seligman, *Essays in Taxation*, pp. 736-747; Withers, *War-time Financial Problems*, p. 55; Studenski, *Public Borrowing*, chap. v.

If in such a case interest rates remained high it would probably be due to the scarcity of capital caused by the war.

A fourth argument against loans is the increasing burden of falling prices. The fact that falling prices due to the usual long-run causes, i. e. increased goods, will not cause an increase in the debt burden considerably weakens this point. Another argument is the one that a large debt decreases the ability of the government to provide for increased social services. This depends upon the size of the debt and the difficulties of transferring funds. To most persons who have thought about this point it ceases to be the bugbear it was once considered. Still another argument is the improvement of the tax system by greater war use of taxes. Against this possible advantage must be set the stimulus to saving by the debt service after the war. It does show that loans have one great disadvantage in the defects they cause in the distribution of wealth. Loans, however, appear to have many compensating advantages on the production side. To sum up, one finds that the stimulus to savings arising out of the debt service qualifies most of the arguments against loans.

IV. SUMMARY

In our treatment of the theory of debt burdens we have found that they consist largely in the failure of capital accumulation to be stimulated and in unfortunate changes in the distribution of wealth. We have seen that the monetary influences upon public debts are much greater than is usually supposed. It also appears that the subject of burdens involves value in the conception as well as in the solution of its problems. The problem of debt retirement is very clearly one of eliminating debt burdens rather than of cancelling nominal claims. Burden theory is absolutely essential to it. Theoretically it must be regarded as the inverse of borrowing, if burdens are homogeneous. H. C. Adams in his famous work centers attention upon rapidity as the chief problem in retirement. The reduction of burdens really requires emphasis on proportions, but Adams has focused it on absolute amounts. A proper theory of retirement would deal with dynamics and the factors of change. Instead of scrutinizing debts so closely, the public financier should examine the effects of institutions for saving, production and tax systems.

CHAPTER XI

Relation of the Theory of Debt Burden to the Theory of Debt Retirement

In the preceding chapter the nature of debt burdens was discussed in the light of contemporary theories of the relationships of taxation, prices and saving. In this chapter an attempt will be made to relate the treatment of burdens to the problems and practices of debt retirement. Among the more important forms that debt burdens may take are, as we have demonstrated, transfer burdens, the undesirable redirection of investments, distribution burdens, monetary burdens, and the burdens of reduced saving. In debt retirement practice what account should be taken of these varieties of burden?

I. Retirement Practice and the Categories of Burden

In the case of burdens arising from the transfer of the debt service the post-war discussion has added very little to our knowledge. Three conclusions seem to follow from this discussion. In the first place, since this burden consists to a large extent of the costs of collection and administration of the taxes raised to pay for the interest and retirement of the debt, these costs should be reduced to the lowest possible point without sacrificing efficiency. This is of course an administrative problem and can be best solved in the time and place where it arises. In the second place, as was pointed out in Chapter IX, the limitation which the debt puts upon social services depends largely upon the extent to which the taxes necessary to pay the debt by their size reduce the ability of the taxpayer to shoulder the additional burdens of the social services. This is usually a transfer problem, since the payment of debt does not necessarily reduce the total income of a country. In regard to this obstruction to the provision of social services, it seems that regardless of the size of debts there must be some minimum for each country below which it would not be desirable to reduce social expenses, and which should be maintained even if to do this the inflation of money is required. The burden of internal debt should never be accepted as an adequate excuse for the curtailment of desirable social expenditures. In the third place, since another important aspect of the burden of transferring the debt service is the economic friction caused by high taxes, these taxes should be adapted to business conditions as well as possible. It is desirable that new techniques be developed for the empirical treatment of the problems raised by the deductive analysis of the effects of taxation.

The question of undesirable redirection of industry, which is a point closely related to the preceding one, also requires more study before any definite conclusions can be reached. Keynes believes that the tendency of debt payment is to increase gilt-edged investments. This is by no means certain, nor is it certain that debt payment increases investment in large companies with a wide reputation. By the questionnaire method such problems could be investigated and the truth or falsity of these assertions demonstrated. So many factors are involved that almost the only place where they are isolated is in the minds of those dealing directly with them—hence the desirability of investigation.

The tendency of debt payment to affect the distribution of wealth was discussed in Chapter VIII, where it was decided that to a large extent the effects of taxation for retirement upon distribution were determined by the relation of debt retirement to saving and to prices. It must not be assumed that debt retirement will necessarily increase the inequality of wealth or that during the period in which it is proceeding especially progressive taxes are required, or that in practice there is necessarily any conflict between the saving and distribution objectives of debt retirement. Of most importance are the conditions under which the debt originated. If bank credit has been used as a basis for the purchase of government bonds and there has been an increase in the rate of saving after a war, it is possible that the debt service perpetuates an inequality of wealth created at the time the debt originated. Of most importance is the fact that even should the debt be retired in the ordinary way through the use of a sinking fund, and if repayment takes place in some measure through an actual increase in savings, there would not be any reduction in the inequality of wealth originally set up by the debt.

For debt retirement policy, therefore, these conclusions seem warranted. First, a thorough investigation of the monetary and banking conditions surrounding the origination of the debt should be made. Second, if these conditions show that the debt has caused considerable inequality, it might be desirable to levy heavier taxes upon the original debt holders. Taxes designed to discriminate against those who have unduly profited from inflation have already been evolved in Germany. If saving accompanies retirement, the inequality will be perpetuated through the reissuance of credit by the banks on the basis of the new capital. If repayment takes place without increased saving but increased local debt allows borrowing for this purpose, then the inequality will be perpetuated in the form of the banks' loans directly to localities, through their purchase of local bonds or through loans to individuals who have in their turn purchased local bonds. If the increase of bank credit is retarded and the increase in capital accumulation either continues at the same rate or is accelerated, then prices will fall, and if through the increased profits of this accumulating capital the bond holder is able to complete the purchase of his bonds, the banks benefit from the increased purchasing power of their profits. The location of the gains in case of such an increase in saving is very difficult. About all that may be said is that these gains may go to the agencies or persons who inflated the exchange medium and that probably banks would get a disproportionate increase in income as a result of the accumulation of capital. In view of this possibility the large profits of banks during and immediately after a war might properly submit to heavy special taxes. A third conclusion that follows from this discussion is that the mere maintenance of the debt does not greatly affect the inequality of wealth and that retirement policy need not include much attention to this question. Far more attention should be paid to the conditions surrounding the origination of the debt. An additional reason for raising a large proportion of the war expenses by taxes is the prevention of the tendencies toward inequality of wealth that arise from paying for a war loan with inflated currency.

It may further be concluded that direct and progressive taxation during the period of debt payment tends to reduce any unfortunate tendencies which have been set up by the debt, and it might be suggested that direct taxes be emphasized after a war as well as the use of taxes to secure funds during a war. It has been suggested that to the extent that taxes fall upon the wealthy saving is discouraged.[1] There is certainly no proof of this except the fact that the rich, having larger incomes, are able to save more than the poor.[2]

[1] See Chapter IX.

[2] When this theory is applied to debt retirement policy it results in the linking of retirement to wages. Thus F. J. Blakemore, a witness before the Colwyn Committee, suggested that each worker be taxed an hour's wage a week to pay the debt. The result, he thought, would be

When taxes return to bond holders in the form of capital and interest, there is a presumption against the theory that taxes for debt payment will reduce saving unless levied upon the poor. This whole question needs still further investigation before any very definite conclusions can be drawn.

The burdens of debt of a more general nature, arising from a fall in prices induced by debt payment or otherwise caused, require that some attention be paid to the price level in the retirement of debt. If it is clear that debt payment, by reducing the loans of a central bank or by reducing the credit base through the repayment of bank loans by individual bond holders, causes deflation, then measures should be taken to prevent too rapid a repayment of the debt or to stimulate borrowing by other government agencies. Furthermore, at no time should debt payment be carried out to such an extent as to affect adversely the efficiency of open market operations when they are desirable.

External debts need not constitute a burden in the sense, sometimes attributed to them, of taking capital from the country. It is true that this is frequently the result of their repayment. On the other hand, if they were originally paid in actual goods, the debtor country was saved the depletion of capital at the time of the public expenditures, and the differences between the external and internal loans depend upon the time at which the depletion occurs and not upon the presence or absence of the depletion. In trying to determine, therefore, how rapidly external as against internal debts should be repaid, the loss of capital need not be treated as though it were a cause for special haste, but transfer

a sinking fund of £78,000,000 a year. (*Colwyn Report, Minutes of Evidence*, p. 201.) The opposite point of view is well expressed by another witness who says, "Since we wish to raise additional sums for debt redemption from owners of invested wealth we think that if there be no Capital Levy, this might well be done by increasing such differentiation." (*Ibid.*, p. 415.)

difficulties and the ability to pay should be given chief consideration. External debts, except for the difficulties of transfer, need not be any more burdensome than internal debts.

In the first chapter it was pointed out that the relations between saving, the price level and debt retirement had not been adequately determined. In the chapters that followed an attempt was made to show how these three factors enter into many of the problems related to the retirement of debt. The conclusion in regard to the general effects of retirement upon saving was that retirement should tend to accelerate saving. If this tendency is not present, what might be called a " saving burden " is created. In view of this conclusion the question arises as to how the effects of retirement upon saving should be related to retirement policy.

II. FOUR WAYS OF RELATING THE SPEED OF RETIREMENT TO THE VOLUME OF SAVING

An examination of the thought of various economists on this point shows that this relation may be effected in any one of four ways: (1) retirement must not reduce the volume of saving, (2) retirement must be adjusted to the volume of saving, (3) retirement must be adjusted to the needs of saving, (4) retirement should promote saving.

In England there were a few men who believed that retirement was progressing too rapidly in 1926. Among these was McKenna, who thought the incentive to save would be reduced by too heavy taxes.[3] Conservatively minded people believed that the poor should be taxed more heavily than the rich in order that taxation for debt retirement might not reduce saving.[4] Many economists have advocated modera-

[3] *Colwyn Report*, p. 333.

[4] *Colwyn Report, Minutes of Evidence*, p. 148. See remarks of Lord Hunsdon.

tion in taxes so as not to discourage saving and some, as we have seen, have had regard specifically to debt retirement. Others have carried this belief further and have assumed that if debt retirement took a reasonable proportion of the volume of savings, saving would not be discouraged. H. C. Adams thought that debt payment should have a proper relationship to the productive powers of the nation. He asked: "What reason can be urged for exhausting the energy that might go to the development of the nation's strength in reducing the burden?"[5] Lowes Dickinson believes that annual debt payments should at no time exceed the annual increases of capital.

Out of this idea comes an attempt to estimate the capital needs of the nation and to adjust the speed of retirement to it. Thus Professor Fred Hall in England speaks of a "sufficient sum of savings and the desirability of adjusting retirement to it."[6] The adjustment between debt retirement and the need for growing wealth was apparently in the mind of the Secretary of the Treasury of the United States when he advocated that "A balance should be maintained between debt reduction and tax reduction."[7] A group of accountants in England attempted to estimate the capital needs of the country and included the growth of population, the replacement of capital, provisions for new undertakings, and an improved standard of living in their calculations. The Federation of British Industries and A. M. Samuel presented similar views. Sir Josiah Stamp also has indicated how calculations may be made to estimate the general tax capacity.[8]

Finally, debt retirement may be considered as a means of

[5] Adams, *Science of Finance*, p. 556.

[6] *Colwyn Report, Minutes of Evidence*, par. 4636.

[7] *Annual Report of the Secretary of the Treasury*, 1926, p. 9.

[8] Stamp, *Wealth and Taxable Capacity*, pp. 134-137.

stimulating saving. Thus the Secretary of the Treasury in 1924 went so far as to say that

Tax collections for the purpose of debt retirement do not lessen a country's capital supply. The funds are put back into productive channels, and moreover the annual interest rate is lessened by the additional retirements. There are limits, however, to taxation even for debt-paying purposes. The disturbing influence of an excessive rate of redistribution through debt liquidation might more than offset the advantages of debt reduction.[9]

Although the strength of the public credit was stressed, the increase of capital through debt payment was virtually implied. The opinions of Bastable, Adam and Withers have already been cited.[10] It is apparent from the previous chapters that if the natural tendency of taxation for the payment of debt is to stimulate saving, then the level of taxation should never be so high or the character of it so burdensome as to prevent the acceleration tendencies. The point at which saving would be retarded by taxation would be more easily determined than the capital needs of a changing economic system. It is also much easier to determine the trend in savings and the rate of saving. In Chapter II, attention was called to the fact that immediately after the war the trend of real saving was sharply accelerated and the void in the capital supply somewhat refilled. Debt payment may be a factor in this acceleration along with high interest rates. Debt retirement policy should be based upon an examination of the rate of post-war saving. If savings are not increasing at a more rapid pace than in the period before the debt was incurred, this may be presumptive evidence that the level of taxes is too high, unless some other completely satisfactory

[9] *Annual Report of the Secretary of the Treasury*, 1924, p. 22.

[10] See Chapter IX.

explanation can be found. Such measures of saving as we have in the United States seem to show an acceleration of savings.[11] Using these measures, not only has the same rate of saving as in the post-war period been resumed, but almost the same level of saving has been reached. This can be readily seen by a glance at the diagram given on page 673 of *Recent Economic Changes.*

If saving is accelerated by debt retirement the price level will have a tendency to fall. This is the counterpart of the rise in the price level when the debt was incurred. A healthy condition of debt creation and payment would involve a loan of savings and a payment of savings. The unproductive use of the debt proceeds would raise prices; the payment of the debt through the stimulation of saving would replace the original capital and bring down the price level. The debt holder would tend to be paid in dollars equal in purchasing power to those he parted with, and if debt holders could be persuaded to retain their claims to the date of repayment, the most recent lenders should be repaid first, the earliest should be paid last.

III. CIRCUMSTANCES IN WHICH DEBT PAYMENT INVOLVES CONFISCATION

There is some truth in the belief that to pay the debt in anything but savings is confiscation if the original loans were made from savings. Confiscation in debt retirement has been much discussed and a variety of meanings have been used. W. W. Paine, testifying before the Colwyn Committee, thought that the term included four possible meanings: the psychological attitude of the tax payer, the size of the tax, taxation without assent and taxation without a *quid pro quo.* Of these various aspects the last is by far the most significant.

[11] *Recent Economic Changes,* vol. ii, p. 673.

Some people have preferred to express this latter aspect in terms of taking capital. If taxes come out of capital, debt is not really paid and the wealth of the lender is confiscated. For example, Sir George Stanhope-Pitt has said: " So long as debt repayment is within the savings of the nation, you are not taking capital. Immediately you exceed that figure you are depriving industry of its lifeblood." [12] A. M. Samuel had much the same belief. Any payment of debt out of capital is bad policy. Taxes used for this purpose which cut into capital are inadvisable. Debt payment should not proceed so rapidly that actual capital is not substituted for the credit instruments retired.[13]

Of these two men Samuel carried the idea of confiscation farthest. He believed that a fall in prices was necessary as a result of the process of repayment and that this fall would come about through payment of the debt out of savings. But he apparently subordinates the notion of debt payment as a stimulus to saving, because when he comes to set up a criterion for the speed of retirement, he merely suggests that debt payment should not proceed more rapidly than the volume of savings. His major belief is that debt payment should not go beyond the annual increment of income into what he terms " capital." [14] As a natural consequence of his belief that some forms of debt payment would involve confiscation, he makes a distinction between debt payment and debt cancellation. Payment is discharged through transfer of savings. Had Samuel gone further to consider debt payment as a stimulus to saving, the connections between price, confiscation and saving would have been completed.

It follows from all this that the capital levy or any other too heavy tax represents the extreme of confiscation. This

[12] *Colwyn Report, Minutes of Evidence*, p. 260.

[13] *Ibid.*, p. 87.

[14] *Ibid.*, p. 74.

comes about from the possible discouragement to saving and the absence of the stimulus to saving over a period of years which would apparently result from the gradual repayment of debt. This fact has been recognized, but not completely related to the various factors involved. In one sense it may be said that the capital levy would increase the burden of debt since no stimulus to saving would have resulted from the debt's existence.

IV. QUESTIONS ASSOCIATED WITH THE SAVINGS ASPECTS OF DEBT PAYMENTS

In the light of these conclusions certain answers may now be given to a number of questions closely associated with the savings aspects of debt payment. One of these refers to the old theories of debt retirement held by Dr. Price. Ross believes that the chief mistake of Price was that he considered sinking funds to be productive. Are sinking funds productive? This question involves an additional one: what is meant by "productive"? Without attempting to answer the latter, it can be said that sinking funds are not passive economic mechanisms when they involve a system of heavy national taxation. To the extent that they do stimulate the amount of saving they are productive, if the term refers to the increase of wealth.

Another related question is whether debts should or should not always be accompanied by the means of their extinction. H. C. Adams believed that all debts should be accompanied by such means.[15] This statement has come to mean that every debt should be accompanied by proper taxation and retirement mechanism. It might be argued from the above discussion that national debts should not only be accompanied by the means of extinction but also by the means of repayment, i.e. such devices as would stimulate the accumulation of capital.

[15] Adams, *Public Debts*, p. 268.

Another question that may be partly answered by these savings considerations is whether debts should be perpetual or not. Regardless of the other factors that may enter into this question, it is true that to the extent that debts are perpetual and that taxes are not raised for their retirement, there is no stimulation to saving and the debt becomes burdensome in the sense that this stimulation is lacking.

A fourth question is, what account should be taken of taxable capacity in the retirement of internal debts? There seems to be too great a confusion as to whether internal debts are or are not burdensome. Internal debts may be considered burdensome, as we have seen, but this burden arises largely from the proportion of the funds transferred and from the effects upon saving. Taxable capacity for internal debts can only be determined by the measurement of the volume of savings, the determination of what proportion of that volume is being annually transferred from tax payer to debt holder, and the effects of the transfer upon saving. What proportion may be transferred without harm, and the effects upon saving, can only be determined by a detailed examination of the conditions at any given time or place. Attention should be given to the factors involved in saving and an investigation of those factors should be made and the tax system adjusted to them. For example, Dalton has suggested the exemption of taxes on undistributed corporate earnings.[16]

V. THE SINKING FUND: ITS FORM AND FUNCTIONS

(a) *The Integration of the Price and Savings Aspects of Retirement in Relation to Sinking Fund Policy*

Since the war the sinking fund has been vindicated as a means of debt retirement in both theory and practice. Of the three other most commonly discussed methods the levy

[16] *Colwyn Report, Minutes of Evidence*, p. 408.

on capital has now ceased to be an important issue, repudiation has only occurred in countries that were very badly off financially (even Germany having revalued her debt), and in some countries little advantage is expected to come from any future conversions. It is upon the sinking funds that the nations of the world have come again to rely for the alleviation of their debt burdens. Furthermore, as was pointed out in Chapter I, there is not much optimism about fortunate changes in price or about the growth of population. What light then does the integration between the price and saving aspects of retirement throw upon sinking fund policy and the methods of retirement suggested since the war?

In the first place, in view of the previous discussion the functions of sinking funds in regard to national debts should now be somewhat clearer. Sinking funds have four functions: to insure payment of the debt, to make payment regular, to establish the form and character of payment and to guide the speed or rate of payment. Possibly a fifth is to maintain national credit. It was shown in Chapter IV that the American fund does indicate the rate of payment and establish conditions of regular payment. The same may be said of the British sinking fund provisions. In France much more is done through the sinking fund laws to insure payment. The degree of persistence in carrying out sinking fund law is greatest in the United States, less great in England, and least in France. The degree of effort exercised through law to maintain sinking fund payment is, however, in the reverse order. In the United States it was not thought necessary to establish a separate constitutional sinking fund body such as exists in France or to lump interest and retirement funds together in a fixed annual charge as in England.

The one most important function of sinking funds is to

set the rate of retirement. The accomplishment of this function has been limited by the great use of the surplus in the United States and the frequent alterations of the fixed charge in Great Britain. It might appear from this that the determination of the rate of retirement is not the most important function. Those who regard the rate of retirement as the central problem, however, would be more likely to attribute this failure in the United States and Great Britain to vacillation in administrative policy. But it is more reasonable to suppose that the sinking fund should not determine the rate of retirement through the mere establishment of a given percentage or annual charge once and for all. Rather should sinking fund laws set up some mechanism by which a varying rate of retirement may be followed, and yet this variation may not be totally arbitrary. Of course there is much to be said for Pigou's opinion that no one can set a definite time limit to the payment of the debt, that the debt should not be paid off more rapidly than is convenient and that this convenience would have to be determined in the course of the payment.[17] But to leave this entirely up to "convenience" is too indefinite and has led in the past merely to the payment of surplus and this in turn to no payment at all. The common solution has been to establish a sinking fund and let "convenience" be represented by the additional appropriation of surplus. It would seem, however, that by the estimation of the trend of savings and by a general investigation of business conditions at the time of the adoption of the sinking fund some rate of retirement might be tentatively determined. Surplus could be applied in addition but this surplus should surely not be as large as the sinking fund. In case the surplus is very large, the sinking fund should either be increased or the taxes lowered.

The sinking fund should not only be set up in relation to

[17] *Colwyn Report, Minutes of Evidence*, par. 6083.

the volume of saving; it should be varied in amount as the volume of saving changes. "Convenience" should be accounted for, but in some definite way. Unless certain other public expenses seem obviously more important or the greater retirement of debt seems likely to cause undue financial difficulty, debt retirement should proceed more rapidly in case of an increased volume of national saving. An index of the volume of saving might be devised. In case this increased two per cent the fund should increase two per cent unless the Treasury could give adequate reason for not doing so. Account should also be taken of the rate of saving. If it was apparent that the trend of saving was not increasing, then the Treasury should seriously consider whether the sinking fund was not too large.

It is, therefore, apparent that the rate of retirement need not be set arbitrarily in the beginning and that some definiteness may be introduced by sinking fund law into the adjustment of debt payment to varying economic conditions. In this way it may be possible to satisfy partly the demand that business conditions be considered in the rate of debt payment. This demand has been made by a great number of persons. Secretary Sherman, for example, long ago contended that the sinking fund should be allowed to lapse in bad times if replaced when good times returned.[18] Pigou believes that debt payment should vary with good and bad times or that at least taxes for retirement should not be increased during a depression.[19] There is, of course, the danger that politics may enter into the debt policy if the connection is not made definite by law. Professor Seligman,[20] Mr. McKenna and the National Chamber of Trade in Great Britain also favor an adjustment of the rate of payment to

[18] Ross, *Sinking Funds*, p. 83 *et seq.*

[19] *Colwyn Report, Minutes of Evidence*, p. 43.

[20] Seligman, *Studies in Public Finance*, p. 80.

variations in business conditions. Witnesses for the last even suggested that retirement should be adjusted to the net savings of the nation.[21] But they treated the whole matter as though the debt funds were not returned to business and held that the capital needs of the community must be taken into account. Schuster in his testimony before the Colwyn Committee said, however, "Debt repayments through the sinking fund should be carried on continuously and quite irrespectively of considerations of good and bad trade." This he advocated in order to insure the regular and continuous retirement of the debt and because the maintenance of the sinking fund was the "best means of maintaining confidence . . ."[22] It was also declared by other witnesses that it would be difficult to anticipate periods of good and bad trade and that a suitable method of adjustment to these periods was the employment of budget surplus.[23] Professor Macgregor also holds the latter view. These objections do not preclude the possibility of some systematic modification of the sinking fund according to the variations in the rate of saving provided some surplus financing is continued. The alteration of the sinking fund could take account of the trend of saving and the surplus of cyclical variations in the conditions of business. Thus the sinking fund should be a guide to the rate of retirement, but it should not be an unintelligent guide. Some adequate and systematic relationship should be set up between the rate and volume of saving and the sinking fund.

Two plans for linking debt retirement with business conditions have been suggested. Bowley advocated the establishment of a joint sinking fund and public works fund of £100,000,000. All of it was to be spent on debt retirement

[21] *Colwyn Report, Minutes of Evidence*, p. 246.

[22] *Ibid.*, p. 9.

[23] *Colwyn Report*, evidence of Cooperative Congress, p. 304.

during good years, but only £45,000,000 during bad years. In the latter the remaining £55,000,000 was to be spent for public works, a committee indicating, some time ahead, the nature of public works to be supplied. The second plan, that of Hobson, was merely to vary the amount of debt retirement with some index of the volume of business.

A number of questions arise in connection with sinking funds which the preceding pages may help to answer. The first of these is: how may the function of guiding the speed of payment and insuring payment both be achieved? The Colwyn Report stated that the sinking fund should be both a guide and a minimum below which debt retirement should not fall. But it is hard to establish such a minimum unless borrowing for sinking fund purposes is prohibited. Borrowing to pay sinking funds has occurred in England, France and the United States since the war, but in the United States only in the most recent years (1930-31). In the United States and England sinking funds may be guides but they certainly do not establish a minimum amount to be paid for debt retirement in any real sense. Mr. Gillett, speaking before the House of Commons in regard to a sinking fund law, said,

As far as the principle of accumulation is concerned there is no doubt that after it has run for a certain number of years, the favorable position created is such that, human nature being what it is, there is always the danger of those lapses from financial virtue which have been so properly stigmatised as raids. I cannot myself visualize accurately a situation where the government in 1978 will be providing £355 millions for the service of the debt while knowing that the government of 1979 will not have to provide a penny. That is hardly how it will work. But still I believe it will be a good guide within the lifetime of many of us here, if we push ahead with a figure of £355,000,000 a year.[24]

[24] Parliamentary Debates, *Official Report*, vol. 219, p. 563.

Whatever one may think of laws to prevent borrowing for sinking fund purposes, they are no longer popular with the leading nations of the world and if debt payment is to be enforced it will not be enforced by this method.

More popular since the war have been the use of special funds and the attachment of special sources of revenue. Germany and Great Britain have used special sinking funds since the war and some economists have advocated them on theoretical grounds. Dalton, for example, thought that special funds would be more difficult to raid because in order to meet the needs of the nation borrowing would be necessary and this would cause much adverse publicity.[25] He preferred this method of enforcing retirement to the attachment of special revenues. France represents the outstanding post-war example of such an attachment.[26] Without discussing the old argument on these two measures and without repeating again our discussion of a third, namely constitutional independence of the sinking fund, it can be said that their employment arises in the main from two conditions, a low state of political *savoir faire* and heavy taxation relative to the growth of national income. If the debt is retired in proper relation to the growth of saving, at least one reason for these measures will have been withdrawn. The other reason for their use is a matter for education to remove. If before this is accomplished the use of these measures is found successful in practice, their use will have to depend upon the conditions present at given times and places.

Another proposal made in England to insure payment is the conversion of the debt into terminable annuities. In Mr. J. St. Loe Strachey's plan these were to run for one hundred years. The Colwyn Committee expressed their

[25] *Colywn Report*, p. 404.

[26] See Chapter IV.

conclusions about Mr. Strachey's plan as follows: "It (the plan) resolves itself into a question whether the demand for a security of this type might be such as to enable the government to issue on terms advantageous to itself. We ourselves are not very hopeful." [27] Cannan also favors the conversion of the whole debt into annuities, as Stafford Northecote tried to do in 1875. On the whole, however, both England and France have made relatively little use of annuities and they are apparently no longer an important means of debt retirement.

(b) *Public and Private Credit Conditions in Relation to Sinking Fund Policy*

A second question with regard to sinking funds is, how should their operations be related to public and private credit conditions? The improvement of public credit has of course been considered one of the most important functions of the sinking fund for a long time. Plehn pointed out that the earliest American sinking funds performed this function even though they did not succeed in retiring the existing debt.[28] Witnesses before the Colwyn Committee asserted that the maintenance and improvement of national credit was one of the main purposes of the sinking fund. Pigou believed that repayment would enable the government to borrow more cheaply. Stamp thought that the price of government bonds would be raised by a plan of consistent debt retirement, that it was desirable to remove debts in order to meet future emergencies, and that taxation for removal should precede the emergencies. It is apparent then that many economists have praised the effect of sinking funds in improving the conditions of public credit. It is, however, possible that too much emphasis may be put upon the

[27] *Colwyn Report*, p. 320.

[28] Plehn, *Introduction to Public Finance*, 3rd ed., pp. 410-411.

improvement of public credit. If taxation for retirement has a tendency to stimulate the accumulation of capital, this will tend to lower the loan price of capital to the government and to the general public. As a matter of fact, the public credit is frequently the effect of the more important factor, i.e. the accumulation of capital. The great loan operations of the United States should show the enormous potentialities of public credit to meet emergencies and should raise the question of whether or not the importance of rapid debt payment to preserve the public credit for emergencies has not been over-emphasized.

The most interesting aspect of the relationship between credit conditions and retirement was indicated in Chapter V: in so far as this retirement stimulates saving the rate of interest will have a tendency to fall. In one sense the burden of debt may be reduced at a progressive rate even without a cumulative sinking fund. It thus appears that if taxation is devised in such a way as to stimulate rather than retard capital accumulation and if every effort is made to keep the rates of interest paid by the government as low as general credit conditions warrant, the general character of the relationship between the sinking fund and public and private credit will be satisfactory.

(c) *The Form of the Sinking Fund*

A third question relates to the form of the sinking fund. Should it be cumulative or non-cumulative, based on a percentage or on a given absolute figure? It should be obvious that in one year the interest and the sinking fund may be lumped together to represent the total burden of debt. If during the first years after a war a nation can support this burden it should be able to do this in later years when times are better. The sinking fund should therefore always cumulate the interest of bonds already paid. This policy has been adopted in the sinking funds of both the United States and Great Britain since the World War. As we pointed out above, the sinking fund might well be made greater as the volume of saving increases. It might also be desirable to include the interest saved by conversion or refunding. Where there is a fixed annual debt charge, as in England, this sort of cumulation is provided. In regard to the percentage base, it would seem that where a debt has been created for unproductive purposes or for a capital investment of indefinite maturity, it would be best to suit payments to general economic conditions and not to a certain percentage of the capital of the debt. A definite amount representing a certain proportion of national savings and determined in the beginning by a careful investigation would seem most reasonable.

(d) *The Sinking Fund and Changing Prices*

A fourth question refers to changes in prices. What account should the sinking fund take of these changes? There should be two important aspects to the answer of this question. These refer to price changes in which the debt plays a part and to price changes independent of debt payment. Since the burdens of debt arise from deflation rather than merely from falling prices, it is necessary, as was pointed out earlier in this chapter, to investigate the causes of falling prices in order to determine whether deflation is occurring. Debt retirement should be retarded if it is plain that it is causing deflation. Where the deflation is not due to debt retirement, should the rate of retirement be adjusted to the deflation? Several possible modes of adjustment have been suggested. One of these is that the amount of payment should be stabilized on a commodity basis. Glenday has suggested that if the price level falls the amount to be paid back should decrease.[29] Keynes has a plan of issuing debt in such a form that the interest and capital are payable in a fixed commodity value. Professor Hall also believes that the fall in prices must be taken into account in determining the amount of debt payment. Dalton favors the issue of debt with a rate of interest variable with the changing price level. This plan, he believes, would make it unnecessary either to decrease the amount of debt during times of falling prices or to issue a greater quantity of paper money in order to prevent a decline in prices. The objections to a variable rate of interest are, he thinks, rapidly decreasing.[30] It seems reasonable to conclude from the preceding chapters that since falling prices do not necessarily represent increased debt burden and since there are objections to variable interest and debt capital, debt policy should advocate measures to prevent or retard deflation rather than tie debt issues to a fixed price level.

Although measures to prevent deflation may be advisable, the conscious use of inflation to pay the debt would not be wise. In Chapter III it was seen that the outstanding example of this practice was provided by Germany in 1923. Alfred Hoare and a Mr. Stilwell have advocated inflation to remove debt in England. Hoare advocated that the government build up a treasury surplus by the issue of paper money and then convert the debt at a lower rate of interest by offering to pay it off in this money. His scheme was first expounded in an issue of *Sperling's Journal* as early as October, 1918. Hartley Withers objected to his plan on the ground that it would penalize thrift.[31] Withers also discussed Stilwell's "Great Plan, How to Pay for the War," which consisted of a large issue of inconvertible paper. Of

[29] *Colwyn Report, Minutes of Evidence*, par. 4777.

[30] Dalton, *Public Finance*, p. 180 *et seq.*

[31] Withers, *War-time Financial Problems*, chap. xv.

these plans he says: "Not only would they defraud the debt holder by paying him off in currency enormously depreciated by the multiplication that would be involved; but they would also by that depreciation throw the burden of the debt on the shoulders of the general consumer through a further disastrous rise in prices. . . ."[32]

Another interesting aspect of the relation of retirement to deflation arises out of the fact that they may represent conflicting aims in public policy. In Great Britain deflation has been pursued as an end in itself. The prestige of returning the pound to its pre-war rate of exchange has, according to some economists, cost her a great deal. M. E. Robinson, for example, believes that deflation was accomplished at the expense of the needs of tax and debt reduction.[33] In an earlier chapter it was seen how ready even a Labour chancellor of the exchequer was to sacrifice debt reduction to the maintenance of the gold standard at pre-war exchange. The choice of these objectives depends upon national preferences but it seems to the writer that from the standpoint of the public debt a case might have been made for devaluation in the early post-war years.

VI. THE REDUCTION OF DEBT BURDEN THROUGH CONVERSION AND REFUNDING

In the preceding chapters very little attention has been paid to the possibilities of reducing debt burden through a reduction in interest by conversion or refunding. The reason for this omission should have become increasingly clear as the discussion progressed but at this point it seems desirable to state it definitely. It is seldom possible for public officials to take advantage of conversion unless the market rate of interest has fallen for government loans and

[32] *Ibid.*, p. 222.

[33] Robinson, *Public Finance*, p. 160.

lower interest rates will be accepted. This fall may not necessarily be due to debt retirement, but, as was pointed out above, it may be. At any rate the advantage due to conversion or refunding is not due essentially to the conversion but to the fall in the rate of interest that makes it possible. Conversions are not so much influences as effects. Furthermore, in post-war debt history relatively small use has been made of conversions. This has resulted to a large extent from the fact that the advantages from conversions do not appear to be very great. Conversion was used in both France and England largely to improve the state of debt maturities. Since 1926, in England, at least, conversions have appeared to have very little further potentiality for the reduction of debt interest. Dalton in his testimony before the Colwyn Committee said that in the ten years after 1924 the following amounts and their respective rates of interest would fall due, totalling altogether £4,106 millions: £165 millions at 5½ per cent, £2,698 millions at 5 per cent, £134 millions at 4½ per cent, £256 millions at 4 per cent, £63 millions at 3½ per cent and £16 millions at 3 per cent. Since the rate of interest could not be expected to fall much below 4½ per cent for such loans he thought that only about £15 millions annually could be saved by conversions. Actually more has been saved, but only by the process of conversion with increased capital.[34] Somewhat more hopeful is Shirras, who has estimated that if the British debt could be reduced to a three per cent basis, £100 millions of interest could be saved a year.[35] Rates of interest in Great Britain have not allowed the country to make such great savings.

Refunding in both France and the United States has, however, very considerably reduced the burden of high interest rates. This has been especially true of the French short

[34] See Chapter III.

[35] Shirras, *Public Finance*, p. 537.

term debt. The history of the progressive reduction of the rates of interest on that debt was outlined in Chapter III. The history of the reduction of interest in the United States is given in writings dealing more directly with the post-war history of debt management.[36] On the whole it seems that conversion has lost in popularity and that the American methods have gained.

There are, as Shirras and others have pointed out, three factors involved in the conversion of debt: prices, interest and taxes. Many economists have cooperated in the course of time to build up a number of criteria for conversion. Among these are: the capital of the debt should not be increased by conversions; conversions should be simple; they should be accompanied by the guarantee of no immediate reconversion; they should lead to consolidation and uniformity of debt and help to reduce the floating debt; and they should help to establish convenient maturities.[37] The Colwyn Committee and most of the witnesses appearing before it supported these criteria of conversion. Cannan and Pigou were particularly outspoken in their criticism of conversion above par. In English Parliamentary debates, Pethick-Lawrence and Dalton have interrogated the government to learn how much increase in capital has resulted from conversion above par. It thus appears that although most of the traditional criteria of conversion have been reaffirmed since the war, that most emphasized in theory, and most ignored in practice, is conversion at par. Conversion at par, it seems to the writer, takes on a new significance in the light of the previous discussion. So long as the policies indicated

[36] See Hendricks, *Fedcral Debt, 1919-1929* and Love, R. A., *Federal Financing*.

[37] See Shirras, *Public Finance*; Bastable, *Public Finance*; Matsushita, *Economic Effects of Public Debts*; Leveque, *Les Conversions de dettes publiques*.

in regard to the sinking fund are followed, the burdens of debt may perhaps be reduced to a minimum, but if the government is forced by the nature of its loans to pay an excessive rate of interest, a new and needless element of burden is injected into the situation. The function of conversion and refunding is to remove as completely as possible this arbitrary element. When the price of government bonds considerably exceeds par the presence of this element may be indicated. Leveque, who has written a comprehensive theoretical work on conversions, concludes that conversions are best at par because they do not increase capital, controvert the borrower's interests or impede future conversions. All of these arguments are sound, but still more important is the fact that if through conversion or refunding bonds are kept near par, the arbitrary element of excessive interest is kept out of the burden of debt. Leroy-Beaulieu thought that every conversion should be made with view to a succeeding one. This means in terms of our interpretation that no conversion should prevent a future adjustment of government to market interest rates. A close contact with the money market is required. This adjustment would be hampered not only by inefficient conversions but by the original issue of the bonds at a discount. Long ago H. C. Adams also pointed out the need of a technique to keep debts at par. Conversions constitute one of these techniques and they should not be used in such a way as to prevent parity.

APPENDIX I

BONS DE LA DÉFENSE NATIONALE OUTSTANDING, 1913-1928

(millions of francs)

Year	Bons de la Défense Nationale	Bons du Trésor	Total
1913	000	410	410
1914	1,619	116	1,735
1915	6,963	43	7,006
1916	12,574	44	12,618
1917	19,522	30	19,552
1918	22,335	580	22,915
1919	46,140	1,912	48,052
1920	48,938	1,961	50,899
1921	58,420	1,942	60,362
1922	56,431	2,639	59,070
1923	54,723	2,997	57,720
1924	54,538	1,870	56,408
1925	45,735	2,393	48,128
1926 (Dec. 31)	49,075	230	49,305
1927 "	43,464	20	43,484
1928 "	35,665	364	36,029

Source: Haig, *Public Finances of Post-War France*, p. 231 (*Chappedelaine Report*, Budget, 1928, Chambre, p. xxxiii and *Experts' Report*, 1926, p. 150).

APPENDIX II

United States Debt

(In Dollars)

Form of Debt	1919	1920	1921	1922	1923	1924
Pre-war Debt and Consols, Conversion and Postal Savings Bonds	883,463,130	883,549,390	....	883,840,470	883,670,230	883,703,790
1st Liberty Loan	1,984,783,330	1,952,458,300	1,952,258,800	1,951,843,750	1,951,764,200	1,951,524,750
2nd Liberty Loan	3,526,377,747	3,325,307,000	3,316,536,550	3,310,597,050	3,199,036,800	3,104,587,150
3rd Liberty Loan	3,904,313,017	3,662,715,800	3,611,560,300	3,473,788,000	3,407,787,250	2,997,199,950
4th Liberty Loan	6,613,907,148	6,394,361,813	6,354,860,350	6,345,383,750	6,328,565,650	6,324,495,550
Total Liberty Loans	16,029,381,248	15,354,836,100	15,235,216,000	15,081,612,550	14,887,153,910	14,377,807,400
Notes: Victory	4,413,933,116	4,246,380,530	3,913,780,350	1,991,183,400		
Loan and Tax Certificates	3,465,136,000	4,573,308,000	2,708,574,451	1,828,787,500	1,031,418,500	807,513,500
Pittman Act Certificates	255,475,000	259,375,000	....	74,000,000		
Special Certificates	15,741,000	24,000,000				
War Savings Certificates	910,684,987	827,419,021	694,105,410			
Matured Debt	2,144,970	6,747,700	10,939,620	25,250,880	98,172,160	30,241,250
Total Interest Bearing	25,975,959,747	24,061,095,361	23,737,352,080	22,711,035,587	22,007,590,754	20,981,586,429
Non Interest Bearing Debt	234,570,522	230,075,349	....	227,792,722	243,924,843	234,292,746
Total Gross including Debt above	26,210,530,269	24,297,918,411	23,813,547,430	23,964,071,722	22,349,687,757	21,251,120,426
Treasury Notes	....	....	311,191,600	2,246,596,350	4,104,195,150	3,735,309,400
Treasury Savings Certificates	....	....	....	679,015,317	237,198,674	413,304,039
Treasury Bonds	....	....	....	....	763,954,300	763,948,300

APPENDIX II—(*Continued*)

Form of Debt	1925	1926	1927	1928	1929	1930
Pre-war Debt and Consols, Conversion and Postal Savings Bonds	765,316,010	765,860,170	766,549,790	768,132,510	770,207,310	772,544,850
1st Liberty Loan	1,951,519,650	1,939,212,300	1,939,158,200	1,939,154,150	1,939,148,900	1,933,533,350
2nd Liberty Loan	3,104,558,750	3,104,527,800	1,306,379,750			
3rd Liberty Loan	2,885,377,350	2,488,272,450	2,147,664,850	1,228,848,600		
4th Liberty Loan	6,324,481,200	6,324,471,950	6,296,906,450	6,294,043,600	6,278,359,550	6,268,251,550
Total Liberty Loans	14,265,936,950	13,856,484,500	11,690,109,250	9,462,046,350	8,217,508,450	8,201,803,900
Victory Notes						
Loan and Tax Certificates	578,685,000	483,279,000	702,095,500	1,252,408,000	1,640,199,500	1,264,354,500
Pittman						
Special						
War Savings Certificates						
Matured Debt	30,242,930	13,327,800	14,707,235	45,331,660	50,751,399	31,715,370
Total Interest Bearing Debt	20,210,906,251	19,383,770,860	17,250,943,965	17,317,695,096	16,638,941,379	15,921,892,350
Non Interest Bearing Debt	275,122,993	246,084,419	244,523,064	241,263,806	241,504,968	231,700,578
Total Gross Debt	20,516,272,174	19,643,183,079	18,510,174,266	17,604,290,562	16,931,197,747	16,185,308,299
Treasury Notes	2,404,241,400	1,612,403,600	2,019,194,550	2,900,000,550	2,861,011,500	2,390,286,500
Treasury Saving Certificates	385,690,091	359,809,690	309,259,325	144,469,036	13,028,019	
Treasury Bonds	1,811,036,800	2,305,933,900	2,763,735,550	2,790,638,650	3,136,986,600	3,136,986,600
Treasury Bills	....	....	....	....	....	155,916,000

Source: Compiled from the *Annual Reports of the Secretary of the Treasury.*

APPENDIX III

Debt Maturities by Years, United States
(in Dollars)

	Over 10 years	Matured Debt	1 year or less	1 to 2 years	2 to 3 years	3 to 5 years	5 to 10 years
1913	....	1,659,550					
1914	257,756,700	1,552,560	....	....	....	63,945,460	
1915	702,671,750	1,507,260	....	....	63,945,460	....	203,121,880
1916	784,737,230	1,473,100	4,300,000	63,945,460	....	118,489,900	
1917	2,257,156,784	14,232,230	349,578,192	....	....	118,489,900	
1918	6,850,582,934	20,242,550	1,744,159,500	....	....	118,489,900	3,228,109,638
1919	14,053,275,251	11,109,370	3,633,804,490	....	....	3,586,334,871	3,958,552,769
1920	12,436,715,510	6,747,700	4,573,308,000	....	5,073,784,371	3,781,205,700	
1921	12,399,641,710	10,939,620	4,126,844,450	3,913,780,350	642,666,525	159,381,144	3,611,560,300
1922	12,381,569,430	25,250,880	4,490,240,681	336,230,834	1,186,107,390	943,099,150	3,473,788,000
1923	13,014,160,129	98,172,160	1,393,029,438	1,129,657,762	1,904,020,096	4,676,777,147	
1924	12,912,903,182	30,241,250	2,101,594,499	1,746,226,026	1,125,680,216	3,272,113,501	
1925	13,960,840,997	30,242,930	1,920,031,629	1,123,716,176	3,034,602,471	122,665,975	
1926	14,439,605,620	13,327,800	2,163,599,170	2,506,665,566	50,000,000	123,000,000	
1927	11,029,775,460	14,707,235	3,226,581,016	252,933,663	101,007,513	1,528,714,650	2,042,954,280
1928	9,749,018,680	45,331,660	2,508,687,926	202,037,708	70,000,000	2,730,048,550	2,097,902,230
1929	5,771,441,230	50,751,399	1,653,227,519	15,000,000	154,700,000	2,575,349,500	6,519,263,130
1930	5,168,458,220	31,715,370	1,420,270,500	1,626,115,500	....	764,111,000	6,343,153,000

Source: Compiled from *Annual Reports of the Secretary of the Treasury.*

APPENDIX IV

Debt Retirement: United States

(In Thousands of Dollars)

	Total chargeable against ordinary receipts	Surplus	Decrease in general fund balance	Total debt reduction
1916	.....	48,478	[2]*82,261*	[3]*33,783*
1917	.....	[d]*853,357*	[2]*897,116*	[3]*1,750,473*
1918	1,134	[d]*9,033,254*	[2]447,487	[3]*9,479,606*
1919	8,014	[d]*13,370,638*	333,342	[3]*13,029,280*
1920	78,746	212,475	893,963	1,185,185
1921	427,123	86,723	[2]*191,976*	321,870
1922	422,695	313,802	277,573	1,014,069
1923	402,850	309,657	[2]*98,883*	613,674
1924	457,999	505,367	135,528	1,098,894
1925	466,538	250,505	17,576	734,619
1926	487,376	377,768	7,833	872,978
1927	519,554	635,810	[2]*24,055*	1,131,309
1928	540,225	398,828	[2]*31,470*	907,614
1929	549,604	184,787	[2]*61,186*	673,205
1930	553,883	183,789	3,105	745,779
Total	4,915,775	19,749,257	[2]160,465	14,993,948

[2] Increase in net balance.

[3] Increase in debts.

[d] Deficit.

Source: *Annual Reports of the Secretary of the Treasury.*

APPENDIX V

The Amounts Applied to Various Sinking Funds of the United Kingdom

(In Pounds)

Sinking Fund	1925	1926	1927	1928
Old Sinking Fund..........	—[1]	—[1]	—[1]	—[1]
New Sinking Fund.........	45,000,000	50,000,000	60,000,000	65,000,000
Capital of Terminable Annuities	1,812,922	1,084,840	1,043,497	1,026,841
Funding Loan Sinking Fund	2,528,280	2,641,781	2,762,196	2,892,013
Sinking Fund for Victory Bonds	2,145,039	2,230,837	2,320,059	2,412,867
Sinking Fund for Conversion Loan	13,238,859	14,386,112	15,099,277	14,701,272
Funding Loan and Victory Bonds for Death Duties...	7,816,000	6,995,000	8,405,000	12,340,000
Other Securities so Surrendered	30,262	117,640	190,963	162,409
Balance Available	12,226,403	9,991,379	22,317,755	15,451,883
Sinking Fund for 4% Consolidated Loan	....	....	....	9,210,000
Depreciation Fund for 4% War Loan	....	7,538,843	2,720,344	1,665,725
Issued for Redemption of External Debt............	....	4,953,566	5,140,906	

[1] No sums fell to the fund because of a deficit.

Source: Great Britain—*Finance Accounts.*

BIBLIOGRAPHY

Books

Adam, Henri, *L'Amortissement de la dette publique*, Girard, Paris, 1916.

Adams, H. C., *Public Debts*, Appleton, New York, 1893.

——, *Science of Finance*, Holt, New York, 1898.

Allen, J. E., *War Debt*, Methuen, London.

Allix, Edgard, *Science des finances*, Rousseau, Paris, 1927.

Angell, J. W., *Recovery of Germany*, Yale University Press, New Haven, 1929.

Baronowski, E., *Probleme des Staatskredites*, Köln, 1929.

Bastable, C. F., *Public Finance*, 1st ed., London, 1892 and 3rd ed. Macmillan, New York, 1903.

Bastiat, F., *Oeuvres complètes*, Guillaumin, Paris, 1862-78.

Beckhart, B. H., *Discount Policy and the Money Market*, Holt, New York.

Birck, L. V., *The Public Debt*, Lincoln MacVeagh, New York, 1927.

Bodet, Alfred, *Les emprunts de guerre 1915-1918*, Texier, Poitiers, 1919.

Bogart, E. L., *War Costs and Their Financing*, Appleton, New York.

Boggs, T. H., *International Trade Balance in Theory and Practice*, Macmillan, New York, 1922.

Brand, R. H., *War and National Finance*, Arnold, London, 1921.

Brown, H. G., *The Economics of Taxation*, Holt, New York, 1924.

Carnegie, A., *Problems of Today*, Doubleday Page, New York, 1909.

Cassel, G., *Nature and Necessity of Interest*, Macmillan, New York, 1903.

Comstock, A., *Taxation in the Modern State*, Longmans Green, New York, 1929.

Cucheval-Clarigny, *Essai sur l'amortissement et sur les emprunts d'état des finances de la France de 1870 à 1891.*

Chapman, J. M., *Fiscal Functions of the Federal Reserve Banks.*

Dalton, Hugh, *Principles of Public Finance*, Routledge, London, 1929.

Dewey, D. R., *Financial History of the United States*, Longmans Green, New York, 1928.

Dexter, P. and Sedgwick, J. H., *The War Debts—An American View*, Macmillan, New York, 1928.

Douglas, P. H., *Real Wages*, Houghton Mifflin, New York, 1930.

Edgeworth, F. Y., *Papers Relating to Political Economy*, Macmillan, London, 1925.

Ely, R. T., *Outlines of Economics*, 5th ed., Macmillan, New York, 1931.

Fisk, H. E., *English Public Finance*, Bankers Trust Co., New York, 1920.
——, *French Public Finance*, Bankers Trust Co., New York, 1922.
——, *Our Public Debt*, Bankers Trust Co., New York, 1919.
Foxwell, H. S., *Papers on Current Finance*, Macmillan, London, 1919.
Gini, Corrado, *A Comparison of the Wealth and National Income of Several Important Nations*, Rome, Provveditorate Generale della Stato Libreria, 1925.
Gonner, E. C., *Interest and Saving*, Macmillan, London, 1906.
Gottlieb, L. R., *Financial Status of Belligerents*, Bankers Trust Co., New York, 1920.
Grady, H. F., *British War Finance*, Columbia University thesis, New York, 1927.
Graham, F. D., *Exchange, Prices and Production in Hyper-Inflation—Germany*, Princeton University Press, Princeton, 1930.
Haig, R. M., *Public Finances of Post-War France*, Columbia University Press, New York, 1929.
Hargreaves, E. L., *National Debt*, Arnold, London, 1930.
Hendricks, H. G., *Federal Debt, 1919-29*, unpublished thesis, University of Illinois.
Hirst, F. W., *Political Economy of War*, Dent, London.
Hollander, J. H., *War Borrowing*, Macmillan, New York, 1919.
Hume, David, *Essays Moral, Political and Literary*, Longmans, London, 1870.
Hunter, M. H., *Outline of Public Finance*, Harper, New York, 1926.
Jèze, Gaston, *Le Remboursement des emprunts publiques*, Paris, 1927.
——, *The War Finance of France*, Yale University Press, New Haven, 1927.
Kempster, J. W., *Britain's Financial Plight*, London General Press, London, 1928.
Keynes, J. M., *Economic Consequences of the Peace*, Harcourt, Brace and Howe, New York, 1920.
——, *Treatise on Money*, Harcourt, New York, 1930.
King, W. I., *Wealth and Income of the People of the United States*, Macmillan, New York, 1915.
Kniffen, W. H., *American Banking Practice*, McGraw Hill, New York, 1921.
——, *Commercial Banking*, 2nd ed., McGraw Hill, New York, 1928.
Lachapelle, G., *Le crédit public*, Berger Levrault, Paris, 1931.
Larrieu, J., *L'Aménagement de la dette intérieure*, Paris, 1931.
Lasch, G., *De la répercussion de la value monétaire sur la dette publique et privée*, Strasbourg, 1924.
Lawrence, J. S., *Stabilization of Prices*, Macmillan, New York, 1928.
Leroy-Beaulieu, P., *Traité de la science des finances*, F. Alcan, Paris, 1912.

Leveque, Paul, *Les Conversions de dettes publiques*, Paris, 1905.
Levrault, Raymond, *Les Caisses d'amortissements de la dette publique d'après guerre*, Ernst Sagot, Paris, 1926.
Love, R. A., *Federal Financing*, Columbia University thesis, New York, 1931.
Lutz, H. L., *Public Finance*, Appleton, New York, 1924.
Mallet, B. and George, C. C., *British Budgets 1914-1921*, Macmillan, London, 1929.
Marshall, A., *Principles of Economics*, 8th ed., Macmillan, London, 1927.
Matshushita, S., *Economic Effects of Public Debts*, Columbia University Press, New York, 1929.
McCulloch, J. R., *Select Collection of Scarce and Valuable Tracts.*
——, *Taxation and Funding.*
Mellon, A., *Taxation: The People's Business*, Macmillan, New York, 1924.
Mill, J. S., *Principles of Economics*, edited by Ashley, Longmans Green, London, 1929.
Moulton, H. G., *The French Debt Problem*, Macmillan, New York, 1925.
——, *Germany's Capacity to Pay*, McGraw Hill, New York, 1923.
National Bureau of Economic Research, *Recent Economic Changes in the United States*, McGraw Hill, New York, 1929.
Pethick-Lawrence, F., *Public Debt*, Labour Publishing Co., London, 1924.
Pigou, A. C., *Political Economy of War*, Macmillan, London, 1921.
——, *Public Finance*, Macmillan, London, 1929.
Plehn, C. C., *Introduction to Public Finance*, Macmillan, New York, 1915.
Reinhardt, H., *Grundfragen der Deutschen Öffentlichen Verschuldung*, Erich Reiss, Berlin, 1929.
Ricardo, D., *Principles of Economics*, Everyman's edition, Dutton, New York, 1926.
Rist, C., *Les finances de guerre d'Allemagne*, Payot, Paris, 1921.
Robertson, D. H., *Banking Policy and the Price Level*, King, London, 1926.
Robinson, M. E., *Public Finance*, Nisbet, London, 1924.
Rogers, J. H., *The Process of Inflation in France*, Columbia University Press, New York, 1929.
Ross, E. A., *Sinking Funds*, Baltimore, 1893.
Seligman, Edwin R. A., *Currency, Inflation and Public Debts*, Equitable Trust Co., New York, 1921.
——, *Essays on Taxation*, 10th ed., Macmillan, New York, 1925.
——, *The Shifting and Incidence of Taxation*, 4th ed., Columbia University Press, New York, 1921.
——, *Studies in Public Finance*, Macmillan, New York, 1925.
Shirras, F., *The Science of Public Finance*, Macmillan, London, 1924.
Silverman, H. A., *Taxation, its Incidence and Effects*, Macmillan, London.

Stamp, J., *Wealth and Taxable Capacity*, King, London, 1922.
Studenski, P., *Public Borrowing*, National Municipal League, New York, 1930.
Taussig, F. W., *Principles of Economics*, Macmillan, New York, 1926.
Vidal, Jean, *De l'Amortissement de la dette de guerre*, Firmin et Montane, Montpelier, 1921.
Walter, H. C., *Foreign Exchange and Foreign Debts*, Methuen, London, 1926.
Westerfield, R., *Banking Principles and Practice*, Ronald, New York, 1924.
Will, R., *Die schwebenden Schulden der europäischen Gross-staaten*, Mohr, Tubingen, 1921.
Withers, H., *War-time Financial Problems*, Dutton, New York, 1919.
Young, E. H., *System of National Finance*, Murray, London, 1924.

PERIODICALS

American Economic Review, June, 1930.
Annalist, August 20, 24, 31, Sept. 7, 1928.
Contemporary Review, January, 1924.
Economica, October, 1921; June, 1930.
Economic Journal, December, 1927.
Economist, August 2, 1924.
Journal of the American Statistical Association.
North American Review, February, 1930.
Proceedings of Academy of Political Science, April, 1927.
Quarterly Journal of Economics, August, 1927.
Revue de Science et de Législation Financières, 1919-23, 1925, 1927, 1929, 1930.

GOVERNMENT PUBLICATIONS

UNITED STATES

Annual Reports of the Secretary of the Treasury, 1919-23, 1925-27, 1929, 1930.
Annual Supplement, Survey of Current Business, U. S. Department of Commerce.
Congressional Record, vol. 57, 1919.
Federal Reserve Bulletins.
Senate Documents, *Interviews on Banking and Currency Systems.*
Office of Internal Revenue, *Statistics of Income.*
U. S. Statutes, 1879-1881, 1929-30.
Treasury Department, *Reports of the Comptroller of the Currency.*
United States National Monetary Commission, *Report 407.*
Statistical Abstract of the United States, 1931.

GREAT BRITAIN

"Colwyn Report", *Report of the Committee on National Debt and Taxation*, Cmd. 2800, and *Minutes of Evidence*, 2 vols. His Majesty's Stationery Office, London, 1927.

Finance Accounts, 1929.

First Interim Report of the Committee on Currency and Public Exchange 1918.

Great Britain and Ireland Statistical Tables, 1928, 1929.

Official Parliamentary Debates.

Official Reports of the House of Commons.

FRANCE

Annuaire Statistique Générale.

Bulletins de Statistique et de Législation.

MISCELLANEOUS

League of Nations *Memorandum on Public Finance.*

Reports of the Committee of Experts appointed by the Reparations Commission.

INDEX

Bei Fragen zur Produktsicherheit wenden Sie sich bitte an:
If you have any questions regarding product safety,
please contact:

Walter de Gruyter GmbH
Genthiner Straße 13
10785 Berlin
productsafety@degruyterbrill.com